Teaching
101

For my students, from whom I've learned even more than from my colleagues or teachers

Teaching
101

Classroom Strategies for the Beginning Teacher

JEFFREY GLANZ

Skyhorse Publishing

Skyhorse Publishing books may be purchased in bulk at special discounts for sales promotion, corporate gifts, fund-raising, or educational purposes. Special editions can also be created to specifications. For details, contact the Special Sales Department, Skyhorse Publishing, 307 West 36th Street, 11th Floor, New York, NY 10018 or info@skyhorsepublishing.com.

Skyhorse® and Skyhorse Publishing® are registered trademarks of Skyhorse Publishing, Inc.®, a Delaware corporation.

Visit our website at www.skyhorsepublishing.com.

10 9 8 7 6 5 4 3 2 1

Library of Congress Cataloging-in-Publication Data is available on file.

Cover design by Scott Van Atta

Print ISBN: 978-1-63220-572-8
Ebook ISBN: 978-1-63220-987-0

Printed in the United States of America

Contents

Preface   ix

Acknowledgments   xvii

About the Author   xxi

Activity 1   xxii

1. Why Does Teaching Matter?   1
    Focus Questions   1
    Analyzing Your Responses   3
    Follow-Up Questions/Activities   9

Activity 2   10

2. What Makes a Good Teacher?   11
    Focus Questions   11
    Teaching Idea #1: Are You a Good Teacher?   13
    Teaching Idea #2: Seven Research-Based Findings
        About the Qualities of an Effective Teacher   19
    Teaching Idea #3: What Makes an Effective Teacher?   20
    Teaching Idea #4: Three Approaches to Teaching   21
    Teaching Idea #5: Four of the Most Essential Concepts
        That Affect Student Achievement   23
    Teaching Idea #6: An Important Quality of a Good Teacher   24
    Teaching Idea #7: Another Important Quality of a Good Teacher   27
    Teaching Idea #8: A Final Quality of a Good Teacher   30
    Teaching Idea #9: A Good Teacher Must Use
        Wait Time Effectively   32
    Teaching Idea #10: Questioning Strategies   33
    Teaching Idea #11: Good Teachers Incorporate
        Literacy Strategies Whenever Feasible:
        Five Literacy Strategies That Work   34
    Teaching Idea #12: Good Teachers Encourage
        Hands-On and Minds-On Learning   36

Teaching Idea #13: Good Teachers Employ K-W-L   37
Teaching Idea #14: Good Teachers Get Parents
    on Their Side: Ten Ways   38
Conclusion   40
Follow-Up Questions/Activities   40

Activity 3   **42**

3. Who Are the Students in My Class?   **43**
Focus Questions   43
Student Idea #1: What Do I Need to Know About My Students? 44
Student Idea #2: All Students Have Five Basic Needs   45
Student Idea #3: Children Need Attention and Much More . . . 46
Student Idea #4: Role of Race, Gender,
    Sexual Orientation, and Social Class   47
Student Idea #5: Hatred, Bigotry, and Prejudice   48
Student Idea #6: Bullying   50
Student Idea #7: Students with Learning Disabilities and Needs 52
Student Idea #8: Are You a Culturally Relevant Teacher?   57
Student Idea #9: Different Ways of Learning   61
Student Idea #10: Differentiating Instruction: But How Can
    I Meet the Needs of All My Students?   63
Student Idea #11: The Challenge of Inclusion   70
Conclusion   78
Follow-Up Questions/Activities   79

Activity 4   **80**

4. How Should I Write Lesson Plans?   **81**
Focus Questions   81
Lesson Plan Idea #1: Understanding the Lesson Plan   82
Lesson Plan Idea #2: Essential Components and Criteria
    of a Successful Lesson   84
Lesson Plan Idea #3: Sample Lesson Plans   101
Conclusion   120
Follow-Up Questions/Activities   120

Activity 5   **124**

5. Can I Effectively Manage My Classroom?   **125**
Focus Questions   125
Classroom Management Idea #1: Basic Terms and Elements   127

Classroom Management Idea #2: Developing
    Your Personal System of Discipline   129
Conclusion   136
Classroom Management Idea #3:
    A Sample Discipline Plan   137
Follow-Up Questions/Activities   148

Activity 6   **150**

6. How Can I Help My Students Learn?   **151**
Focus Questions   151
Helping My Students Idea #1: Simple Strategies
    for the Early Grades   157
Helping My Students Idea #2: Simple Strategies
    on How to Improve Learning   158
Helping My Students Idea #3: Simple Strategies
    on How to Improve Study Skills   162
Helping My Students Idea #4: Simple Strategies
    on How to Read Material from a Chapter or Book   166
Helping My Students Idea #5: Cooperative Learning   167
Conclusion   171
Follow-Up Questions/Activities   175

Activity 7   **176**

7. How Should I Assess and Grade My Students?   **177**
Focus Questions   177
Assessment Idea #1: Assessment Basics   178
Assessment Idea #2: Some Fundamental
    Principles of Assessment   182
Assessment Idea #3: Constructing Classroom Tests   193
Assessment Idea #4: Using Portfolio Assessment   200
Conclusion   205
Follow-Up Questions/Activities   205

Activity 8   **206**

**8. How Can I Best Incorporate State
and District Curriculum Standards?**   **207**
Focus Questions   208
Standards Idea #1: What Is Curriculum Development?   210
Standards Idea #2: Suggestions for Implementing Standards   216

Conclusion   225
Follow-Up Questions/Activities   225

Activity 9   **226**

**9. How Can I Begin to Incorporate Technology
Into My Teaching?**   **227**
Focus Questions   228
Technology Idea #1: A Few Simple Ways to Integrate
   Technology for Beginners and More   230
Technology Idea #2: Criteria for Evaluating Web Sites   237
Technology Idea #3: Criteria for Evaluating Software Programs   240
Technology Idea #4: Practical Integrated
   Projects With Microsoft Office   243
Technology Idea #5: Use of PowerPoint in the Classroom   246
Technology Idea #6: New Technologies   249
Conclusion   256
Follow-Up Questions/Activities   257

Closing Comments   **259**

Appendix A: Annotated Bibliography   **261**

Appendix B: Some of the Best Web Sites for Teachers   **275**

Appendix C: Self-Assessment Instrument   **277**

Appendix D: Teacher's Suggestions Exchange Forum   **287**

References   **289**

Index   **293**

Preface

In the opinion of fools, it is a humble task, But, in fact, it is the noblest of occupations.

—Erasmus

Tell me and I'll forget; show me and I may remember; involve me and I'll understand.

—Chinese Proverb

Education's purpose is to replace an empty mind with an open one.

—Malcolm S. Forbes

Welcome to *Teaching 101*. I am gratified that you, the reader, have found this book so practical and valuable. I have updated the book to make it even more user-friendly. This edition of *Teaching 101* is premised on three important principles highlighted in each of the above quotations. First, teaching is an esteemed profession. Be proud as a teacher because your influence is enormous, probably beyond your expectations. Second, this book emphasizes an active approach to learning. Successful teachers go beyond lecture and giving directions; they inspire by involving students in the learning process. This book includes many interactive activities to involve you, the reader. Third, as represented by the final quotation, the purpose of education, as advocated in this edition, is to expand one's intellectual horizons through critical reflection and openness to lifelong learning. What else do these quotations convey to you?

Response: _____

_____

(Share thoughts with a colleague.)

Listed below are the contents included in *Teaching 101*.

1. Updated citations and references, including Web sites

2. Checked complete text for readability (consequently, some text was deleted and/or added)

3. Relevant quotations, explanations, and exercises

4. An introductory activity sheet at the start of each chapter to prompt important thinking about upcoming ideas

5. A chapter on assessment in the text

6. A section on bully prevention in Chapter 3

7. Two new detailed and excellent lesson plans as samples for readers in Chapter 4

8. Substantially revised Chapters 8, on curriculum development, and Chapter 9, on technology.

9. An appendix (Appendix D: Teacher's Suggestions Exchange Forum)

Please feel free to e-mail (glanz@yu.edu) any suggestions for improvements to *Teaching 101*.

* * *

On the first day of class, I tell my 30 eager prospective college students a story. After all, isn't that what good teachers do? That is, tell stories. This is a famous story, I explain, told at Harvard Law School, in which 175 eager, albeit anxious, first-year law students await their first professor in their first course. A middle-aged, scholarly-looking gentleman dressed in a dapper blue suit enters the huge auditorium through one of the doors adjacent to the stage. The professor walks across the stage without looking out at his audience. He places his ledger on the podium and peers out at his students and selects his victim. "You," pointing to a male student in the rear of the auditorium, "state the facts in the case before you." Nervously and hurriedly, the 175 students read the case they had only moments before ignored. The student selected by the professor offers no response. Once again the professor repeats his request. The student again freezes. Again the request is made. "State the facts in the case before you." The student gives an inadequate answer. Stoic and silent, the professor nonchalantly reaches into his pocket and takes out a dime and says "Take this dime, call your mother (it's an old story!), and tell her to pick you up because you'll never become a lawyer." Shocked, yet thankful they weren't called upon, the 174 other students anxiously await the student's reaction. No response. "You heard what I said. Take this dime and tell your mother to pick you up." The student rises and walks slowly toward the stage. Hushed silence pervades the auditorium. Suddenly the student stops, looks up at the professor and shouts "Sir, you are a bastard." Without batting an eyelash, the professor looks up and says, "Go back to your seat; you're beginning to think like a lawyer."

"This story," I inform my class, "epitomizes the purpose of law school, which is to instill habits of skepticism, verbal aggressiveness, and the readiness to challenge the authority of a lawyer." I continue by conveying my expectations and hopes for them this semester. "My purposes in teaching this course are very different from that professor at Harvard. I do, however, want to help you begin to *think and act* as a teacher . . . to respect teaching as a noble profession." That is my goal for you, too, my reader. To think, act, and be proud that you are a teacher. As a new teacher, you face daunting tasks and inevitable challenges. The problems and pressures you encounter are unique. At every turn you may be belittled, criticized, and unappreciated. Those who do not teach can never really know all that you encounter and experience. As one of my nonteaching acquaintances once queried: "How tough can it be? You teach a half a year, have all holidays and summers off, and leave work when the sun is still shining?!" Go on, explain . . . ugh . . . . Do you feel the same way? Respond to the Likert-type statements in Form P1 to reflect on and express your feelings about your profession and some of the reasons why you decided to teach.

Form P.1   RESPOND

RESPOND				
SA = Strongly Agree ("For the most part, yes") A = Agree ("Yes, but . . .") D = Disagree ("No, but . . . ") SD = Strongly Disagree ("For the most part, no")	*SA*	*A*	*D*	*SD*
1. I feel upset when others criticize or belittle teachers and teaching.				
2. I became a teacher and remain one because I love children (my students).				

(Continued)

(Continued)

SA = Strongly Agree ("For the most part, yes") A = Agree ("Yes, but . . . ") D = Disagree ("No, but . . . ") SD = Strongly Disagree ("For the most part, no")	SA	A	D	SD
3. I consider those who go into teaching, for the most part, committed and dedicated professionals.				
4. I would recommend that my son or daughter become a teacher if he or she is inclined to do so.				
5. I went into teaching, for the most part, because of the emotional satisfaction provided.				
6. I'm disturbed when the media misrepresent teachers and teaching.				
7. I consider myself a professional on a par with lawyers and medical doctors.				
8. I'm uncomfortable when I have to defend why I went into teaching.				
9. Teachers should receive more recognition and remuneration.				
10. I chose to become a teacher because I want to make a difference in the lives of my students, not because I'll have summers off.				

If you checked *Strongly Agree* (SA) for most, if not all of the items, then you value your chosen profession, understand why it's so vital to society, and are upset when others misunderstand or denigrate teaching. And now for another story.

Many years ago when I was a fourth-grade teacher with only a few years of teaching experience, I attended a conference, unrelated to education, in Austin, Texas. Between conference sessions, I walked into a cocktail reception area and found myself in a small group with three other conference attendees. Not knowing each other, the first question one of the fellows posed was "What do you do?" An athletic, tall, tan-skinned gentleman dressed in a rather expensive black suit proclaimed proudly that he was an anesthesiologist. The next gentleman, anticipating his turn, announced boldly and arrogantly, "I am a *successful* attorney" (notice the added adjective) "working on Wall Street." Intent to outdo the first two contributors of this dull yet intense conversation was a short, stocky middle-aged man who stated emphatically, "Well, I own a chain of high-tech companies throughout North America" (fortunately for him, this conversation took place many years prior to the recent demise of dotcoms and related tech companies). Their eyes then turned toward me. I must admit I hesitated for a moment. I swallowed and looked as confident as I could saying, "I am a teacher." They stared at me in deathly silence. The seconds felt like minutes. Then, I think it was the lawyer who muttered, "Uh hum . . . " Clearing his throat nervously, he quickly changed the topic to discuss the weather. The discomfort was palpable. Although I'm usually reticent in such situations, a fearless attitude overcame me that afternoon. Perhaps it was wanting, or needing, to "give it" to those snobbish, elitist "gentlemen," or perhaps I felt an obligation to the profession I loved so much. I stated loudly and clearly, "Excuse me, but may I ask how you became a lawyer?" Momentarily stunned, the fellow retorted, "Well, of course, I attended the finest law school." "And," I added, "who taught you how to conduct research, write a brief, and to do 'lawyering' in general?" "Well, my professors of course." To which I quickly responded, "Oh, you mean teachers." At that point, I placed my drink on the nearest tabletop and disdainfully walked away from the smoke-filled room with so much negative energy.

Teaching is certainly noble, as the quote by Erasmus at the beginning of this preface indicates. Teachers have the privilege of caring for youth by helping them develop the necessary academic and social skills for success-ful living. As Elliot Eisner, an insightful educational critic, insightfully posits (and I'm paraphrasing), "The purpose of teaching is not to help students do well in school but, rather, to do well in life." Teachers, then, are in an optimal, influential position to make a difference in the lived experiences of their students. As such, teaching is indeed important and should receive its due recognition.

I wrote this book because I believe that teaching is a spiritual and intel-lectual calling. Teaching is both a science and an art. I believe that teach-ers are born great, but I also believe that one can become a great teacher. How to do so is not as easy to answer. Books on becoming a teacher flood the market. Many of these texts are used in college courses for preparing prospective teachers. Most, if not all, of these books are lengthy and cover many topics that are not necessarily critical for the K–12 practitioner. A new book is needed that culls the essential principles and ideas about teaching in an easy-to-read, concise yet thoughtful and still comprehensive manner. *Teaching 101* is such a text. I have tried to distill essential ideas and practices into a concise text that is reader-friendly, easy to understand, and practical.

CAUTIONARY NOTE: This book cannot really convey "all" you will ever need to know about teaching. I've culled what I thought was the most essential as a start. As you progress in your wonderful career, you necessarily will deepen your knowledge, understanding, and practice. As a teacher, you need to be a lifelong learner. Always seek to improve and learn. Read education journals and magazines like *Educational Leadership*. Join organizations like the Association for Supervision and Curriculum Development (ASCD) (http://www.ascd.org/). Attend professional development training sessions at your college, school, or district office.

Teaching 101 identifies, describes, and explains essential theories and practices for excellence in teaching and being a successful teacher. This book is primarily written for new teachers, whether they are contemplating the career, just starting out, or within the first several years. The ideas and principles contained here are necessarily generic and relate to teachers at all levels K–12. *Teaching 101* is written in workbook format to facilitate easy reading and use. Charts, photos, boxed text, questionnaires, and practice exercises will make for easy, enjoyable, and meaningful reading.

Teaching 101 includes the following chapters:

- *Why Does Teaching Matter?* A short and hopefully inspirational beginning to help you understand the importance of education and teaching, as well as the impact we have as teachers.
- *What Makes a Good Teacher?* A practical overview of specific knowledge, skills, and dispositions that good teachers possess.
- *Who Are the Students in My Class?* Some of the differences in student learning styles and needs of students.
- *How Should I Write Lesson Plans?* A nuts-and-bolts approach to designing lessons.
- *Can I Effectively Manage My Classroom?* Simple and effective suggestions and guidelines to successfully promote positive student behavior in the classroom.
- *How Can I Help My Students Learn?* An analysis of several key metacognitive strategies that promote learning drawing on brain-based learning strategies, including study skills instruction and cooperative learning.
- *How Should I Assess and Grade My Students?* Simple yet concise guidelines on developing a system of assessment in your classroom.
- *How Can I Best Incorporate State and District Curriculum Standards?* Suggestions for teaching to the numerous statewide and local standards-based reforms while at the same time developing creative, interdisciplinary lessons.

- *How Can I Begin to Incorporate Technology Into My Teaching?* Suggestions for using technology to best promote student learning.

Teaching 101 begins with an Activity sheet, then includes Focus Questions at the start of each chapter and Follow-up Questions/Activities that you are encouraged to answer or undertake. You also will find a number of interactive tools ("Reflect," "Respond," and "Recollection") that provide background, reinforce ideas, and/or extend practice that I hope you respond to by writing responses or thinking deeply. These interactive tools will engage and challenge you to reflect on new material and help deepen your appreciation of the complexities of teaching; that is, teaching well. *Teaching 101* also includes four useful appendixes: Appendix A contains essential readings; Appendix B contains key Web sites that will provide practical ideas, information, and teaching suggestions; Appendix C contains a self-assessment instrument for use as a reflective tool to assist you in becoming an even better teacher; and Appendix D contains information on how to keep abreast of the latest research and practices in teaching.

This book will acquaint you, the prospective and/or new teacher, with ideas about teaching that are essential for success. The book also will reinforce or ingrain information you might already know. *Teaching 101* will encourage you to develop and maintain a professional outlook. No other profession is more important than the one you've chosen. You have an awesome responsibility to really make a difference in the lives of others. Take the questionnaire that follows to self-assess your own motivations, goals, and perspectives.

Share your responses with explanations with a colleague. Do others share your views? Explain.

Acknowledgments

I have learned much from my teachers, even more from my colleagues, but, most of all, from my students.

—Passage from the Talmud (ancient Hebrew text)

This work stands on the shoulders of many others that have contributed to the literature of teacher education. I owe a great debt of gratitude to my teachers. Two teachers stand out in my mind as influencing me the most during those precollege years. I thank Mrs. Barris, my Hebrew language high school teacher who taught me one of the most valuable lessons in life. One year she gave me the "Ayin Award" for highest achievement in Hebrew language. Now, you might think that I could speak Hebrew fluently. I can't now and I didn't then. In our class there were Israeli boys and girls who were fluent. Yet, she gave me the award. "Why?" I asked her. She responded with an invaluable lesson of life. "Jeffrey, sure they speak fluently, but you try harder and get higher marks on written tests." I learned that *effort* pays off. I have tried to instill that virtue, more than any other, in my students through my teaching. I also acknowledge Mr. Walter Benjamin, my high school geometry teacher. He was the first teacher to acknowledge my potential to succeed despite messages from other teachers to the contrary. Thanks as well to the following individuals who influenced my teaching style: Arno Bellack, Carmen Benardo, Gary Griffin, Dorothy Hennings, Gregory Holtz, Dwayne Huebner, James Sanders, and Harvey Sober.

Colleagues have perhaps inspired me even more. Their closeness and friendship meant all the difference. Deep appreciation is extended to Michael Andron, Tom Banit, Mapy Chavez-Brown, Dawn Cuccinnello, Connie Donvito, Chaim Feuerman, Helen Hazi, Gerry Melnick, Jim Reilly, Karen Shawn, Jeffrey Shurack, Dan Stuckart, Susan Sullivan, Myra Weiger, and Xiaobo Yu, as well as Lisa Glanz, my wife and colleague.

I am most grateful to my students, because it is they who challenged me, stimulated my thought, and motivated me to excel. Many, many students stand out in my mind. This book would not be possible if not for the thousands of students I have taught over the years at elementary, middle, and high schools, as well as colleges. I'll try to mention some, but fear leaving out so many more. I apologize in advance if I left you out. Daniel, a fourth-grade student in my first year of teaching, you were the first student who presented a difficult challenge. We succeeded, Daniel, and I even named my firstborn after you, though you are unaware of it. Thanks to former students Tzipie Brown, Nechama Henya Kaplan, and Faigy Leffler, who worked with me on a master's degree project in 1996 to develop a guidebook for beginning teachers. I have, thanks to you, used some of that material here. Thanks to Sharon Bertram, Ivonne Caceres, Rivkah Dahan, Lorin Edelman, Amanda Hamrah, Laura Giumarra, Barbara LaMort, Marissa Meduri, Clinia Miller, Shirley Nichols, Erika O'Rourke, Barbara Persky, Dolores Querques, Amy Quinn, Vivian Rodriguez, Nicholas Sansone, Rachel Schwab, Gilda Spiotta, Rivka Teitelbaum, Anthony Vavallo, Moises Vazquez, Nadia Wagner, and Leslie Williams-Jenkins. Thanks to Marissa Ankiewicz and Lauren Pollock for sharing their wonderful lesson plans. Thanks to Randall Dancan, owner of Eden Enterprises, for some adapted material in Chapter 2.

I have unwittingly drawn on the works of many others. My notes are many, and often they do not include a precise source. Nothing is new, not even the ideas in this book. Someone once said that every good teacher steals an idea or technique from someone else. That is certainly true here. I have tried to reference and acknowledge all who are deserving, but I may have inadvertently missed someone or something. If I have done so, please let me know so I can make the correction in the next edition of this work.

Many thanks to Robb Clouse, former Senior Editor of Corwin, who believed in this project and my ability to make it happen. Thanks also go to Arnis Burvikovs, Senior Acquisitions Editor, for believing in the importance of this work and seeing it to fruition. Special thanks to my graduate research assistant at Yeshiva University, Audrey Menachem, whose keen insight and intellect were invaluable in helping write this edition. Her assistance in revising the chapter on technology in particular was invaluable, along with assistance in general editing and in tracking down references and permissions. A great deal is owed to many other individuals who have contributed to the publication of this book. While I certainly acknowledge their contribution, any deficiencies that exist are my sole responsibility.

The publisher gratefully acknowledges the contributions of the following individuals:

Nancy L. Cook, Associate Professor of Education
Hope College
Holland, MI

Edward Garcia Fierros, Associate Professor
Graduate Teacher Education Coordinator
Villanova University
Villanova, PA

Jennifer Crissman Ishler, Assistant Professor of Education
Pennsylvania State University
State College, PA

Kathy Rank, Fourth-Grade Teacher
Bennett Intermediate School
Piqua, OH

Lois Rebich, Instructional Support Teacher
Ross Elementary School
Pittsburgh, PA

Elena Vo, Lead ESOL Teacher
Glenn C. Jones Middle School
Buford, GA

Julie Wakefield, Social Studies Teacher
Robert McQueen High School
Sparks, NV

Shawn Susan White, Social Studies Teacher
Weston McEwen High School
Athena, OR

Jennifer Wilson, Third-Grade Teacher
Grant Ranch School
Littleton, CO

Cookie Winburn, Instructional Coach
Richland School District Two
Columbia, SC

Diane Woodford, Fifth-Grade Teacher
Covington Elementary School
South Sioux City, NE

About the Author

 **Jeffrey Glanz** received his BA and MS from the City University of New York and an MA and EdD from Teachers College, Columbia University. He taught at the elementary and middle school levels for fifteen years before serving as an assistant principal in an urban elementary school. He taught at the secondary level, as well as in other nonformal school settings. Dr. Glanz currently serves as the Raine and Stanley Silverstein Chair in Professional Ethics and Values in the Azrieli Graduate School of Jewish Education and Administration at Yeshiva University. He formerly served as Dean of Graduate Studies and Chair of Education at Wagner College in Staten Island, New York. Dr. Glanz was Executive Assistant to the President at Kean University and was named Graduate Teacher of the Year in 1999 by the Student Graduate Association. He was also the recipient of the Presidential Award for Outstanding Scholarship in the same year. Dr. Glanz has authored twenty books on various educational topics, including coauthoring *Supervision That Improves Teaching and Supervision in Practice,* in its third edition with Corwin. He is also the author of Corwin's *The Assistant Principal's Handbook: Strategies for Success,* going into its second edition. He is a prominent national speaker on topics that include instructional leadership, educational supervision, and teaching strategies. You may contact him at glanz@yu.edu and peruse his Web site at http://www.yu.edu/faculty/glanz/.

ACTIVITY 1

1. Think of the best teachers you've ever had. What did they do or say that made them so effective? Record your response below and share your thoughts with a colleague.

_____

_____

_____

_____

_____

_____

_____

_____

_____

_____

2. Think of the worst teachers you've ever had. What did they do or say that made them so ineffective? Record your response below and share your thoughts with a colleague.

_____

_____

_____

_____

_____

_____

_____

_____

_____

_____

Why Does Teaching Matter?

A teacher affects eternity; he can never tell where his influence stops.

—Henry Brooks Adams

A conversation between Sir Thomas More and Richard Rich, a younger associate, regarding Richard's future plans: More: "Why not be a teacher? You'd be a fine teacher. Perhaps even a great one." Rich: "And if I was, who would know it?" More: "You, your pupils, your friends, God. Not a bad public at that . . . "

—Bolt (*A Man for All Seasons*, 1962)

Focus Questions

1. What comes to mind when you think of the word *teacher*?

2. When did you first know you wanted to become a teacher?

3. What impact can a teacher have on the life of a student?

4. Why do you think teachers are undervalued members of society? Justify a position in which teaching is as *noble* as law or medicine.

5. How can teaching serve as a spiritual endeavor or a calling?

L ife *is* a ceaseless journey. Who we are, what we decide to do, and how we do it are influenced by a multitude of factors. We are a composite of our genetic makeup, the influence of our parents, our environment, our experiences, and even social and political forces. Our personal strengths and weaknesses, likes and dislikes, educational decisions, opportunities presented to us, help we receive from others along the way, and the many personal choices we all make influence our thoughts, speech, and actions. Why does someone go into teaching? Dan Lortie (1977), in a classic sociological study of American teachers, examined several primary reasons why people he interviewed became teachers. Aside from the more mundane explanations relating to material benefits and the desire to interact with people, Lortie and other researchers who came after him discovered that more fundamental and profound influences included the desire to engage in work that is personally and socially meaningful.

Teaching is personally and socially meaningful.

Recollection

I always wanted to become a teacher. I recall how I used to force my sister, four years my junior, to sit and take a test I prepared for her. Despite her protestations, I made her sit to take the exams. I'm not proud of what I did, but I do recall the intense joy I felt using my red pen to mark her answers wrong and to award a grade. The sense of power and authority I felt was uplifting. I regret, of course, coercing my sister in those days (happily, she has forgiven me). I've matured since then, fortunately, to realize that teaching is not a matter of serving as an authority figure but, rather, helping another human being to achieve new insights and potential. I've come to realize that helping someone else is both personally and socially important.

What are your first recollections about considering teaching as your career? Why have you decided to teach? Why does teaching matter?

_____

_____

_____

_____

_____

_____

_____

_____

Form 1.1   RESPOND—Is teaching for you?

RESPOND Is teaching for you?				
SA = Strongly Agree ("For the most part, yes") A = Agree ("Yes, but . . . ") D = Disagree ("No, but . . . ") SD = Strongly Disagree ("For the most part, no")	SA	A	D	SD
1. I get asked for help a lot, and I have a hard time saying no.				
2. When I meet a person, I'll give that individual the benefit of the doubt; in other words, I'll like him until he gives me a reason not to.				
3. People usually like me.				
4. I'm happiest interacting with people and aiding them in some way.				
5. People tell me I have a great sense of humor.				
6. I'm good at smoothing over others' conflicts and helping to mediate them.				
7. I believe that respect for authority is one of the cornerstones of good character.				
8. I feel I'm good at supervising a small group of people, and I enjoy doing so.				
9. I want my life to mean something.				
10. I am more spiritual than most of my friends.				

ANALYZING YOUR RESPONSES

Note that the items are drawn from one of my previous books (Glanz, 2002) *Finding Your Leadership Style: A Guide for Educators,* published by the Association for Supervision and Curriculum Development. For a more detailed analysis, please refer to that work. Suffice it to say here that if you answered SA or A to the items in Form 1.1, you are well suited to teaching as a career. Don't allow any one survey to sway you one way or another, but effective teachers, generally, are naturally inclined to help others; are caring, sensitive individuals; and possess a strong desire to make a difference.

Education is much more than transmitting some set of prescribed cultural, societal, or institutional values or ideas. Education is an ongoing, spirited engagement of self-understanding and discovery. Etymologically, the word *education* comes from its Latin root *educare*, meaning to draw out or to lead. That is, in fact, our goal as educators—to draw out that unique latent potential within each student. As Smith (cited in Slattery, 1995, p. 73) poignantly explains, "education cannot simply tell us what we are, but what we hope to become." When we teach our students, regardless of the subject, we serve as a catalyst for them to reach their potential. A fundamental human quest is the search for meaning. The process of education becomes a lifelong journey of self-exploration, discovery, and empowerment. Teachers play a vital role in helping students attain deep understanding. As Rachel Kessler (2000) concludes in her *The Soul of Education,*

> Perhaps most important, as teachers, we can honor our students' search for what *they* believe gives meaning and integrity to their lives, and how they can connect to what is most precious for them. In the search itself, in loving the questions, in the deep yearning they let themselves feel, young people can discover what is essential in their own lives and in life itself, and what allows them to bring their own gifts to the world. (p. 171)

As educators, we affirm the possibilities for human growth and understanding. Education embodies growth and possibility, while teachers translate these ideals into action by inspiring young minds, developing capacities to wonder and become, and facilitating an environment conducive for exploring the depths of one's being. The capacity for heightened consciousness, the emphasis on human value and responsibility, and the quest of becoming are quintessential goals. Teaching thus becomes not only meaningful and important, but also exciting.

Extraordinary times call for extraordinary teachers. We need teachers who can challenge others to excellence, and teachers who love what they do. We need teachers who help students achieve their potential, and teachers who help students understand why and how to treat others with respect, dignity, and compassion.

Haim Ginott (1993) made the point that education is more than teaching knowledge and skills in dramatic fashion when he related a message sent by a principal to his teachers on the first day of school:

Teachers

- Challenge others to excellence
- Love what they do
- Help students achieve their potential
- Help students understand why and how to treat others with respect, dignity, and compassion

Dear Teacher:

I am a survivor of a concentration camp. My eyes saw what no man should witness:

Gas chambers built by *learned* engineers.

Children poisoned by *educated* physicians.

Infants killed by *trained* nurses.

Women and babies shot and burned by *high school* and *college* graduates.

So, I am suspicious of education.

My request is: Help your students become human. Your efforts must never produce learned monsters, skilled psychopaths, educated Eichmanns.

Reading, writing, arithmetic are important only if they serve to make our children more humane. (p. 317)

The challenges of teaching are certainly awesome. Overcrowded class-rooms, lack of student interest, absenteeism, lack of preparedness, high incidence of misbehavior, and lack of parental support, compounded by social problems such as drugs, unstable family life, teenage pregnancy, poverty, child abuse, violence, and crime, give pause to think. But think again. If not for these challenges, the rewards of teaching would not be so great. Our work matters. We make a difference. Listen to the words of praise this fourth grader has for her teacher:

Cherished Memories of Mrs. Siblo

As the flowers blossom

The weather gets warmer

And time is still passing.

June has approached quicker than ever.

Another school year is coming to an end;

And I won't have Mrs. Siblo as my teacher ever again.

I feel kind of sad to say goodbye

To the greatest teacher that once was mine.

Before I go to achieve another full year,

I want you to know that the memories

I have of you will be cherished

And remembered every year.

As we were passing through the halls of PS 42

We were, quiet and not talking,

For we knew better, Class 4–227.

You made me laugh, you made me feel bright,

You guided me to always do right.

You taught me math,

And led me down the right path.

You taught me to spell

And use vocabulary well.

You taught me punctuation and capitalization.

You taught me reading,

And that was a great feeling.

Your evil eye is sweet, and kept me on my feet.

You were not an artist,

But you sure tried your hardest.

All the good you have taught me,

All the hard work we've shared,

Mrs. Siblo, you are indeed the greatest teacher

I've once had

I sure am going to miss you, I cannot tell a lie.

I better end this poem now before I start to cry

With my heart filled with memories and gratitude,

I will always remember you.

You made an impression that will stick with me,

Even while I earn my master's degree.

Dana Criscuolo
PS 42, Eltingville
Staten Island, New York

Source: Reprinted with permission of Dana Criscuolo.

Not convinced? Listen to Dov Brezak (2002) relate the tremendous power of expressing and showing we care, that we do make a difference:

> One public school teacher in New York decided to give a tribute to all her students. She called them to the front of the class, one at a time, and told each one of them how he or she had made a difference to her and to the class. Then she presented each of them with a blue ribbon imprinted with gold letters that read, "Who I am makes a difference."

> Then, as a class project, she gave each student three more of the blue ribbons, and instructed the class to use the ribbons to show similar recognition to others. Students were to report back to the class on their experiences a week later.

> One of the boys in the class went to a junior executive he knew and thanked him for his help in planning his career. The boy attached a blue ribbon to the executive's shirt, and then gave him the two ribbons that were left. "We're doing a class project on recognition," he explained, "and we'd like you to find someone to honor. Present that person with a blue ribbon, and ask him or her to use the other ribbon to honor someone else as you honored him."

> Later that day, the junior executive went in to his boss, who was known as a grouchy fellow. He asked his boss to sit down, and he told him that he admired him deeply. He asked if he could place the blue ribbon on his jacket. Surprised, his boss said, "Well, sure!" Then the junior executive gave his boss the extra ribbon. "Would you take this ribbon and honor someone else with it?" And he explained about his young friend's class project.

> That night, the boss came home and sat with his 14-year-old son. "The most incredible thing happened to me today," he told his son. "One of my junior executives came in, told me he admired me, and pinned this blue ribbon that says, 'Who I am makes a difference,' on my jacket. He gave me an extra ribbon, and told me to find someone else to honor.

> "I want to honor you. My days are really hectic, and when I come home, I don't pay a lot of attention to you. Sometimes I scream at you for not getting good enough grades in school, or for the mess in your bedroom. But somehow tonight I just wanted to sit here and tell you that you make a difference to me. Besides your mother, you are the most important person in my life. You're a great kid, and I love you."

> The startled boy cried and cried, his whole body shaking. Finally he looked up at his father, and through his tears he said, "I was planning on committing suicide tomorrow, Dad, because I didn't think you loved me. Now I don't need to."

Margaret Mead once said, "Never doubt that a small group of thoughtful, committed citizens can change the world, for indeed it is the only thing that ever has." It is up to each of us to change our world, touch a life, and to make a difference. We are involved in what Gary Zukav (2000) calls "sacred tasks." In his words,

> Your sacred task is part of the agreement that your soul made with the Universe before you were born. When you are doing it, you are happy and fulfilled. You know that you are in a special and wonderful place. . . . When you are not doing your sacred task, you are miserable. (p. 241)

Teaching is a sacred task.

People have different sacred tasks. For some, starting a business might serve as a path for fulfillment; for others, it might be to raise a family or cook. For us, it is teaching. Sharing, guiding, assisting, communicating, praising, encouraging . . . touching another's soul. Moving them to realization and understanding. Recognize your sacred task. Never forget why you are a teacher. Each of us entered teaching to make a difference in the lives of our students. We see the uniqueness of each child and try our utmost to light that spark of potential that lies dormant within. We realize that our task also is not just to help our students do well in school, but, more important, to succeed in life. We encourage our children by teaching them to be caring, moral, and productive members of society.

In the end, our destination is to create a vision of possibilities for our students; a journey of self-discovery. I am reminded of Robert Browning's observation that "a man's reach should exceed his grasp or what's a heaven for?" Browning gives us a moral message and serves as a moral compass. As we work against tough odds, we persevere. In doing so, we inspire our students to achieve excellence. We play a vital role. We shape lives. We touch the future. Christa McAuliffe was right.

The Boris Pasternak poem from *Dr. Zhivago* is a fitting conclusion to this chapter. Or shall I say a beginning—a beginning of hope and possibility, of responsibility and vision.

You in others—this is what you are.

Your soul, your immortality, your life in others.

And now what?

Our legacy is the future.
Our students are the future.

You have always been in others and you remain in others.

This will be you—the spirit that enters the future

And becomes a part of it.

Our legacy is the future, our students. And that's why teaching matters.

Follow-Up Questions/Activities

1. Interview an experienced teacher and ask why he or she has remained a teacher.

2. Read some biographies of great teachers such as Anne Sullivan Macy (teacher of Helen Keller), Jaime Escalante, and so forth.

3. How are teachers portrayed in movies and television? Are these portrayals realistic? Explain. (See Bolotin & Burnaford, 2001). Movies such as: *Lean on Me, Coach Carter, Freedom Riders, Akeelah and the Bee, Teaching Mrs. Tingle,* and *Matilda*

4. Describe a teacher you know who personifies the ideals espoused in this chapter. What sets him or her apart from others?

5. How can the ideas and ideals discussed in this chapter assist you in refining your educational philosophy?

ACTIVITY 2

In Google or your favorite search engine, type in *good teaching*. You'll find a lot of material. Record your findings below and then share your findings with a colleague.

_____

_____

_____

_____

_____

_____

_____

_____

_____

_____

_____

_____

_____

_____

_____

_____

_____

_____

_____

_____

_____

_____

_____

_____

_____

_____

_____

_____

_____

_____

_____

_____

_____

What Makes a Good Teacher?

In teaching you cannot see the fruit of a day's work. It is invisible and remains so, maybe for twenty years.

—Jacques Barzun

Teaching involves much more than transmitting information. It includes representing complex knowledge in accessible ways, asking good questions, forming relationships with students and parents, collaborating with other professionals, interpreting multiple data sources, meeting the needs of students with varying abilities and backgrounds, and both posing and solving problems of practice.

—Marilyn Cochran-Smith

Focus Questions

1. In your opinion, what makes a good teacher?
2. What are the qualities you would want a student teacher in your classroom to possess?
3. What is the one characteristic that marks a good teacher?
4. What specific skills must a good teacher possess?
5. What values, or dispositions, should teachers possess or espouse?

What are some of the important knowledge, skills, and dispositions essential to good teaching? Although the literature in teacher education attests to the various complexities, and even difficulties, in defining an effective teacher (Darling-Hammond, 2000; Good & Brophy, 1997), we have accumulated much knowledge over the years to identify common behaviors that characterize good teaching (Stronge, 2002). Drawing from this extant literature in teacher education and based on thirty years as a teacher, administrator, and teacher educator, I have included in this chapter some practical ideas, strategies, and techniques.

As the information is presented, try to note whether the particular item or statement refers to *knowledge*, a *skill*, or a *disposition*. At the end of the chapter, you will be asked to compile a list. This list will assist you in organizing all the ideas you'll learn in this book. I have included fourteen teaching ideas or items accompanied by brief descriptions of how to use the idea or concept in practice. In the first edition to the book. I included a lot more information that might have overwhelmed, but I think in the case of a beginning teacher "less is more, or better." The list is not exhaustive, of course, but it does highlight some key areas essential to good teaching.

Let's begin this chapter on "what makes a good teacher" by challenging you to reflect on your career and what actually made you a good teacher. "But I just started teaching," you may say. "How can I undertake such a reflection when I have just begun?" Read on.

Reflect

Imagine that it's your retirement dinner. For some of you that may be thirty years away, for others, less time. Still, imagine that for this celebration, three former students of yours have been invited to relate what you have meant to them. What would you want them to say about you? Jot down your ideas in the space below. Read on, and we'll analyze your responses shortly.

_____
_____
_____
_____
_____
_____

TEACHING IDEA #1:
ARE YOU A GOOD TEACHER?

We all know about the challenges of teaching. What do good teachers do to overcome these challenges? What makes a good teacher? Are you one? Do you feel you make a difference? Here are a few guidelines that might help you evaluate yourself.

Reflect

Provide the best possible education

Use different modes of teaching

Make a difference

Show interest in students

Treat all students alike

Accept criticism

Keep personal problems personal

Don't give up

Learn from everyone

1. Good teachers take the time to reflect on what they do. They think about their failures as much as they consider their successes. They try to improve themselves by reading, attending conferences, and seeking advice from others.

2. Effective teachers are not always popular. A teacher's job is not necessarily to win a popularity contest. It is to provide students with the best possible education.

3. Outstanding teachers use many different modes of teaching. The lecture method isn't always in the best interest of the student.

4. Good teachers believe and feel that they can make a difference. In the words of researchers, they have "high self-efficacy." Though they may not see immediate results, they know what they do counts.

5. Teachers who show genuine and continuous interest in their students will motivate those students to higher achievement.

6. Good teachers treat all of their students alike, regardless of their academic level, ethnicity, or economic status.

7. Effective teachers can accept criticism as well as praise.

8. Good teachers can separate personal problems from their work at school.

9. Effective teachers don't give up on a child. They try and try and try.

10. Successful teachers seek input and guidance from their students, colleagues, supervisors, parents, and friends.

In summary, a good teacher is one who listens, understands, and cares about students. Respect, encouragement, and persistence are essential qualities. Take a look at what you recorded for the previous reflection exercise when you imagined your retirement dinner at which three students would relate what you meant to them. I bet not one of you wrote, "He taught me the causes of the Civil War" or "She taught me how to solve algebraic equations." When we think about it, what really matters is how we affect our students as individuals, as human beings. You more likely want those students at your retirement dinner to recall how you treated them with respect, never gave up, encouraged them, or instilled values of courage or determination. These are the true reasons we go into teaching. Certainly, imparting content is important and essential. But, what matters most are those dispositions or values we impart intentionally or unintentionally. These endearing values and virtues are what good teaching is all about.

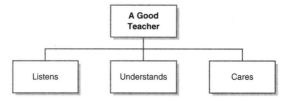

Respond

What are some of the major findings of the vast literature on teacher effectiveness? In your opinion, list five of the most important conclusions we can make about teacher effectiveness. (See some answers below.)

1.

2.

3.

4.

5.

Suggested Answers to the Above "Respond"

Here are five of the most important conclusions I think we can make about teacher effectiveness.

1. *The teacher has the greatest impact on student achievement.* The teacher is the decisive element in the classroom in much the same way that a surgeon is the most critical element to the recovery of a patient in the

operating room and the mechanic in the auto shop. In other words, teachers make a difference when it comes to student learning in a classroom. That's why *Teaching 101: Classroom Strategies for the Beginning Teacher* places so much emphasis on teacher self-efficacy; that is, the belief that you make a difference.

2. *Our memories and experiences as students in school play an important role in terms of how we conduct ourselves in the classroom.* Whether or not we are aware of it, the way we were educated and treated as students during our formative and formal years of schooling may influence our behavior and actions toward our students. For example, if you were largely taught in a deductive manner through the lecture method (i.e., teacher talks and students listen—passive learning), you are likely to teach the same way. This does not mean you necessarily will teach this way. What it does indicate is that the way you were taught may influence the way you perceive and understand teaching and learning. Remaining cognizant of such an influence while learning alternative ways of presenting information (e.g., cooperative learning, use of technology, discussion, Socratic dialogue) can go far toward thwarting such a potential negative influence. Of course, the converse may also yield positive results. The point here is that we need to examine carefully those experiences of our past to determine how they may or may not influence our behavior as teachers. That's why *Teaching 101* challenges you to reflect on your experiences and teachers who may have had a particularly positive, or not so positive, influence on you. Analyze your responses to the following reflect activity. Share your responses with a colleague; keep a reflective journal. How might your recollections influence your behavior in the classroom? See the recollection that follows.

Reflect

These next several reflective activities are critical in building a memory bank so that you may become conscious of certain influences, good and bad, that affect your behavior in the classroom and, importantly, how you treat and teach your students.

1. Think about your earliest recollections of your formal schooling. What do you recall? Can you recall names of teachers and significant others? What kinds of memories do you have about going to school, say from nursery through elementary school? Then, what about throughout all your formal schooling experiences through

(Continued)

(Continued)

graduate school? (Write your responses, share them with a colleague, and compare them with the ones discussed in this book.)

_____

_____

_____

_____

2. Next, recall the teachers you admire, the ones you would consider to be *good* or *great* teachers, teachers you would want to emulate. Write all you can about them. What makes them particularly memorable and admirable? From their actions, how would you describe their philosophy of teaching? What pedagogical strategies did they incorporate that were particularly successful? Why would you want to emulate their actions? How would you do so?

_____

_____

_____

_____

3. Next, recall the teachers you least admire, the ones you would consider *bad* or *harmful* teachers, teachers you would not want to emulate. Write all you can about them. What made them particularly ineffective?

_____

_____

_____

_____

Recollection

I recall the first time I screamed at one of my children for some petty infraction that I no longer remember. I do recall, however, the moments after the incident. My child walked away dejected, and I stopped in my tracks. "Oh my, I can't believe I said that to him. It's precisely the same thing my uncle said to me when I was growing up. I had vowed never to say that to my child. . . . And I did."

How does this recollection relate to our previous discussion of the influence of our experiences on the way we may act as teachers? Share your recollections below:

_____

_____

_____

_____

_____

_____

Let's continue with three other of the most important conclusions I think we can make about teacher effectiveness.

3. *Our beliefs, attitudes, and philosophies about teaching, learning, and students influence how we perform in the classroom.* What we do "behind the classroom door" (Goodlad, 1970) is influenced greatly, not merely by what we espouse but rather what we think and believe (Osterman & Kottkamp, 1993). That's why *Teaching 101* challenges you to examine your belief systems and their impact on behavior. See Form 2.1, RESPOND—Beliefs Inventory.

4. *Teachers who undergo intensive, long-term teacher preparation programs that include significant field experiences are better prepared to face the realities of teaching than those not similarly trained.* For example, see Darling-Hammond, Chung, and Frelow (2002) and Cochran-Smith (2002). Teacher preparation does not end with student teaching. Induction programs and mentorships play a vital role in sustaining teacher effectiveness. Were you offered guidance and constructive feedback in student teaching? Are you given the emotional and technical support you need to remain successful in the classroom during your early years of teaching? If not, seek assistance. Take responsibility for your own development as a professional educator. Seek a mentor. Take a graduate course. Enroll in a master's degree program. Attend conferences, workshops, and other professional development sessions.

5. *Teachers who are effective classroom managers dramatically increase their likelihood for success.* How many teachers have you seen who are very knowledgeable, and even great communicators, but simply fail because of their inability to deal appropriately with student misbehavior. The inability to deal effectively with misbehavior is the number one reason why beginning teachers leave the profession. Are you adequately prepared to deal with student misbehavior? Do you have a systematic, well-thought-out discipline plan? Do you have a variety of preventive, supportive, and corrective discipline techniques at your disposal? Read Chapter 5.

Form 2.1 RESPOND—Beliefs Inventory

RESPOND Beliefs Inventory				
SA = Strongly Agree ("For the most part, yes") A = Agree ("Yes, but . . . ") D = Disagree ("No, but . . . ") SD = Strongly Disagree ("For the most part, no")	SA	A	D	SD
1. I really believe that all students can learn.				
2. Students can learn only at their own rate.				
3. Some students need special instructional accommodations.				
4. Male and female students are equally capable of learning mathematics.				
5. Students of all ethnic and religious groups should be afforded the same opportunities to learn.				
6. Teachers can help change a bureaucratic school or district.				
7. I'm only as good as my training.				
8. I am the decisive element in the classroom.				
9. I constantly need to learn and grow to become a better teacher.				
10. I believe that students learn best by doing, by active learning.				
11. I believe that good teachers encourage critical thinking.				
12. Cultural diversity and multicultural education are essential components in any good curriculum.				
13. A good teacher must care for students.				
14. Good teachers are involved in the community outside school.				

TEACHING IDEA #2: SEVEN RESEARCH-BASED FINDINGS ABOUT THE QUALITIES OF AN EFFECTIVE TEACHER

Based on the preceding information, here are seven research-based findings (Stronge, 2002) about the qualities of a good teacher:

1. The single greatest influence on students in a classroom is the teacher. "Teachers have a powerful, long-lasting influence on their students" (p. vii).

2. Certified and experienced teachers who have specific knowledge, skills, and dispositions are more effective in terms of promoting student achievement than unlicensed and/or inexperienced teachers. "Experienced teachers differ from rookie teachers in that they have attained expertise through real-life experiences, classroom practice, and time" (p. 9). Research demonstrates that teachers with more experience plan better, apply a range of teaching strategies, understand students' learning needs, and better organize instruction.

3. Teachers who practice the art of reflection are more effective than those who do not. "Effective teachers continuously practice self-evaluation and self-critique as learning tools" (p. 20). Research indicates that reflective teachers keep a journal of sorts, meet with a colleague to discuss classroom practice, and maintain high expectations for students.

4. Teachers who possess good classroom management skills increase instructional in-class time. "An effective teacher plans and prepares for the organization of the classroom with the same care and precision used to design a high-quality lesson" (p. 25). Research confirms that effective classroom managers minimize discipline problems, increase instructional time, maintain clear rules and procedures, and have developed a systematic classroom management plan.

5. Teachers who carefully and methodically plan and prepare for instruction are more effective than those who do not. "Organizing time and preparing materials in advance of instruction have been noted as important aspects of effective teaching" (p. 37). Research proves that instructional planning leads to appropriate lesson objectives, use of a variety of instructional prompts (such as advance organizers or multimedia), higher level questions during a lesson, less student misbehavior, and greater student attention.

6. Teachers who employ instructional strategies that increase time-on-task are more effective than those who do not. "Along with the importance of time allocated to instruction by the teacher, the time the students spend 'on-task,' or engaged in the teaching and learning activity, is an important contributor to classroom success" (p. 48). Research verifies that teachers who engage learners use more positive reinforcement strategies, vary the types of questions they pose, distribute their questions to many students, tend to provide step-by-step directions to students, and come to class well prepared.

7. Teachers who differentiate instruction by employing a variety of teaching strategies and attending to the needs of all learners are effective in promoting learning. "Effective teachers tend to recognize individual and group differences among their students and accommodate those differences in their instruction" (p. 57). Research supports teacher use of various grouping strategies (such as cooperative learning), individualized approaches, careful monitoring and assessment of student progress, and an understanding of the specific learning needs of students.

TEACHING IDEA #3: WHAT MAKES AN EFFECTIVE TEACHER?

Some Areas of Competence: A Self-Assessment

1. *Content (subject and general knowledge)*—Are you content knowledgeable?

2. *Pedagogical (teaching theory, learning theory, curriculum theory)*—Do you possess pedagogical expertise?

3. *Self*—Do you know yourself well (e.g., your strengths, limitations, and so on)?

4. *Interpersonal (students, parents, administration, community)*—Do you relate well to others? How do you know?

5. *Questioning*—Do you pose varied, thought-provoking questions when appropriate?

6. *Planning (consequences of poor planning = behavior problems, lack of learning, monotonous presentation, lack of respect of teacher, and so on)*—Do you always plan for instruction?

7. *Classroom Management*—Are you having difficulty with classroom management and implementing an effective discipline plan?

8. *Communication*—Are you a good communicator? How do you know?

9. *Predisposition to Act in a Positive or Negative Way Toward Others*— Categories:

    a. *Toward Self*—Assess your strengths, limitations, needs, likes/ dislikes, self-esteem (feelings of adequacy). How do you know your assessments are accurate? Reflect/introspect, talk to others, keep a journal, read self-help books—what have you learned about yourself during fieldwork and student teaching experiences?

    b. *Toward Children*—Do you like kids? Do you have any biases (e.g., ethnic, religious, gender, social class)? Do you have high or low expectations for students?

    c. *Toward Peers*—How do you feel toward and work with colleagues, parents, administrators, custodians, and others?

    d. *Toward Subject Matter*—Are you enthusiastic about what you teach?

Reflection

Turn to a colleague you trust and share your personal responses or reactions to each of the questions above. Do you have any areas in which you think you may need improvement? What do you intend to do to build more knowledge and skill development? Read on.

TEACHING IDEA #4: THREE APPROACHES TO TEACHING

Rather than relying on one approach, good teachers use a variety of teaching approaches. Compare and contrast the three most common approaches outlined below. How and when do good teachers use them?

	Lecture	*Discussion*	*Teacher-Directed Socratic*
Purpose	Transmit knowledge Achieve content mastery Present information in direct manner	Opportunity for students to voice their opinions, analyze, compare their views	Lead students to a particular conclusion through guiding, critical questions
Process	Teacher active Students passive	Teacher facilitates, guides discussion, drops leading questions, ensures participation Students more active	Teacher less active— drops leading questions Students more active (seek answers to questions)

(Continued)

(Continued)

	Lecture	Discussion	Teacher-Directed Socratic
Methodology	Direct/deductive	Indirect/inductive	Direct—teacher directly poses questions Indirect—teacher poses questions to facilitate student self-discovery
Time Reference	Short duration	Unlimited/continuous	Unlimited/continuous
Quantity of Students	Large groups	Average groups	Very small groups Often one on one
End Result	Exact information accumulated/obtained Knowledge often memorized	Nonexact—there might be more than one answer Ability to understand issue under discussion	Exact—students discover answers independently through teacher-posed questions and self-discovery
Conclusion	Overused method of teaching When would you use? When wouldn't you use?	Use to encourage student critical thinking When would you use discussion? How would you encourage all students to participate?	Use to engage the student one on one to help clarify a problem When would you use Socratic teaching?

Summary

Each of these three approaches can be used together. For instance, in a lecture, you can conduct a discussion and when a student has difficulty understanding a specific issue you can enter the Socratic mode for a brief time. An effective teacher is able to use lecture, discussion, and Socratic teaching when warranted.

Reflection

Stand in front of a mirror (yes, I know, this sounds ominous). Now role play a lesson in which you incorporate all three approaches. Make sure you use correct "wait time." What is that? Read on.

TEACHING IDEA #5: FOUR OF THE MOST ESSENTIAL CONCEPTS THAT AFFECT STUDENT ACHIEVEMENT

Good teachers are aware of crucial factors that promote student learning. Research into teaching effectiveness consistently points to four concepts that are critically important in promoting achievement. How do these four ideas relate to your practice as a teacher? What can you do to ensure that all of the concepts below are incorporated in your classroom?

1. *Academic allocated time* (AAT) is the amount of time you assign for various subjects; for example, reading, math, science. Research studies consistently affirm strong relationships between the amount of time you allocate for a particular subject and student achievement. Common sense dictates that if you don't spend time learning and practicing something then learning will suffer. However, merely allocating time is insufficient. What a teacher does with the time allocated for mathematics, for instance, is critical.

2. *Academic instructional time* (AIT) refers to the actual amount of time you spend in various subjects. Instructional time is influenced by external interruptions (such as excessive announcements over the school loudspeaker and constant interruptions from the main office, including monitors coming into class for attendance reports and the like). Minimizing these external interruptions goes far toward increasing the possibility for greater AIT. Internal factors are also significant. For instance, if you have difficulty controlling student behavior, AIT will be negatively affected. Therefore, to increase AIT, schools must minimize classroom interruptions and you, as the teacher, should have a system of rules and procedures that deal effectively with disciplinary problems and other disruptions.

Can you think of another policy (school or classroom) that will improve AIT? Answer: Reduce rates of tardiness and absenteeism.

3. *Academic engaged time* (AET) is the time a student actually spends attending to academic tasks. Often referred to as *time on task,* this factor is most essential for promoting academic achievement. You can allocate time for, say, math and you can spend time instructing your students in the subject, but you won't see results unless they are on-task. According to Allan Ornstein (1990), "Students of teachers who provide more academic engaged time (as well as actual instructional time) learn more than students of teachers who provide relatively less time" (p. 76).

4. *Academic success time* (AST) is the time students are successfully engaged in learning. You can allocate time, provide instructional time, ensure on-task behavior, but are they successfully on-task? How do good teachers ensure that students remain successfully on-task? Here are some suggestions:

    a. During student independent work, you should spot check by circulating around the room providing situational assistance.

    b. At times, administer a quiz.

    c. Call on nonvolunteers to ascertain their attention and comprehension.

    d. Implement your discipline plan (see Chapter 5) with consistency.

    e. Use cooperative learning grouping (see below).

    f. Group students who have specific problems in a content area.

    g. Constantly remind students to stay on-task.

    h. Reward on-task behavior.

    i. Make your lessons appealing.

    j. Meet the needs of all students by providing equal attention to all.

Can you think of other ways?

Okay, now you understand these critical concepts that good teachers know about. How can you actually put them into practice?

_____

_____

_____

_____

_____

TEACHING IDEA #6: AN IMPORTANT QUALITY OF A GOOD TEACHER

Form 2.2   RESPOND—Good Teachers Are . . . Part 1

RESPOND **Good Teachers Are . . . Part 1** (Responses are discussed after the questionnaire.)				
SA = Strongly Agree ("For the most part, yes") *A = Agree ("Yes, but . . . ")* *D = Disagree ("No, but . . . ")* *SD = Strongly Disagree ("For the most part, no")*	*SA*	*A*	*D*	*SD*
1. I acknowledge another point of view when data indicate that the other's position is more accurate.				

SA = Strongly Agree ("For the most part, yes") A = Agree ("Yes, but . . . ") D = Disagree ("No, but . . . ") SD = Strongly Disagree ("For the most part, no")	SA	A	D	SD
2. When I make up my mind about an important educational issue or matter, I easily alter my stance if information is presented contrary to my stance.				
3. In making decisions, I can absorb varied positions and pieces of evidence, and I usually remain neutral before I render my final decision, even in cases in which I may have vested interests.				
4. Despite natural inclinations, I would not favor someone from my ethnic group in rendering a decision about an educational matter.				
5. I am not stubbornly close-minded when I know I'm right.				
6. I do not consciously make prejudgments about people.				
7. I am usually consulted because people consider me fair and nonjudgmental.				
8. I value honesty in words and action, and I have an unwavering commitment to ethical conduct.				

Good teachers are impartial. Impartiality is defined in this context as behavior that is free from prejudice and bias in which no one individual is favored over another. Bias undermines good teaching because it interferes with an impartial review of information and people. Were you the teacher's pet? Do you have a "pet"? If so, how do the other students feel? Let's examine your responses to the questionnaire above. The eight statements indicate your proclivity to act impartially as a teacher. Each of these statements clearly provides an example of an impartial leader. Analyze each statement to better understand the extent to which you possess this character trait.

    1. *I acknowledge another point of view when data indicate that the other's position is more accurate.*

A paradigm is a lens that affects what we perceive and how we interpret meaning. All of us view and understand the world through our lens. People in the 16th century, for instance, believed the earth was the center of the universe. They understood the world through an inaccurate paradigm. Galileo advocated a Copernican theory that suggested that the sun, not the earth, was the center. Galileo, as you know, was threatened with torture to change his position. Certainly, we don't confront such onerous challenges, but we too suffer from paradigm inflexibility; that is, the refusal or inability to accept alternate points of view.

> 2. *When I make up my mind about an important educational issue or matter, I easily alter my stance if information is presented contrary to my stance.*

Open-mindedness is the willingness to entertain alternate viewpoints. Can we change our minds whenever there is good reason to do so? Open-mindedness doesn't represent an "anything goes" attitude. Rather it entails the willingness to critically examine different possibilities and presupposes a measure of tolerance. An impartial leader shows intellectual respect for others and their opinions.

> 3. *In making decisions, I can absorb varied positions and pieces of evidence, and I usually remain neutral before I render my final decision, even in cases in which I may have vested interests.*

Ask yourself, "What are my vested interests" If I had a vested interest in seeing a program implemented, for instance, could/would I remain neutral toward opposing viewpoints? Do I have paradigm flexibility; that is, the ability to consider multiple perspectives?"

> 4. *Despite natural inclinations, I would not favor someone from my ethnic group in rendering a decision about an educational matter.*

Feeling comfortable around those who are like us is natural. When I enter a reception area at a conference where I don't know anyone, for example, I will tend to gravitate to people most like myself (for me, that's white, male, and Jewish). Such behavior is normal. However, I must remain vigilant to not favor others simply because they are very much like me. Rendering decisions as educational leaders must not entail gender, religious, sexual orientation, social, or racial bias.

> 5. *I am not stubbornly closed-minded when I know I'm right.*

Open-mindedness is easier when one is undecided or uncertain about a particular issue. Let's say you feel you are right about something. Can you still maintain an open-minded stance? An impartial educational leader can.

6. *I do not consciously make prejudgments about people.*

The key word is *consciously*. As human beings, it is normal to prejudge people. For example, when you meet someone for the first time you inevitably, without intending to do so, will observe their dress, manner of speech, and physical appearance. These stimuli automatically register. Impartial leaders are aware of such reactions, acknowledge them, and purposely counter them in order to remain open-minded.

7. *I am usually consulted because people consider me fair and nonjudgmental.*

Do people consider you fair and nonjudgmental? Ask a colleague or two.

8. *I value honesty in words and action, and I have an unwavering commitment to ethical conduct.*

What have you done recently that would confirm such honesty and commitment to ethical conduct? Be specific. If you have difficulty coming up with an instance or two, then perhaps you are not as committed to these ideals as you might think.

Are you impartial?

TEACHING IDEA #7: ANOTHER IMPORTANT QUALITY OF A GOOD TEACHER

Form 2.3 RESPOND—Good Teachers Are . . . Part 2

RESPOND **Good Teachers Are . . . Part 2** (Responses are discussed after the questionnaire.)				
SA = Strongly Agree ("For the most part, yes") A = Agree ("Yes, but . . .") D = Disagree ("No, but . . .") SD = Strongly Disagree ("For the most part, no")	*SA*	*A*	*D*	*SD*
1. When I hear about another's suffering, I am emotionally moved.				
2. I demonstrate my compassion toward others (not part of my immediate family) by going out of my way to truly offer assistance.				

(Continued)

Form 2.3 (Continued)

SA = Strongly Agree ("For the most part, yes") A = Agree ("Yes, but . . .") D = Disagree ("No, but . . .") SD = Strongly Disagree ("For the most part, no")	SA	A	D	SD
3. I often think about the welfare of others and wish them the best of luck.				
4. I would give the "shirt off my back" to assist a friend.				
5. I value commitment to the development of the individual within the school/district, and I value treating all individuals as significant stakeholders in the organization.				
6. Others would characterize me as a person who is kind, caring, nurturing, and sensitive.				
7. I openly give recognition for outstanding professional performance because I sincerely want to acknowledge their contributions.				
8. I am sensitive to the social and economic conditions of students, as well as to their racial, ethnic, and cultural backgrounds.				

Good teachers are empathetic. Why is empathy such a vital virtue? If you have empathy, you have compassion for others. Caring for others communicates that they are important, worthwhile, and esteemed individuals. Treating people with such compassion will encourage them to respond in kind, to you and to others. Such behavior inspires them to do their utmost to help others. What more can a teacher hope for?

1. *When I hear about another's suffering, I am emotionally moved.*

Are you so immune to others' tragedies that you no longer are emotionally concerned? Empathetic people are not merely intellectually aroused by the sufferings experienced by others. They "feel" their pain. Can you relate a time when you felt that way?

2. *I demonstrate my compassion toward others (not part of my immediate family) by going out of my way to truly offer assistance.*

Empathy may entail just listening to another's travail. A higher level of empathy is actually doing something to assist that person. Empathetic people don't hesitate to go out of their way to do so. When was the last time you went out of your way to help someone in a school situation?

3. *I often think about the welfare of others and wish them the best of luck.*

Empathetic people don't feel pity or sorrow for someone. Sympathetic people do that. Empathetic people think about and, if they are religious, pray for others.

4. *I would give the "shirt off my back" to assist a friend.*

Empathetic people are doers.

5. *I value commitment to the development of the individual within the school/district, and I value treating all individuals as significant stakeholders in the organization.*

Empathetic people are people-oriented and treat all people (custodians, teachers, students, parents, and colleagues) with kindness and benevolence.

6. *Others would characterize me as a person who is kind, caring, nurturing, and sensitive.*

This is the definition of an empathetic person.

7. *I openly give recognition for outstanding professional performance because I sincerely want to acknowledge their contributions.*

Empathetic leaders care for people by recognizing and rewarding their achievements. They do so not because it's required, but because they feel it's the right thing to do.

8. *I am responsive and sensitive to the social and economic conditions of students, as well as to their racial, ethnic, and cultural backgrounds.*

Empathetic leaders are concerned about all facets of peoples' lives and the conditions that affect them.

Are you empathetic?

TEACHING IDEA #8: A FINAL QUALITY
OF A GOOD TEACHER

Form 2.4   RESPOND—Good Teachers Are . . . Part 3

RESPOND **Good Teachers Are . . . Part 3** *(Responses are discussed after the questionnaire.)*				
SA = Strongly Agree ("For the most part, yes") *A = Agree ("Yes, but . . .")* *D = Disagree ("No, but . . .")* *SD = Strongly Disagree ("For the most part, no")*	*SA*	*A*	*D*	*SD*
1. I possess above-average levels of energy in almost any endeavor I undertake.				
2. I'm a highly motivated, devoted, and ardent individual.				
3. Strong values and a commitment to actualize them motivate me.				
4. Though not a fanatic, I have a strong commitment to see things through to the end once I make up my mind to do something.				
5. People often tell me that I am passionate in whatever I do, as opposed to someone who is usually blasé and laid-back.				
6. I dislike laziness and procrastination.				
7. I tend to see the glass "half full" as opposed to "half empty."				
8. Others would characterize me as resilient, alert, optimistic, and even, at times, humorous.				

Good teachers are enthusiastic. The number one quality of a good teacher is enthusiasm. Students often complain that their teacher is boring. Can you recall sitting in a class where the teacher was not enthusiastic, to say the least, about his or her work? Can you recall what a difference an enthusiastic teacher made? What about the same for teachers you've known? Enthusiasm demonstrates passion for one's work. When one is passionate one usually enjoys what he or she is doing and one usually succeeds.

Moreover, such enthusiasm is inspiring. Consider some of the world's great leaders. I think you'll agree that two of the most important qualities they possess are energy and optimism. They inspire others to action.

1. *I possess above-average levels of energy in almost any endeavor I seek to undertake.*

Have you ever met someone who appears dull and disinterested most of the time? Ever meet someone who appears energetic and interested most of the time? Some people can maintain high levels of energy while undertaking almost any endeavor. Later in this chapter, I'll suggest a way to boost your energy level.

2. *I'm a highly motivated, devoted, and ardent individual.*

How do you know you are so? Are you motivated, devoted, and ardent in your current role? Why or why not? If not, what makes you certain that you would be so in another role?

3. *Strong values and a commitment to actualize them motivate me.*

One of the important ways to engender enthusiasm is to believe in something profoundly. If you believe in something deeply, it is almost impossible not to exhibit enthusiasm when engaged in that activity.

4. *Though not a fanatic, I have a strong commitment to see things through to the end once I make up my mind to do something.*

Excessive enthusiasm can be annoying, if not dangerous. Those people who are committed to a project eagerly will pursue it vigorously.

5. *People often tell me that I am passionate in whatever I do, as opposed to someone who is usually blasé and laid-back.*

Do people often tell you that? If they do, you possess enthusiasm.

6. *I dislike laziness and procrastination.*

Someone who is engaged, committed, and resolute will not exhibit these negative behaviors. Have you ever engaged in a project or activity that you disliked or were not committed to? You would likely exhibit laziness and procrastination when compelled to undertake such projects or activities.

7. *I tend to see the glass "half full" as opposed to "half empty."*

Optimistic people are naturally enthusiastic. Working to enhance your sense of optimism will increase your enthusiasm. Of course, we cannot maintain optimism and enthusiasm in all that we do all the time. But the critical idea here is that the degree to which we can maintain a positive outlook relates to our ability to enthusiastically pursue our goals.

8. *Others would characterize me as resilient, alert, optimistic, and even, at times, humorous.*

If people do, then you are an enthusiastic leader. One of the best ways, in general, to gauge the degree to which you possess any of these virtues is to ask others to assess for their opinion.

Are you enthusiastic?

TEACHING IDEA #9: A GOOD TEACHER MUST USE WAIT TIME EFFECTIVELY

Wait time is an instructional strategy that refers to the amount of time students have to think during questioning. Research indicates that providing between 7 and 10 seconds for students to think before the instructor answers a question or calls on someone else improves student accurate participation.

Benefits include (see http://www.agpa.uakron.edu/p16/btp.php?id=wait-time)

1. Length of student responses increases

2. Student initiated and appropriate responses increase

3. Student failure to respond is reduced

4. Student confidence in responding is increased

5. Student speculative responses increase

6. Student-to-student interaction increases, and teacher-focused instruction decreases

7. Student evidence to support statements increases

8. The number of student questions increases

9. Participation of "slow" students increases

10. The variety of student responses increases

Here's how I use wait time: I pose a question. I do not call on anyone for about 7 seconds, even if someone raises a hand immediately. I allow think time. What happens if after 7 seconds no one responds? I ask myself, "Do I need to rephrase the question?" If so, I do and start again. If not, I ask students to pair off and share thoughts about possible answers. I give them 60 to 90 seconds. This technique always yields results. Students give their answers. Not always, however, are the answers right, but at least they had time to reflect and respond. Try it out next time.

TEACHING IDEA #10: QUESTIONING STRATEGIES

What's the difference between convergent and divergent questions? Have a colleague note the questions you ask. How many were convergent? Divergent?

Table 2.1 Convergent/Divergent Questions

Good Teachers Know the Difference Between Convergent and Divergent	
Convergent	Divergent
Where did the Korean War start?	What are four products of Israel?
What are the four main products of Israel?	How does computer chip production in Israel affect computer export prices in our country?
Who wrote A Tale of Two Cities?	How does Dickens contrast the experiences of the rich and poor?
Which planet is closest to the sun?	How would you compare living conditions on Mercury and Earth?
What are the two elements of hydrogen peroxide?	How is hydrogen made?
What is the definition of a quadrilateral?	How have quadrilaterals influenced architecture?

(Adapted from http://honolulu.hawaii.edu/intranet/committees/FacCom/guidebk/teachtip/askq5/; URL is no longer functional.)

Observe a colleague teaching a lesson and listen only to the questions. How many were convergent and how many divergent? Were the questions framed clearly? Did your colleague use good wait time? Read on.

TEACHING IDEA #11: GOOD TEACHERS INCORPORATE LITERACY STRATEGIES WHENEVER FEASIBLE: FIVE LITERACY STRATEGIES THAT WORK

These ideas are based on the work of Fisher, Frey, and Williams (2002).

1. **Read-Alouds:** I believe that reading to students is not an activity reserved for the early childhood grades, but that students in all grades through high school benefit immeasurably from read-alouds or shared reading. Select a book that interests students and set aside a time each day to read to them (between 5 and 20 minutes).

   - Students can listen, read along, or respond to questions prepared in advance on a worksheet or on a chalkboard.
   - Ask questions from time to time, but avoid using this time to "test" students. Allow them the opportunity to simply listen.
   - After each book is completed, encourage students to develop some sort of project based on the book. Allow them complete freedom to express their thoughts and ideas. If students prefer not to do anything, that's okay. Reward students who do develop projects by posting their work in appropriate settings and venues. Let students develop a project of their own.

2. **Graphic Organizers:** Graphic organizers provide students with visual information that extends class discussions or work with texts.

   - Encourage all students, especially visual learners, to demonstrate their understanding of a particular topic by visually presenting their thoughts and ideas.
   - Provide homework and testing options to show or depict in any way that they have learned the material.

3. **Vocabulary Instruction:** Regardless of the content taught, teach vocabulary.

   - Keep a section of the chalkboard titled, for example, "Our New Words."
   - Encourage students to record all words they do not understand. At the same time, when a new vocabulary word is encountered in class, write the word on the board.
   - Review each day the newly learned words.
   - Use role plays, storytelling, or any other nontraditional method to help students use the newly learned words in context.
   - Avoid at all costs the traditional ways of reviewing words, including writing them countless times, learning to spell them, writing them in sentences devoid of context, and so on.

4. **Writing to Learn:** Encourage students to write, even in small amounts.

   - Allow class time for writing activities.
   - Encourage journal writing time.
   - Utilize "Minute Papers" in which students use class time to record, for instance, what they have just learned or questions they still have.

5. **Reciprocal Teaching:** Many forms of this very important teaching strategy can be used. I have found reciprocal teaching particularly effective during and after learning content-laden material.

   - After some time of having presented relatively difficult material, tell students to close their notebooks and texts and to find a partner to "pair and share."
   - Inform students that one of them should be designated as Student A and the other Student B.
   - Let Student B tell Student A everything he or she just learned. Student A cannot ask any questions. Student A records information. As Student B relates the information, Student A pays attention to any errors or omissions.
   - After about five minutes, have Student A share with Student B any errors or omissions. Allow about three minutes.
   - Then have students open their notebooks and texts to determine if the information they related to each other is correct.
   - Each pair shares experience with whole class.

Today, literacy is essential development in every subject. How might you incorporate some of the above-mentioned strategies in teaching science, math, and social studies? Share ideas with a colleague.

TEACHING IDEA #12: GOOD TEACHERS ENCOURAGE HANDS-ON AND MINDS-ON LEARNING

How do people learn best? John Dewey (1899) said that people learn best by doing. Hands-on instructional tasks encourage students to become actively involved in learning. Active learning is a pedagogically sound teaching method for any subject. Active learning increases students' interest in the material, makes the material covered more meaningful, allows students to refine their understanding of the material, and provides opportunities to relate the material to broad contexts.

More specifically, students who are encouraged to "gather, assemble, observe, construct, compose, manipulate, draw, perform, examine, interview, and collect" (Davis, 1998, p. 119) are likely to be engaged in meaningful learning opportunities. Students may, for example, gather facts about the rise of Nazism in Germany by exploring the Internet and composing essays about key figures in the National Socialist Party. Students may become involved in cooperative group activities aimed at learning more about resistance efforts to Nazi oppression. Students may record their observations about reading selections and react to video segments in personal reaction journals. Students may construct posters demonstrating anti-Semitic propaganda, while teams of students may interview Holocaust survivors at a local senior citizen residence.

Many of us would applaud such efforts because students are actively involved in meaningful and relevant learning activities. However, as O. L. Davis, Jr. (1998) has reminded us, hands-on "activities that do not explicitly require that pupils *think* about their experience" can simply mean "minds-off" (p. 120). Davis explains further:

> Raw experiences comprise the grist for thinking. They are necessary, but not sufficient, instructional foci. For the most part, hands-on activities must include *minds-on* aspects. That is, pupils must think about their experience. They must, as Dewey noted, reflect about what they have done. Consciously, they must construct personal meanings from their active experience. (p. 120)

Constructivist learning theory that supports both hands-on and minds-on activities is essential in teaching any subject. According to constructivist theory, people learn best when they are given opportunities to construct meanings on their own. How best to accomplish this lofty goal becomes paramount. Simply leaving students "on their own" is a wholly inefficient and ineffective way of stimulating reflective thinking. Teachers *must* guide students and provide thought-provoking questions or frameworks as they engage in these hands-on activities. Davis amplifies this key instructional component: "Indeed, for hands-on activities to qualify as educationally appropriate tasks, teachers must work with pupils before, during, and after these engagements so that pupils maintain a minds-on awareness of their unfolding experiences" (p. 120).

Reflection

How can you encourage hands-on and minds-on learning? List five ways.

TEACHING IDEA #13:
GOOD TEACHERS EMPLOY K-W-L

Begin your class by employing the K-W-L strategy developed by Donna Sederburg Ogle (1986). K-W-L is a strategy that models active thinking needed before, during, and after learning. The letters *K, W,* and *L* stand for three activities students engage in when learning: recalling what they *know,* determining what they *want* to learn, and identifying what they have *learned* (see Form 2.5).

Teachers should encourage students to write out what they know about a given topic, what questions they want answered, and what they have learned after a particular unit of instruction. I begin a new unit by asking students to write all they know about the topic. Once students are conscious of their prior understandings, new information and meanings may replace prior knowledge that may be based on factual errors or misinterpretations. Moreover, students who realize how little they know about the topic may develop higher levels of motivation and eagerness when learning the new content. One student in my class wrote in her journal: "I never realized how little I knew about. I'm anxious to learn as much as I can this year."

Students then brainstorm specific topics they want to learn about and questions they want answered. Teachers who involve students in charting the nature of content to be learned are more likely to encourage attention and learning.

After each major unit and as a culminating activity of the course, the final stage of K-W-L is employed. I ask students to list what they have learned. Students individually or in small groups record their responses and then share their information with the class.

The K-W-L activity is valuable because it activates students' own knowledge of the topic under study. Students are provided the opportunity to share in the development of topics and objectives. Finally, they are encouraged to summarize or review what they have learned.

Form 2.5 K-W-L Strategy Sheet

What I Know	What I Want to Find Out	What I Learned

TEACHING IDEA #14: GOOD TEACHERS GET PARENTS ON THEIR SIDE: TEN WAYS

1. Make a special effort at the beginning to reach out to parents.

2. Capitalize on eagerness of parents to assist in any way.

3. Make parents feel welcome and accepted.

4. Tap into diverse interests and talents of parents.

5. Give them options or ways of helping out.

6. Start a parent e-mail chat group.

7. Listen to parents.

8. Call them even when there is no trouble.

9. Ask them for assistance; be specific.

10. Give them specific instructions for assisting their child with homework and projects.

Opening the channels of communication is key!

One of the reviewers for this second of *Teaching 101* suggested I include a phone call dialogue script for the first "scary" call you will have to make to a parent at some time. So here goes. Of course, feel free to add your own flare.

Teacher: Hi, this is Ms. Bedell, your daughter's fourth-grade teacher.

Parent: Yes, is everything all right?

Teacher: Your daughter, Megan, is very bright and has a great personality. She's lively and I'm certain she'll become successful at whatever she does in life. The issue, though, for now is that she is just a bit too excitable and I'm having some trouble keeping her focused on her work so that it's not distracting to others.

Parent: Well, thanks for your positive thoughts about Megan's future. I'm concerned though she's being disruptive. What exactly does she do?

Teacher: Let me give you one example. During our math lesson today, students were doing some worksheets at their desks, but Megan remained out of her seat most of the time trying to speak with her friend across the room. By the time I called the class together to review the material, she hadn't completed but half the work.

Parent: Oh . . . (sounding worried).

Teacher: But I have a suggestion. Why not have a few words to Megan about your expectations for staying on task until she finishes all her work. When she does finish, tell her to come over to my desk and I'll give her some extra special tasks to do to keep her active mind occupied and challenged. She's very smart, you know.

Parent: Thank you so much for calling. Keep us informed of her progress.

Teacher: My pleasure, and thank you for being so receptive.

The precise words you use are not important. But notice what the teacher did. She started out the conversation pleasantly and offered something positive to point out about the student. You can always find something positive to say about a student, even if it's inconsequential. Doing so will win over the parent, and that's the whole "battle," if you will. Look over the script again and note two other things the teacher did effectively. Share your ideas with a classmate.

Don't be afraid of parents. Win them over with sincere caring, and they'll serve as a great asset.

CONCLUSION

This chapter included a number of ideas (14 starters) that can be categorized as essential *knowledge, skills,* and/or *dispositions.* Certainly, these ideas or strategies, by themselves, are insufficient and do not encompass all there is to know about good teaching. But, I thought I'd present some diverse and important concepts to get you started. There is certainly much more to learn about good teaching, which you will, I am sure, acquire with continued experience, the advice of good mentors, and continued study perhaps in graduate school or in-service work in schools (PD—professional development).

For now, please complete Form 2.6 by summarizing what you learned in this chapter about what makes a good teacher:

Form 2.6

Knowledge	Skills	Dispositions

The list you developed from this chapter is certainly not exhaustive. Add to your list on your own.

Follow-Up Questions/Activities

1. What else do you need to know about good teaching practice?

2. Interview a good teacher and discover what makes him or her so good. In other words, what does the teacher attribute to his or her success?

3. Keep a journal that notes, in part, what ideas from this book you intend to try out in the classroom.

4. Interview some students to ask them what they consider makes a good teacher.

5. Take the Self-Assessment Instrument in Appendix C to assess your competence in these four areas: (1) planning and preparation, (2) classroom environment, (3) instruction, and (4) professional responsibilities. This activity will help do two things: (1) reflect on the extent to which you are engaging in meaningful teaching practice to become a good teacher, and (2) reflect on teaching practices that will inform your personal educational philosophy.

ACTIVITY 3

1. List the characteristics of good students. Share your findings with a colleague.

_____

_____

_____

_____

_____

_____

_____

_____

_____

_____

_____

2. Interview five K–12 students. Ask them what they would want the teacher to know about them. Record responses below. Describe the students without divulging who they are. What lessons did you learn? Share with a colleague.

_____

_____

_____

_____

_____

_____

_____

_____

_____

_____

_____

_____

Who Are the Students in My Class?

Take the attitude of a student, never be too big to ask questions, never know too much to learn something new.

—Og Mandino

If students don't learn the way we teach, let us teach the way they learn.

—Motto of E. C. Lee Elementary School,
Aberdeen, South Dakota

Focus Questions

1. Why is knowing and understanding students' backgrounds important in helping them learn?

2. What would you need to know about a student in order to help him or her learn better?

3. What strategies or techniques might you employ to diagnose students' needs in your classroom?

4. How is it possible to meet the diverse needs of all your students?

5. Would you rather teach a group of students of similar abilities as opposed to a more inclusive group? Explain why or why not.

I gaze upon the 20 eager young faces as I stand before them on the first day of class. They look so innocent, filled with expectations and hope. They want to learn about me. Am I nice, am I fair, will I treat them with dignity? I see each face and silently wonder, "Can I reach each one of these souls? What are their fears and hopes? What are their ambitions? What do they need? Can I really help them?" Each of my students has so much potential. I will try my best.

Indeed, each student is precious. Each has so much potential. That is why teaching is such an awesome responsibility. We ask ourselves, "Will I make a difference to each of them? What will they say about me at my retirement dinner? What memories will they have of me?" I know you, the reader, want to do your best (otherwise, why would you be reading this book?). You must believe you can positively affect each student you encounter, even though you may feel you are not making any progress. With such a positive outlook or disposition, you are ready to get to know your students and really make a difference. This chapter reviews eleven key ideas or elements you need to keep in mind when working with your students. The ideas here are not exhaustive, but it's an important start.

STUDENT IDEA #1: WHAT DO I NEED TO KNOW ABOUT MY STUDENTS?

All students have special needs. Although we need to serve the needs of students who have been officially designated as *learning disabled,* we must realize that all students have *special needs.* Isn't that true? Think about your own child or neighbor's child. Each child is unique and each of them has special needs.

Children are unique.

All students learn in different ways and at different paces. The days when teachers simply talked and students dutifully listened are over, as if they ever really listened anyway! Good teachers use multiple strategies and ways to reach students because teachers know that each student processes information differently. Some are good auditory learners while others learn best through visual stimulation. Good teachers also know that students learn at different paces. Just because Charlie "gets it" immediately doesn't mean that Sally, who doesn't immediately connect, is necessarily slower. She just may need some additional think time or special assistance.

How do students learn best?

Some students may have difficulty paying attention. Aside from those students who have serious processing problems, all students, at different times, may tune out. Think about yourself at church or at a lecture. Ask yourself, "What can I do to encourage students to attend to the tasks at hand?" You may have to gently remind Melissa, "Can you answer that question?" You may have to restate or rephrase a question for them. Rather than accusing them of daydreaming, frame your redirect in a positive way. What might you say?

All students tune out occasionally.

All students are motivated. Ever hear someone say, "Well, he's just not motivated?" That is simply not true. All students are motivated, though they may not indeed be motivated to learn what you are trying to teach them. The first step is to realize that all people are driven to act in some way and it is our task to tap into that natural motivation. How can you as their teacher use their natural energies in positive ways to connect them to the content in your class?

All students can be motivated.

Who they are makes a difference. Your students' social, cultural, and ethnic backgrounds, as well as gender, may influence how others treat them. Can you provide instances wherein a student's social class, culture (particularly for English-language learners), ethnicity, and gender negatively affected their academic or social progress?

STUDENT IDEA #2: ALL STUDENTS HAVE FIVE BASIC NEEDS

William Glasser (1975) identifies five basic needs that we all strive to meet. As I review these needs, consider how you might take these needs into consideration in planning your classroom activities and interacting with your students:

1. *Belonging—All people have a need to belong.* That's why so many kids are involved in gang behavior. They are striving to fulfill their craving to belong. If they don't receive that sense of belonging at home or in school, they often resort to potentially negative ways to satisfy this need. Do your students feel needed? Is there a group to which they belong in class/school? How can you encourage them to feel like part of the class? Can they share their ideas and feelings? Can they participate in group activities?

2. *Security—Who doesn't want to feel secure?* If you worked in a neighborhood that lacked proper security for your car, could you go about your day without worry? Of course not. You'd have your car on your mind all day. Similarly, your students need to know that your classroom is a place where they can feel secure and safe. They need an environment free from ridicule and violence. Is your class a pleasant environment? Is it nicely decorated? Do you greet your students each day with a smile and pleasant countenance?

3. *Power—All of us need to feel empowered.* A student who defies your authority, for example, may be communicating, perhaps unconsciously, a desire for attention. Students have a need to feel in charge. Never take a student's verbal attack personally. Engage them in meaningful, productive activities in which they feel they are contributing to the classroom in positive ways. Selecting students as monitors is one way to empower them. Can you identify two other ways to empower your students?

4. *Freedom—Who likes to be told what to do all the time?* All of us need a sense of control over our situation. In what ways can you encourage students to feel that they have some freedom? You could, perhaps, allow them input into what gets taught for a particular lesson or allow them to develop a special assembly or project. By promoting and supporting student freedom, you will satisfy one of their innate needs.

5. *Fun—School and fun?!* Isn't that an oxymoron? How can you make your classroom a place where kids can enjoy themselves and have fun (yes, while they learn)?

Who are the students in your class? They are human beings who crave to fulfill these essential needs. Do they consider your classroom a place where they can satisfy them?

STUDENT IDEA #3: CHILDREN NEED ATTENTION AND MUCH MORE . . .

Children need ample attention and guidance from us. Each child has special needs that are unique. It is our responsibility to satisfy these needs for our students. Here is a sampling of activities that will address these needs:

- *Active games*—playing with family and friends
- *Stories, jingles, and rhymes*
- *Imaginative play*—"pretending to be"
- *Language*—listening to and talking with others
- *Music*—enjoying and being creative with songs and rhythms
- *Tools and materials*—making things of their choice

Activities that address their senses are as follows:

- *Seeing*—observing things at home, on the street, in stores, and other places
- *Hearing*—listening and identifying sounds at home, in nature, and other places
- *Tasting*—describing differences among foods
- *Smelling*—identifying different odors
- *Touching*—feeling many kinds of materials, objects, and so on

Our children have many needs that we must to pay special attention to. If a child is to develop as a healthy human being, the child needs to have more than the basic needs. Some of these other needs are the need for love, friendship, joyfulness, flexibility, sense of humor, optimism, sensitivity, resiliency, honesty and trust, curiosity, playfulness, creativity, laughter, tears, compassion, imagination, song, dance, open-mindedness, the sense of wonder, explorativeness; the need to know; the need to work; the need to learn; the need to organize; the need to belong; and so on.

Each child is unique and each child has unique needs. We, as adults, must meet the needs of each individual child to the best of our ability. By creating an atmosphere of openness, and by listening, watching, and teaching, we must meet the needs to ensure the full growth and development of every child.

Reflection

How do these ideas help you better understand your students? Share ideas with a colleague.

STUDENT IDEA #4: ROLE OF RACE, GENDER, SEXUAL ORIENTATION, AND SOCIAL CLASS

Asking the question "Who are the students in my class?" requires us to consider the impact that race, gender, sexual orientation, and social class have on our students. Race matters, as do gender and class. Our students' backgrounds and the way they have been treated by society as a result influence their behavior. Have we as a society used race, gender, and class to classify and stigmatize our students? Find a colleague and discuss the following questions.

1. What ways might teachers overtly and/or unintentionally discriminate in their classrooms? Describe and discuss.

2. What ways might schools overtly and/or unintentionally discriminate? Describe and discuss.

3. What are some prejudices teachers might have about some people or groups and how might they affect their behavior in the classroom? Describe and discuss.

4. What groups or individuals might be targeted for discrimination? List them.

5. What are some ways teachers might promote equality, opportunity, and justice? Describe and discuss.

STUDENT IDEA #5: HATRED, BIGOTRY, AND PREJUDICE

He was a 49-year-old black man living in Jasper, Texas. Three white men (John William King, Shawn Allen Berry, and Lawrence Russell Brewer) chained the man to the back of a pickup truck and dragged him behind the truck until his body came apart. The three men left the right arm and head in the ditch beside the road where they fell off, and left the remainder of the body near a black cemetery.

He was a gay University of Wyoming student who was found beaten and tied to a fence post on the Wyoming prairie.

He was a Jewish physician who performed abortions in Buffalo. He was shot with a high-powered rifle through his kitchen window in front of his wife and children.

The names of James Byrd, Matthew Shepard, and Barnett Slepian have been etched in our consciousness ever since their brutal murders several years ago. These horrific crimes are poignant reminders that hatred is ever present and, perhaps, endemic to American culture and society.

Have you ever hated someone? I think we all have felt intense anger toward someone. How did we react? Did we shout at them, hit them, plan revenge, or did we merely conjure up images of retaliation? Occasionally, our passions and our tempers get the better of us. We lose control. Yet, you may argue, you would never resort to such extreme acts of hatred as described above. Granted.

What about our tendencies toward bigotry and prejudice? If you are Christian, have you ever harbored ill will toward a Muslim? What about resentment toward Jews? If you are Israeli, have you ever thought badly about Arabs? What about intolerance and hate between Indians and Pakistanis, Asians and Westerners, Swedes and Norwegians, Hispanics and Caucasians, Caucasians and African Americans, Serbs and Kosovars?

Why is it that our fear, suspicion, and hatred of others different from us have overpowered our good sense and moral commitments to civility, good-will, justice, and tolerance? When we think of Columbine, we now know that these kids were bullied. School violence is on the rise and we as educators must consider the way students treat others who are different.

Who are the students in your class? Are they potential victims? Perpetrators? What can you do?

Recollection

Hatred

My father was a survivor of the Holocaust. He denounced hatred of all kinds. Clearly, he had his reasons.

Once he and I were traveling on the Staten Island Ferry. A Hispanic family was seated across from us. They were poorly dressed and had difficulty with the English language, a situation that was all too familiar to me since my parents were immigrants, too.

Several young, rowdy hoodlums were mocking them. My father gazed furiously at these ruffians. I observed the look and the response it elicited. These obnoxious boys timidly responded by walking away while muttering "dirty Jew bastards."

My father later told me, never to hate others for how they speak or look . . . only judge people by their actions, no matter who they are or what they look like.

It was an invaluable lesson I carry with me to this very day.

Have you encountered hate? How can you teach your students not to hate? See the story about little Keisha that follows.

This short, true story is told by the founder of Teaching Tolerance of the Southern Poverty Law Center. I paraphrase:

I'm not a parent but through the years I've loved many children. One of them was a four year old named Keisha, the most volatile of all four year olds I taught in day care. Easy to anger and slow to calm down, Keisha spent

(Continued)

(Continued)

at least part of every day crying. One day I was holding her hand waiting for a class, all white, to leave the library. As our all-black class waited at the entrance, Keisha noticed the difference. "I hate white people. My mommy hates white people and I hate white people." She spoke rather matter-of-factly without a trace of hatred. Then it dawned on her. "Teacher, are you white?" "Yes I am; do you like me?" "I love you," she said and grinned. "I love you too." For Keisha at four, it was not yet necessary to reconcile her love for her teacher and her hatred of white people.

STUDENT IDEA #6: BULLYING

You should remain cognizant of the fact that statistics indicate that 30 percent of Amercan students are involved in bullying, as victims, perpetrators, or both (Coloroso, 2004). According to Rona Novick (2000), bullying is the deliberate use or abuse of power to cause harm to another student. Research indicates that victims of bullies are characterized as shy, anxious, possessing low self-esteem, and having poor social skills (see, e.g., Card, 2003). Serious consequences result after persistent and unremediated bullying. Among them are serious physical, social, and emotional scars. Victims tend to deepen their introvertedness and often become "quietly" emotional. Left unattended, depression can result. Being teased and bullied can lead, in some cases (and we've seen them played out in the news too many times since Columbine) to the victims lashing out against not only their bullies but others, perhaps bystanders.

But what about the bullies themselves? It's a myth that bullies lack self-confidence themselves and that's why they bully others. The truth is that these children are aggressive, undisciplined, and crave power over others (Smith, Cowie, Olafsson, & Liefoogle, 2002). Another myth is that the problem exists primarily with boys—not true.

Can you recall some of your childhood experiences? Perhaps you yourself were victimized, perhaps you were a perpetrator (now reformed of course!) or a bystander. Research and literature on bullying has proliferated in recent years. Here are some practical suggestions for how you as a beginning teacher can help a potential victim, as well as deal with bullies, and even bystanders. Note that schools, on a larger scale, should implement schoolwide bully-prevention programs. Again, the suggestions that follow are for, you, the classroom teacher.

1. *Teacher Awareness*—Get to know your students outside the class-room. Watch how they interact at recess, in the school yard, and after school. Who are the social isolates in your class? Who are naturally

aggressive students? Listen to the content of what students say to each other. Even seemingly playful banter or teasing may be early signs. Nip them in the bud before they worsen. Don't tolerate disrespect among students for other students. Teach by example. Treat all students with dignity and respect.

2. *Conduct classroom discussions about bullying*—Read books on bullying with the class. Discuss case stories of bullying and its effects. Allow students to share their experiences. As a class, establish rules for treating each other respectfully. Set rules for reporting incidents to school officials.

3. *Don't blame the victim*—Victims are victims and are blameless. The onus of responsibility is on the bully! Bullies might defend themselves by rationalizing, if caught, that "well, he was looking to get beat up," or "she provoked me." Do not tolerate such excuses. Report incidents to the assistant principal, guidance counselor, school psychologist, and, or school social worker, if available. Empathize with the victim.

4. *Insist on a bully-free environment*—Establish a well-managed classroom with rules for proper behavior and consequences for misbehavior. Insist on civility, at the least. Strive though for mutual respect and caring.

5. *Empower bystanders to take action*—Discuss why bystanding is intolerable. Explain that they need not physically intervene to take action, but they can put group peer pressure on a bully or bullies or inform school official secretly if necessary. As the teacher or school official, make sure you keep the informant's information secret. Be discrete. Make sure no one finds out who provided the information on the incident in question.

Bullies have problems. They can benefit from anger management interventions. Ask your assistant principal or principal if bully-prevention programs exist in your school or district. If not, suggest that they look into effective programs.

Bullying is a complex social phenomenon that demands our attention. We haven't discussed many topics including, among others, specific bully-prevention programs, adult attitudes that may perpetuate bullying, family issues that might contribute to bullying, and techno-bullying.

As a new teacher, you are realizing that you are not merely *teaching a subject*. Rather, you are a *shaper of lives*. It's our most rewarding yet challenging responsibility. Do everything you can to help all youngsters achieve their very best, academically, socially, and emotionally. They'll remember you most for your caring, not for specifically what content you taught them.

STUDENT IDEA #7: STUDENTS
WITH LEARNING DISABILITIES AND NEEDS

You undoubtedly will encounter students who have varying degrees of difficulties with learning. Some students will have been officially designated as LD, or *Learning Disabled*, while others remain undiagnosed. As a classroom teacher, your responsibility is not of course to undertake the diagnosis (that should be left to specialists); rather your responsibility is to remain cognizant of potential problems and to develop ways of presenting materials appropriate to the special learning needs of students. You should be aware that students with learning problems may have

1. Difficulty paying attention

2. Poorly developed study skill strategies for learning

3. Poor motor skills

4. Difficulties in oral language skills

5. Difficulties in reading, written language, and mathematics

6. Poor time-management and organizational skills

7. Problems with social behavior

8. Difficulty adjusting to change

9. Immature speech patterns and delayed speech development

10. Difficulty sounding out words

11. Difficulty remembering names of familiar things

12. Trouble listening and following directions

13. An inability to tell time or know right from left

14. Poor self-image

Any others?

For each of the problems noted above, provide a strategy or technique that you could employ that might help.

_____

_____

_____

_____

_____

A Short Quiz on Students
With Disabilities (True or False)

_____1. The student with learning disabilities has average or above average intelligence.

_____2. The potential for a child with learning disabilities to succeed is present.

_____3. Ways to increase learning must be developed for the individual child.

_____4. Learning disability programs support the regular classroom and are not a replacement for the regular classroom.

_____5. Students with learning disabilities need to learn to function in a regular classroom setting.

_____6. Students with learning disabilities almost always need their self-concept improved.

_____7. If the problem is not recognized or diagnosed, it will not go away on its own and will continue to interfere with learning.

_____8. The child with learning disabilities can learn with assistance from school and home.

Answers: All true

What Are Learning Disabilities?

The term *learning disability* is one of the most misunderstood in education today. It's difficult to come up with a universally accepted definition of what a learning disability is. We do know that the child with learning disabilities appears normal physically, is of average or above average intelligence, and is one who fails to learn at the expected rate. It is believed that one out of every 15 school-age children in the United States has a learning disability.

A learning disability refers to one or more significant deficits in the learning process. A child with a learning disability most likely will demonstrate a discrepancy between expected and actual achievement in specific subject areas. The school and/or parent may be able to ascertain if a child has a learning disability by observing one or more of these traits:

1. *Hyperactivity*—The child is unable to sit still and concentrate on one thing for a period of time.

2. *Distractibility*—The child has a short attention span and cannot concentrate if surrounded with noise.

3. *Perception*—The child has poor visual and/or auditory skills.

4. *Language*— The child lacks verbal skills and is unable to put ideas into complete sentences.

Once a child is identified as being learning disabled, the school can play a big part in remedying the problem. The school can provide a quality program by attending to the needs of students with learning disabilities. Most, if not all of these students can function effectively in the regular, inclusive classroom if teachers are adequately prepared. The goals for the student with learning disabilities are the same as for the regular student, with one exception: the method of instruction, including the rate of presentation and reinforcement techniques, will vary depending on the student and his or her assessed needs. At times, the teacher may have to form homogeneous groupings in order to provide the child with learning disabilities extra help and support. Still, I am not in favor of segregating these students into "special" classes because of the negative effects on the students' self-esteem that may result. Teachers, in my opinion, can utilize an array of strategies (including differentiating instruction; see discussion later in this chapter) to accommodate the learning needs of all students. If you, the reader, ask more experienced teachers if inclusion is feasible, I doubt you will receive much positive feedback. Many older teachers were simply not trained to think inclusively and were certainly not given the appropriate pedagogical tools to differentiate instruction to accommodate all students' instructional and emotional needs.

The Underachiever

Have you observed a student not paying close attention in your class? Have you seen a student who does not complete assignments, is not working up to potential, or is not motivated to succeed in school? One or all of the above could be symptoms of an underachieving child. There are techniques that can be used in the classroom to help the underachiever.

If a student is getting a slow start on work we can help by doing the following:

1. Keep track of how much time passes before the student starts a task. If the student starts sooner than usual, offer praise as a reward.

2. When a task is assigned, use a timer and state that the task must be started before the timer goes off. Have some type of reward ready if all students start before the timer goes off.

3. Have the student work in an area with fewer distractions.

4. Give the student a simpler or shorter task than usual. Later, you can increase the difficulty or length of task as soon as the student progresses.

If the student isn't completing any assigned tasks, consider trying one of these options:

1. Break the task down into smaller units. It's important for the student to receive some form of success.

2. Do not let the student go to another task until the first task is completed. Avoid nagging the student to finish the task.

3. Make up a daily assignment card listing all tasks assigned. Have the student check off each assignment completed. This will show him or her what progress is being made.

The goal of working with an underachiever is for the student to be able to work independently with a reasonable amount of success. It may be necessary to rearrange your schedule to fit the needs of this student, because this type of student will need more rest breaks and added personal help. Helping an underachiever can be a very rewarding experience

The Accelerated Student

Meeting the needs of all students is imperative, including the advanced, gifted (I hate that word because all students in my view are "gifted" in some way; see Armstrong's book in Appendix A), or accelerated learner. If a teacher is prepared to differentiate instruction to accommodate the learning needs of students, then the needs of the accelerated learner can be met. Here are a few suggestions.

1. *Utilize homogeneous grouping*—Once you have identified above average learners, provide them opportunities to work with students of similar abilities on special activities and projects.

2. *Utilize their talents through peer tutoring*—Train and allow these accelerated learners to assist "slower" (different) learners in specific

learning activities. Students receiving the assistance will benefit, but so too will the advanced learners. They will benefit emotionally because they are helping fellow students. You are teaching them that all students are unique and should be valued. They, too, will learn the material better. I always say that if you want to really understand something, teach. These arguments in favor of peer tutoring can be shared with resistant parents who insist that such an activity detracts from the educational experiences of their children.

3. *Provide enrichment activities and individualized attention*—Do not ignore these accelerated learners by teaching to the "middle." Plan specific lessons for their needs. Plan on meeting and working with them individually.

The English Language Learner (ELL)

Our schools, as you very well know, are becoming more diverse than ever. The numbers of students for whom English is not the primary language is increasing. Helping second language learners is critical (Herrell & Jordan, 2004). I believe that we need to immerse these students into the mainstream as soon as possible. These students may initially need separate instruction from a licensed ELL teacher. After a short time, however, instruction should be provided in the mainstream, within the inclusive classroom. The "pull-out" philosophy must be, in my view, replaced with the "push-in" philosophy.

What are some teaching strategies you can employ?

1. *Total physical response*—Act out concepts and ideas by physically showing them what you mean by, for instance, *stand, sit,* or *eat.* Using as much visual stimulation as possible is key.

2. *Modeling*—Do not tell them that what they said or wrote is "wrong." Rather, model for them the proper way to say something. If a child says, "They was go." Say, "Oh, they were going to the park?" They'll respond, "Yes, they were going to the park." In written work, do not mark their entire composition with corrections. Focus on one or two main corrections (e.g., tense problems).

3. *Content area instruction*—ELL students generally need two years to become proficient in *basic interpersonal communication skills* (BICS). To develop such proficiency, they may need the help of a licensed ELL teacher, even in a pull-out situation. Once, however, they pass a language proficiency exam that assesses their BICS level, they should be placed in a regular class to work on *cognitive academic language proficiencies* (CALP). During this time you should

help the student build vocabulary much the same way you would help any other student. ELL students may, of course, need remedial work in that their vocabulary development may be several years behind their classmates. Providing them with lower level textbooks that are age-appropriate is advisable. In sum, by building vocabulary, you will build their confidence in their language skills and, thus, have a positive impact in the content areas.

My wife, Lisa, is an ELL teacher and she related these humorous and cute anecdotes.

- I had just concluded teaching a unit on American idioms to fourth graders. I wasn't sure how much they really understood these "strange" sayings. A few days later the teacher next door was yelling at her class. All the children stopped to listen. Then I said, "There's no one like Mrs. K." Carlos immediately responded, "Oh, no one can fill her shoes!" I was so pleased. Thanks to Mrs. K, I knew at least one child knew how to use an idiom.
- While working on a project with first graders, I noticed that Jose looked puzzled as he stared down at his paper. "What's wrong Jose?" "I have a dilemma," he explained. Shocked at his use of the word, I asked, "What is your *dilemma*?" Jose answered, "I don't know if I should color or cut first." Then I knew he understood the meaning of the word.
- A group of fifth graders from Albania was working on a writing assignment. One girl came over to me and told me that another girl, Olga, had used a bad word. I called Olga over and asked her what word she used. She responded, "bitch." I told her that that word was not a nice word to use. She looked devastated and apologized. I asked her how she had used the word. She said, "In the summer I go to the bitch."
- The same group of students was looking at a map of the United States. One of the students suddenly exclaimed, "Oh, oh, look my country." "Where, where?" I asked. "Right there," she responded, pointing to the map. "No honey," I said trying to keep a straight face, "that's Alabama."

STUDENT IDEA #8: ARE YOU A CULTURALLY RELEVANT TEACHER?

Maria Rodriguez is a middle school teacher in an urban Los Angeles school district and Mark Ramler is a high school teacher in a suburban district in Washington, D.C. Both teachers are aware that in almost 20 years about

40 percent of the nation's school-age children will represent people of color. They also know that schools have not met the educational needs of culturally diverse students very well. Although Maria and Mark come from different cultural backgrounds, they share a common pedagogical approach that emphasizes culturally appropriate and relevant teaching strategies. Mark and Maria are sensitive to and cognizant of the extent to which a student's cultural background may influence learning and attitude toward school in general. They are responsive to their students by incorporating elements of the students' culture in their teaching.

Culturally responsive teachers (Irvine & Armento, 2003) make special efforts to get to know their students really well. Mark and Maria ask their students to share stories about their family and cultural heritage. Students are encouraged to express themselves openly about their culture. Students obtain a tremendous sense of pride and a feeling of being appreciated. Maria assigns her students a homework assignment to write a story about their family. Sensitive to the fact that "family" may mean something different to different students, Maria encourages an accepting, warm atmosphere in her class conducive to student participation. She, in fact, shares her cultural background with students, which serves to ease their apprehensions and encourages them to share as well. Mark realizes that culturally relevant teaching is much more than reviewing the contributions of Dr. Martin Luther King, Jr., on his national day of observance. Mark's culturally responsive pedagogy is integrated in his curriculum and lessons on almost a daily basis, not just around holidays or special commemorations. He refers to King's work when, for instance, students don't appreciate a policy established by the school administration. He uses their anger as a teaching opportunity to share how Dr. King worked the system to effect the changes he desired. Then, Mark asks his students, "How might we work with administration to change that policy?"

Culturally responsive teachers know that students' culture (values, beliefs, and norms) might clash with institutional values, beliefs, and norms. Some students who do not volunteer in class, for example, might be perceived as lazy or learning disabled. Other students are taught not to look up into the eyes of an authority figure. Maria once overheard another teacher chastise an Asian girl for not looking at her when she spoke to her. The teacher said, "I know in your culture you don't look up when spoken to but you're in America now, look up at me." Culturally aware teachers take into consideration a student's cultural norms. Students feel appreciated and respected. Academic success is more likely when teachers are culturally sensitive.

Below are some suggestions for paying attention to social and cultural customs culled from Kottler and Kottler (2002, p. 20) in their *Children*

With Limited English: Teaching Strategies for the Regular Classroom. Pay attention to

- Verbal communication (pronunciation, patterns of speech, tempo of speech, and so on)
- Nonverbal communication (eye contact, meaning of gestures)
- Proxemics (spatial distance between people)
- Social values (peer group influences)
- Intellectual orientation (e.g., is frequent questioning valued or discouraged?)

In her book, *The Dreamkeepers,* Gloria Ladson-Billings (1994) compares culturally relevant teaching with what she terms assimilationist teaching. An assimilationist believes that ethnic groups should conform to the norms, values, expectations, and behaviors of the dominant social and cultural group. Culturally relevant teachers believe that all students can learn, albeit at different paces and in different ways. Assimilationist teachers believe that failure is inevitable for some students. Ask yourself, "Which teaching approach is better aligned with my preferred style?" Explain your response.

Misperceptions About Culturally Relevant Pedagogy

1. *Misperception:* Culturally responsive pedagogy is a new and special pedagogy that is relevant only to low-income, urban students of color.

Reality: Traditional pedagogy has always been culturally relevant. Middle-class and Euro-American students' culture is the accepted norm in most schools. Can you list some ways in which middle-class students' culture is acceptable in schools? How can schools appreciate the culture of all students?

_____

_____

_____

_____

2. *Misperception:* In schools with diverse students, only teachers of color are capable of demonstrating culturally responsive pedagogy.

Reality: Most teachers are white. It's unrealistic and undesirable to equate culturally relevant pedagogy only with teachers of color. All teachers, regardless of their ethnic background, are capable of incorporating this kind of pedagogy. All it takes is a sensitivity and an appreciation of its importance. Are you capable of teaching in culturally relevant ways? Explain. What factors might create difficulties in incorporating culturally relevant pedagogy?

_____

_____

_____

_____

3. *Misperception:* Cultural responsive pedagogy is primarily a teaching method.

Reality: Yes it is, but it's much more. Culturally relevant teaching is an attitude about teaching, students, the ways they can learn, and outside factors that influence successful learning. Why are you inclined or not inclined to teach this way? Explain. What training might you need to incorporate culturally relevant pedagogy?

_____

_____

_____

_____

4. *Misperception:* Culturally relevant teachers must become expert in a variety of cultures.

Reality: That's not possible, nor is it necessary. All that teachers need to know and believe is that culture plays a vital role in terms of understanding student behavior and learning. Do you really believe that culture makes a difference in student achievement? Explain. What argument can be offered to oppose culturally relevant pedagogy?

_____

_____

_____

_____

Source: Ideas drawn from Irvine & Armento, *Culturally Relevant Teaching* (2003), pp. 13–14.

STUDENT IDEA #9:
DIFFERENT WAYS OF LEARNING

By paying attention to the variety of ways your students learn, you can individualize instruction appropriately and, thus, meet their learning needs. Students will learn better when you pay attention to their learning preferences.

Sensory Modality Style

Some students learn best when you stimulate their senses—auditorily, tactily, and visually. Many students learn best when they are presented with visual stimulation. They learn best when you incorporate videos, pictures, charts, graphs, and other such material. These students learn through observation. Teachers who prepare *advance organizers* and use sensory aids help such students. Auditory learners prefer hearing information. They like listening to a story or a recording. You can help these students learn by, for instance, placing material on an audiotape, video, CD, and so forth. Tactile-kinesthetic learners enjoy the physical stimulation of touching things. Present information to these students through the use of manipulatives or role playing. Using a multisensory teaching approach is very beneficial. Therefore, when you plan a lesson ask yourself, "How can I incorporate as many senses as possible to assist these learners?"

Global/Analytical Styles

These learning styles take into consideration how your students process information. Global learners use the right hemisphere of their brain, which stresses spatial and relational processing. Global learners prefer to learn by considering the whole picture first and then breaking down the information into smaller parts. When they do so, they begin to recognize patterns and see relationships. On the other hand, analytical learners, using the left hemisphere of the brain, learn from parts to whole. When presented with new information, for example, these students seek out the details first. They are analytical thinkers. How do you prefer to learn? Do you first need to be given the context or whole picture, or do you prefer to get right into the details? Find out how many global versus analytic learners you have in class and provide for their learning preferences. How you do so is up to you. Can you think of ways to address both learning needs in a single lesson? Explain.

Field-Independent/Field-Dependent Styles

Students solve problems in different ways. Some students are able to separate information from its context or background. They are field independent in that they can work independently, are intrinsically motivated, and prefer an analytic approach to learning. Others are field dependent in that they need and prefer background information and context. They like to work with others, are extrinsically motivated, and take a global approach to learning.

True or false: Field-independent students like to work alone. Teachers can assist them by assigning research projects.

True or false: Field-dependent learners prefer cooperative learning, field trips, and learning with hands-on manipulatives.

Both statements are true.

Impulsive/Reflective Styles

Some students are quick to respond, to guess solutions or solve problems. They have high energy. On the other hand, others are more reflective. They take their time in responding. They are thoughtful and considerate learners. Teachers must be patient with these learners. Using wait time appropriately will help. I know someone I work with who needs a lot of time to think. I tend to move and go quickly. As I'm on my fifth point, she'll comment and go back to the second point. I didn't allow her to process. What might I have done?

Teach your visual learners using pictures, videos, graphs, charts, magazines, transparencies, LCD projections, computers, SMART Boards, diagrams, drawings, flash cards, handouts, television, and so on.

Teach your auditory learners using tapes, videotapes, lectures, stereos, oral directions, oral review, explanations, discussion, songs, and so forth.

Teach your kinesthetic learners using manipulatives, sense of touch, role playing, plays, demonstration, physical movement, real experiences, field trips, projects, pantomimes, and so on.

> **Reflect**
>
> We've learned thus far that students have varied needs and preferences, and that teachers should be aware of the role of race, gender, sexual orientation, and social class that may impact student learning. Teachers, as culturally relevant educators, accept and consider the student's culture in developing relevant curricula. Teachers must attend to the needs of the student with learning disabilities, the English language learner, the

underachiever, and the accelerated learner. How is it possible for a teacher to teach a class of such heterogeneous abilities? What strategies would you employ in a class of mixed abilities and needs? Jot some practical strategies below and then read on.

_____

_____

_____

_____

_____

STUDENT IDEA #10: DIFFERENTIATING INSTRUCTION: BUT HOW CAN I MEET THE NEEDS OF ALL MY STUDENTS?

Kids of the same age aren't all alike when it comes to learning.

—Carol Ann Tomlinson

Teachers must learn and know how to accommodate the varied and different learning abilities and styles of diverse students. Although I think schools were always diverse and the skill of differentiation (providing appropriate instruction to diverse learners in a diverse classroom) was always important, today it's even more important because students in your classroom come from many more diverse backgrounds and cultures. Differentiation is also important because today's classroom is more likely than ever to include students of varying abilities.

What Is Differentiated Instruction?

- Differentiated instruction can occur when teachers are aware and able to consider and deal with different learning needs and abilities of their students.
- Differentiated instruction is possible when teachers find opportunities for every student to succeed.
- It occurs when teachers can multitask.
- It occurs when teachers can manage a classroom well to allow for "structured chaos" but also know how to minimize excessive noise and disruptions.

- It occurs when a range of activities is provided: whole-class instruction, small-group activities (e.g., pairs, triads, quads), individualized activities (e.g., learning centers, independent study), and student-teacher conferences (e.g., working on contracts for learning).
- It occurs when teachers allow students to express themselves in diverse ways (e.g., artistically, musically, technologically, scientifically, athletically).
- Differentiated instruction allows students to express themselves in different ways (e.g., traditional compositions/essays, speeches, drama, music, building models).
- It considers assessment as an ongoing, integrated process.
- It can occur when a class works together to explore a particular topic or unit of study.
- It occurs when students discuss ideas freely and openly, giving all students a chance to participate in the discussion.
- It occurs when the whole class listens to individuals or small groups about how they plan to learn or study a particular topic.
- It occurs when students work in small groups.
- It occurs when the teacher works with selected students.
- It occurs when teachers consider that students learn differently and must construct meaning on their own.
- It occurs when teachers allow students to take responsibility for their own learning.
- It occurs when teachers use peer tutoring (i.e., advanced learners on particular topics work with students not as advanced).
- It occurs when teachers realize that different students have different strengths and weaknesses.
- It occurs when teachers provide for flexible grouping. For example, sometimes Maria will need remediation in reading by working with the teacher in a homogeneous group, but during math she is able to work independently because her skills are average or above average.
- It occurs when teachers realize students will complete work at different paces and that the teacher must plan for and provide learning activities for students who complete work before others.
- It occurs when students can plan activities on their own.
- It occurs when students can form their own interest groups to explore a topic of interest.
- Differentiated instruction allows for Web-questing (see Appendix B).
- It incorporates cooperative learning, multiple intelligences (see below), and diverse learning styles.

- It provides for literature circle opportunities (i.e., students read a common book and then form a group on their own to discuss the book, and then perhaps develop a common project based on the reading).

Differentiated instruction is NOT for teachers who cannot multitask or who prefer students to sit quietly and pay attention to "teacher talk."

Differentiated instruction means dividing your time among many students, giving quality time to each. That reminds me of a story. There were two famous educators who attended a wedding of a common friend. One stayed for only 30 minutes, while the other stayed for several hours. When the first educator left, everyone was happy and expressed appreciation to him for having attended. Much later, when the second educator was about to leave, someone asked him, "Why are you leaving already? You just came!"

The one who stayed longer at the affair asked his colleague, "What is your secret? How is it that you come for only a short time and everyone is happy, yet I stay for a long time and no one is satisfied?"

"It's really very simple," said the other. "I spend only a half hour but during those 30 minutes my heart is totally involved in the occasion. You may stay longer, but from the moment you walk in, you can't wait to leave. It's clear that your heart isn't in it. No wonder people say you've just come—they never really felt you were present!"

How can you make your students feel that you have given them complete attention?

How many of the following points can you check off?

_____ 1. I call on students equitably.

_____ 2. I care for all students.

_____ 3. All students, regardless of ability, can learn from one another.

_____ 4. I am attuned to the different learning needs and abilities of my students.

_____ 5. I display the work of all students, regardless of ability or achievement (which also reminds me of a story; see next page).

_____ 6. I help students appreciate, tolerate, and accommodate their similarities and differences in learning, culture, and interest.

_____ 7. I celebrate the successes of all students.

_____ 8. I consciously incorporate multiple intelligences whenever feasible.

_____ 9. I consciously incorporate learning styles whenever feasible.

_____10. I preassess students' knowledge prior to instruction so that I can develop appropriate lessons.

_____11. I use a variety of assessment strategies throughout the unit of instruction.

_____12. I am flexible in terms of allowing students to demonstrate different ways that they have learned the material (in other words, I give students choices about how to express their learning).

_____13. I offer different homework options.

_____14. I give different kinds of tests.

_____15. I grade holistically, not relying on one sole test or measure.

_____16. In questioning all students, I prompt and probe equitably.

_____17. I give the same wait time to slow learners as I do to advanced learners.

_____18. I use a variety of grouping procedures, including whole-class instruction and small grouping.

_____19. I use peer tutoring as necessary.

_____20. I find ways for all students to excel.

_____21. I use a variety of teaching strategies.

_____22. I take into consideration students' interests and needs in planning instruction.

_____23. I give students texts that are at varied levels and readability.

_____24. I incorporate technology into instruction wherever feasible and useful.

_____25. I differentiate instruction most of the time.

Now for a quick, true story: When I was an assistant principal, I entered Mrs. Smith's classroom one morning and marveled at her beautifully decorated room. I was happy to notice several bulletin boards displaying student work. On closer inspection, I saw boards titled "Our Best Spellers," "Our Best Math Work," "Our Best Writers." I spoke with Mrs. Smith afterward and asked if she didn't agree that all students need to be, and should be, acknowledged in some way. She agreed and asked me to return the following week, which I did. As I perused the bulletin boards again I noticed that she indeed had included all students' work and she removed the word *Best* from each board. She posted Sarah's score of 45 on her math test, Renaldo's 55 in spelling, and Jean's 60 in writing! Ugh . . .

Postscript: She later assured me that these students would do better next time. Smart teachers find ways for all students to excel and achieve in positive ways.

Using Multiple Intelligences as You Differentiate Instruction

Differentiated instruction acknowledges that each student comes to class with a variety of learning preferences or styles. Each processes information differently. Each student also has a different intelligence, according to famed Harvard researcher Howard Gardner (2000). He identifies eight different intelligences that are common to all people and which vary in degree. They include

1. *Verbal/Linguistic*—Verbally or linguistically intelligent students make varied use of language. They are good with words. They enjoy journal writing, compositions, essays, word games, and reading. These are your future journalists, storytellers, poets, lawyers, and so on.

2. *Logical/Mathematical*—Logically or mathematically intelligent students reason well, see cause-and-effect relationships easily, and see numerical patterns. They enjoy experiments, number games, critical thinking, and mental calculations. These are your future mathematicians, scientists, accountants, and computer programmers.

3. *Visual/Spatial*—Visually or spatially intelligent students think in pictures and images. They have the ability to perceive, transform, and re-create different aspects of the physical world. They enjoy art activities, imagination games, maps, videos, and problem solving. These students are your future architects, photographers, artists, pilots, and mechanical engineers.

4. *Musical/Rhythmic*—Musically or rhythmically intelligent students are sensitive to pitch, melody, rhythm, and tone. They enjoy singing, listening, musical games, audios, and musical instruments. They are your future musicians.

5. *Interpersonal*—Interpersonally intelligent students have the ability to notice and make distinctions among other people. They are people-oriented. They enjoy conversing and interacting with others. They enjoy cooperative learning, role playing, simulations, and teaching. They are your future politicians, salespeople, and teachers.

6. *Intrapersonal*—Intrapersonally intelligent students have the ability to understand themselves very well and understand others' feelings. They can "feel" the other person's needs and desires. They enjoy individualized instruction, independent study, and reflective practices. They are your future therapists, counselors, theologians, and social workers.

7. *Bodily/Kinesthetic*—Bodily kinesthetic intelligent students can handle their body and objects skillfully. They enjoy physical activities, games, drama, and manipulating objects. They are your future athletes, craftspeople, physicians, and mechanics.

8. *Naturalist*—Naturalisticly intelligent students have a keen understanding of their environment. They enjoy working outdoors, in gardens, in botanical gardens, with animals, and so on. They are your future gardeners, botanists, pet owners, and the like.

Take this quiz and identify the correct intelligence based on the preceding list.

1. I can use both inductive and deductive reasoning to solve problems. I like to categorize information, find sequences, and determine cause-and-effect relationships. I love to work on projects that don't involve too much essay writing or oral speech presentations._____

2. I work well with others in pairs or teams. _____

3. I learn best by watching first. I love art projects and to build models. I also like role-playing activities. _____

4. I'm very sensitive to sounds and prefer to express myself using songs.

   _____

5. I like to think a lot. I need time to think and reflect about what I'm doing. I like to be alone sometimes and prefer journal writing.

   _____

6. I love pantomime, charades, and building things. _____

7. I love to debate and argue to make my point. I enjoy reading and to teach others. _____

8. I enjoy plants and I am fascinated with natural phenomena. I have three pets. _____

Answers: 1. logical/mathematical, 2. interpersonal, 3. spatial/visual, 4. musical/rhythmic, 5. intrapersonal, 6. bodily/kinesthetic, 7. verbal/linguistic, 8. naturalist

The following story illustrates how students with different intelligences can work together well.

> Sarah, Jason, Jose, and Robert were working together on a project. Sarah (verbal/linguistic intelligent) was a very serious, diligent reader who loved to write. Jason (interpersonal, intelligent), was very popular and knew how to interact well with other students. Jason was well liked by classmates. Jose (musical/rhythmic intelligent) was very artistic and loved music. Robert (logical/mathematical intelligent) was well organized and enjoyed crunching numbers. Each student worked in the group according to his or her abilities. Each offered a unique contribution. Robert planned the project and offered general oversight and direction, while Jason kept the group socially intact and happy. Jose did all the artistic work and wrote a song to introduce the project. Sarah did a considerable amount of the writing.

Can you think of ways you can integrate multiple intelligences into your lessons? How does knowledge of multiple intelligences assist in differentiating instruction? Explain by giving examples from your classroom.

Reflection

Given the increasing numbers of diverse students with varied learning needs, differentiation is so critical for success in today's classrooms. You must realize that differentiation is more than just dividing your time among many students. It is also about offering choices on how to learn and ways that can engage learners in ways they learn best. What choices would you give your students? How can you maximize student interest in the way they learn best? Share ideas with a colleague.

STUDENT IDEA #11:
THE CHALLENGE OF INCLUSION

The ultimate rationale for inclusion is based not on law or regulations or teaching technology, but on values. What kinds of people are we and what kind of society do we wish to develop? What values do we honor?

—A. Gartner and D. K. Lipsky

Inclusion is a belief system. It is a process of facilitating an educational environment that provides access to high-quality education for all students (Allan, 1999; Barton, 1998; Capper, Frattura, & Keyes, 2000; Huber, 2002; Kochhar, West, & Taymans, 2000; McLeskey & Waldron, 2001; Wolfendale, 2000). Effective teachers believe that all children can learn together in the same schools and the same classrooms, with services and supports necessary so that they can succeed. Maintaining high expectations for all students, believing in their potential, providing needed services to fully participate are essential. No child should be demeaned, nor should students have their uniqueness ignored or belittled. Students with disabilities should be educated with students without disabilities as much as possible. Special classes or removal of children from the regular education environment should occur only when the nature or severity of the disability is such that education in the regular classroom cannot be achieved satisfactorily with the use of supplementary support services (Elliott & McKenney, 1998; Morse, 2002).

Practices that are inclusionary are based on democratic thought and are a hope for the future. Such hopeful thinking is reflected in the writings of Clough and Corbet (2000), Freire (1974; 1994), Kohl (1998), Macedo (1994), McLaren (1994), and Oakes and Lipton (1999).

As a classroom teacher, you are expected to develop educational programs that serve a diversity of students, including those with disabilities. Special education laws since 1975 (Public Law 94-142), including the more recent Individuals with Disabilities Education Act (IDEA) amendments, have challenged teachers to help all children learn side by side, though they may have varied educational needs (Kochhar, West, & Taymans, 2000). In this chapter, we have introduced some teaching strategies to assist you (e.g., differentiated instruction). Some suggestions for making inclusion work for you follow.

Special Services/Supports

- *Exhibit all students' work*
- *Focus on strengths*
- *Promote friendships*
- *Teach acceptance*

1. Make sure that students have not simply been "dumped" into your classroom without special services and supports provided by the administration or special education team in your school or district. Seek advice from your vice principal, mentor, or a colleague.

2. Make each child in your class feel special by acknowledging the good work they all do and ensuring that, for instance, you post work up on classroom or hall bulletin boards from all students.

3. Focus on what children can do rather than always on what they cannot. For example, let each student demonstrate on an occasion a special talent he or she may have (e.g., karate, art, singing, juggling).

4. Encourage and implement activities that promote the development of friendships and relationships between students with and without disabilities. For example, use cooperative learning strategies (see Chapter 6).

5. Teach all your students every day to understand and accept individual differences.

Here is a true story that happened to someone very close to me.

Students With Disabilities—"It's unfortunate, but we simply can't accommodate your child's 'peculiar' learning style."

Sara spoke at a relatively young age. Born to professional educators, Sara was continually exposed to a rich and varied literate environment. Despite her seemingly precocious development, Sara experienced difficulty in her early grades, 1 through 3, keeping up with her classmates. In grade 5, she had problems with retention of information and could not learn as many scientific facts as other students. Sara came home each evening with much homework. The work was frustrating her and she would inevitably cry. As the school year progressed, the workload also increased as did her frustration levels. Sara asked her parents to send her to another school. "I hate my school; the kids tease me and they call me 'dummy.'" Despite extra help at home with a special tutor, Sara's educational and social woes continued. At a parent-teacher conference, her parents were told that Sara "tries hard but just can't keep up." A meeting with the principal proved memorable. After praising Sara's sweet demeanor and fine character traits, the principal suggested that perhaps finding another school would be in Sara's best interests. "It's unfortunate, but we simply can't accommodate your child's 'peculiar' learning style."

Shocked by the principal's naivety, if not ignorance of current peda-
gogic and learning theories, the parents reluctantly registered their
precious Sara into a private school that provided resource room
assistance as well as inclusion class options.

Many schools neither recognize nor appreciate that all children learn
differently, or if they do, they take little or no action to match pedagogical
strategies to varied learning styles. The one-size-fits-all approach to pedagogy and curriculum is ingrained in the minds and actions of many educators.
Teachers, until recently, have not been prepared to teach a diverse group of
students with varied learning styles. Research consistently demonstrates
that most classrooms, especially at the middle and high school levels,
"use traditional instructional methods such as lecture, assigned readings,
drill, and independent practice" (Lauria, 2005, p. 68). Though many
students do thrive in traditional classroom settings, many more do not (see,
e.g., Dunn, et al., 1990). Extensive research has been conducted that
demonstrates that poor academic achievement is often a consequence of a
teacher's inability to match instructional strategies to a child's learning
styles preferences (Dunn & DeBello, 1999). Students whose learning
styles do match the teacher's instructional approaches are often excluded
from classroom discourse.

Reflection

What's your reaction to the scenario above with Sara? How would you
accommodate her in your class?

_____

_____

_____

_____

Assess Your Attitudes Toward Inclusion

Inclusive education means that all students with disabilities are mainstreamed and become the responsibility of the general education class
teacher, who is supported by special education specialists and services.

NOTE: I'd appreciate if you'd e-mail me your responses to the following self assessment
as I'm conducting a study on the topic of inclusion; thanks (glanz@yu.edu). Or, mail
them to the publisher, Corwin (see address information inside front cover of this book).

I teach primarily in a: _____ private school _____ public school

Grade level I teach: _____

I am primarily a: _____ general education teacher _____ special education teacher

Number of students in my class on average: _____

Number of students in my school: _____

If not currently teaching, the grade level I taught the most: _____

My gender: _____ male _____ female

Age: _____ 21–30 _____ 31–40 _____ 40+

Teaching experience: ____ less than 1 year ____ 1–4 years ____ 5–9 years ____ 10–14 years ____ 14+ years

I am a parent of a child with a disability: ____ yes ____ no

I have a friend or relative who is disabled in some way: ____ yes ____ no

I currently or have previously taught in an inclusive classroom: _____ yes _____ no

On a scale of 1–10 with 10 being expert, I would rate my knowledge of disabilities as: _____

My definition of *disability*:

_____

_____

_____

Circle any or all of the categories or types of students with disabilities that are currently in your class(es):

    emotional   physical   learning   visual
hearing   other (please specify)

Check response(s) that best explains how students with disabilities are placed in classes in your school:

_____ no systematic procedure is used _____ students with disabilities are segregated for most of day in a resource room _____ students are mainstreamed regularly _____ we have an inclusion model in our school (heterogeneously grouped) _____ other (please explain)

(Continued)

(Continued)

For each statement below, indicate the extent to which you agree or disagree with the statement by circling the appropriate number.						
Strongly agree = 6 Agree = 5 Agree somewhat = 4 Disagree somewhat = 3 Disagree = 2 Strongly disagree = 1						
I have a high level of understanding of inclusive education.	6	5	4	3	2	1
Students' progress should be assessed according to ability as shown by classroom performance rather standardized tests.	6	5	4	3	2	1
It is important to make instructional modifications for students who need assistance.	6	5	4	3	2	1
My school has a broad continuum of special education services for meeting the needs of all students.	6	5	4	3	2	1
Inclusion of students with mild disabilities into regular classes is generally an effective strategy.	6	5	4	3	2	1
I have input into the type of students with disabilities who are placed in the regular classroom.	6	5	4	3	2	1
Keeping academic expectations consistent for all students is important.	6	5	4	3	2	1
Maximum class size should be lowered when including students with disabilities.	6	5	4	3	2	1
The inclusion of students with disabilities into regular classrooms can be beneficial to the other students in the class.	6	5	4	3	2	1
I have support from my supervisor(s) to try new ideas and implement creative strategies.	6	5	4	3	2	1
Students should be serviced in general education classes regardless of disability.	6	5	4	3	2	1

It is important to keep behavioral expectations the same for all students.	6	5	4	3	2	1
Teachers in my school strongly support inclusive education.	6	5	4	3	2	1
Pull-out programs in resource rooms are the best way to service students with disabilities.	6	5	4	3	2	1
General education teachers must spend a great deal of time with students with disabilities.	6	5	4	3	2	1
Students should be grouped in ways that allow a wide variety of abilities in each class.	6	5	4	3	2	1
I would welcome a child with no hands in my class.	6	5	4	3	2	1
Slow learners should receive special help outside the general education classroom.	6	5	4	3	2	1
Opportunities for staff development are provided by my school and meet my needs for professional growth.	6	5	4	3	2	1
Inclusion in the general education classroom will harm the educational progress of the student with a disability.	6	5	4	3	2	1
Placement of a student with a disability into a general education classroom is disruptive to students without disabilities.	6	5	4	3	2	1
I would certainly be eager to team teach with another teacher in an inclusive classroom.	6	5	4	3	2	1
I would welcome students with severe disabilities into my classroom, as long as specialist assistance would be available, if needed.	6	5	4	3	2	1
My supervisor is not at all familiar or supportive with inclusive practice.	6	5	4	3	2	1

(Continued)

(Continued)

I am professionally prepared to teach an inclusive class.	6	5	4	3	2	1
I would welcome additional professional development to help better serve students with disabilities.	6	5	4	3	2	1
I am knowledgeable and skillful at differentiating instruction.	6	5	4	3	2	1
Parents of students with disabilities, generally, are in favor of inclusion.	6	5	4	3	2	1
Parents of students without disabilities, generally, are in favor of inclusion.	6	5	4	3	2	1
Administrators, generally, are in favor of inclusion.	6	5	4	3	2	1
Students with disabilities, generally, are in favor of inclusion.	6	5	4	3	2	1
Students without disabilities, generally, would not mind to have students with mild or even severe disabilities included in the general education classroom.	6	5	4	3	2	1
Teachers, generally, oppose inclusion.	6	5	4	3	2	1
Given my school's vision and philosophy, inclusive practice would never be welcomed.	6	5	4	3	2	1
Most teachers cannot teach to different student learning styles.	6	5	4	3	2	1
Inclusion is not fair to general education students.	6	5	4	3	2	1
Although I'm committed to social justice and I care about all students, including students with disabilities in my classroom is unreasonable.	6	5	4	3	2	1
Excluding children with disabilities, no matter what the disability, is unethical.	6	5	4	3	2	1

Learning disabled children can learn when their learning needs are accommodated in the general education classroom.	6	5	4	3	2	1
I'd welcome a hearing impaired child in my classroom, and I am able or would try my utmost to accommodate to that child's learning needs.	6	5	4	3	2	1
Pushing services into the classroom takes away from the child's mandate to receive individualized instruction.	6	5	4	3	2	1
A balance of push-in and pull-out services is most beneficial for young students with special needs.	6	5	4	3	2	1
Students with *mild* learning disabilities *should* be educated in classes together with non–learning disabled students.	6	5	4	3	2	1
Students with *severe* learning disabilities *should* be educated in classes together with non–learning disabled students.	6	5	4	3	2	1
Gifted students *should* be educated in classes together with nongifted students.	6	5	4	3	2	1
General education teachers should be required to make the accommodations and remediate as necessary for ALL students in their classes.	6	5	4	3	2	1
Those who have learning disabilities *should not* be educated in the same classes as non–learning disabled students.	6	5	4	3	2	1
I have a child of my own who is disabled in some way.	6	5	4	3	2	1
I believe in inclusion and would be willing to teach in an inclusive classroom.	6	5	4	3	2	1
I believe in inclusion, but it's unrealistic in Jewish day schools and yeshivot.	6	5	4	3	2	1
The needs of students with special needs are best served through special, separate classes.	6	5	4	3	2	1

(Continued)

(Continued)

The challenge of being in an ordinary classroom will promote the academic growth of the child with special needs.	6	5	4	3	2	1
Placing a child with special needs in a general class will hinder academic growth of general education students.	6	5	4	3	2	1
Inclusion offers mixed group interaction that will foster understanding and acceptance of difference.	6	5	4	3	2	1
The child with special needs probably will develop academic skills more rapidly in a special classroom than in a general education classroom.	6	5	4	3	2	1
Including children with special needs will promote their social independence.	6	5	4	3	2	1
Inclusion is likely to have a negative affect on the emotional development of the child with special needs.	6	5	4	3	2	1
Students with special needs should be given every opportunity to function in the general classroom setting, where possible.	6	5	4	3	2	1
I favor full inclusion.	6	5	4	3	2	1
I am against full inclusion.	6	5	4	3	2	1
I favor mainstreaming.	6	5	4	3	2	1
I am against mainstreaming.	6	5	4	3	2	1

CONCLUSION

The students in your class are unique individuals that deserve special attention. I'm certain that you must realize the awesome responsibility you face each day. Trying to understand the needs of each child can seem overwhelming, if not impossible. Don't hesitate to ask specialists, or even parents for assistance. The more information you have about a student, the more likely you will best meet that child's educational needs. Don't get discouraged. Sometimes you won't see much progress or even receive acknowledgment for your efforts. Persist. You are a professional who realizes your primary task is to make each student feel accepted and special. In time, you will develop new ways of meeting each student's needs. Take time to enjoy your students. They are worth it.

Follow-Up Questions/Activities

1. Each of us has experienced learning challenges. Describe some difficulties you have or have had with learning. How can this knowledge help you to deal with students you encounter who also have learning difficulties?

2. What would you do if you discovered that one of your students had difficulty paying attention (e.g., was always fidgety in class)?

3. How would you, or do you, foster inclusion and differentiate instruction in your classroom?

4. Make a list of each child in your present class and identify one learning strength and one learning weakness for each. Specify what new approach you may have learned in this chapter or book, thus far, to assist you in helping this child.

5. Write an essay titled "Who Are the Students in My Class?" Share your essay with a colleague. Have this colleague describe your class to you. What additional information might your colleague need to have?

ACTIVITY 4

Go to Google or your favorite search engine and type in *lesson plans*. You'll find a lot of material. Record your findings below and then share your findings with a colleague. Describe anything useful that you found.

_____

_____

_____

_____

_____

_____

_____

_____

_____

_____

_____

_____

_____

_____

_____

_____

_____

_____

_____

_____

_____

_____

_____

_____

_____

_____

How Should
I Write
Lesson Plans?

What we hope ever to do with ease, we must learn first to do with diligence.

—Samuel Johnson

Teacher planning is the thread that weaves the curriculum, or the what of teaching, with the instruction, or the how of teaching. The classroom is a highly interactive and demanding place. Planning provides for some measure of order in an uncertain and changing environment.

—H. Jerome Freiberg and Amy Driscoll

Focus Questions

1. What are three reasons why lesson planning is so critical?

2. Why do experienced teachers also have to plan?

3. What are the most critical elements of a lesson?

4. Homework is a controversial topic. Some educators are in favor of homework while others are opposed. What's your stand?

5. True or false: Planning occurs before, during, and after a lesson.

LESSON PLAN IDEA #1:
UNDERSTANDING THE LESSON PLAN

Lesson planning—the term suggests many different connotations. So many teachers would say it implies a necessary but unpleasant chore. Others might describe it as burdensome paperwork, an outline for instruction, or even a helpful guide. No matter whether required or not, no matter whether written elaborately or briefly, lesson plans are a part of all teachers' weekly tasks. Without a plan, instruction becomes a random assortment of activities with little rhyme or reason.

Lesson planning is usually associated with only a written design developed by the teacher. Actually, it involves two activities.

1. Mental planning

2. Keeping a written plan book

In mental planning, teachers consider questions, reflect on the topic, and envision what might occur in subsequent lessons. Mental planning is an important and legitimate prerequisite for the written plan. It takes into consideration such things as the textbook, a list of prescribed skills, and library materials. It's not unlike an athlete who mentally prepares by envisioning a successful shot. You too need to envision what your lesson will accomplish, what you want students to learn and know at the end, and how you will go about achieving your objectives.

The plan book is a shorthand outline of what will develop in the classroom based on the mental planning. The written plan serves as a reminder of topics, concepts, skills, and activities that the teacher wants to be sure to use at some point. Basically, it's the teacher's road map. Different schools require different plan books and plans. This chapter merely highlights the main parts of a lesson.

Lesson plans are most effective when the interrelationships of skills are fostered. Most of us can agree with the premise that schooling should offer children opportunities to make connections, to think, and to expand learning. It is false to assume that just because students learn various skills that they automatically will know how to use them in relationships. It's also false to assume that texts make the connections for us. Some textbooks do only a fair job in structuring for continuity. Thus, it becomes the teacher's responsibility to develop lessons that expand thinking and interrelate skills. For example, teachers can develop reading lessons that help students to learn that punctuation, context, and phonics clues can all be used together to interpret the written word. Subjects such as science, reading, and social studies can be interrelated. For example, a story about Columbus can be related to map-reading skills taught in social studies and to navigation by constellations in science. Children need to be encouraged to make connections between various lessons, between subjects, and between in-school and out-of-school life.

Another good practice is to develop long-range as well as short-range goals. Having long-range goals (monthly, quarterly, or yearly) helps teachers maintain an overall perspective and helps to serve as a guide for day-to-day instruction.

It is very important to use teacher judgment when writing short-range objectives. Some subject objectives and daily plans, such as reading and mathematics, are greatly influenced by texts. Texts do not always provide the continuity necessary for effective learning. Also, text suggestions often need to be modified to fit individual classroom situations. Teachers should make changes in textbook guides based on criteria such as the following:

- Do these students already know this material? Does it need reviewing?
- Will this activity fit into the amount of time I have?
- How can I relate to what the students know?
- Could I do part of this activity as independent work for the group to complete while I work with another group?

When determining objectives and writing lesson plans, you should consider students' learning styles. Some students are fast, others slow; some are easily motivated, others difficult to motivate; some do well in large groups, others in small groups; some do better with written work, others with oral work. By taking such learning characteristics into consideration, you can develop strategies that are appropriate for various classes.

It is a good habit to include the method of evaluation. The primary purpose of testing is to determine the extent of student mastery of the objectives, not to determine grades. For any lesson to be productive, you must receive feedback as to how well the objectives are being met. To receive useful feedback, you should spend sufficient time incorporating good evaluation measures as part of lesson planning.

Some other helpful points for effective daily plans include the following:

- Estimate the time required for various activities; plan enough—don't get caught short (students are more apt to get in trouble when they have too much free time on their hands); have additional activities in reserve for those occasions when your regular lessons are completed early.
- Jot down any changes you would like to make for future use while they are fresh in your mind.
- Check off items as they are completed.

- Be flexible and make adjustments as you go. (You, as a teacher, know best how to adjust your lesson plans based on your evaluation of students' progress. Sometimes you need to move slower and give more instruction before proceeding to new objectives.)

The actual format of lesson plans is not as important as the process of developing the plans. Use whatever format is most workable for you, as long as it is clear and easy to follow (unless, of course, you are required to use a certain format). As implied by the points already described, consider using the following process when writing lesson plans:

1. First, analyze students' learning styles.

2. Next, specify long-range goals (may be monthly, quarterly, or yearly). These long-range goals should determine your daily lesson plans.

3. Then specify objectives.

4. After objectives are stated, select or design activities and materials.

5. Include how students will be tested to determine the effectiveness of instruction.

6. After instruction, evaluate activities and make revisions as necessary.

No matter whether your planning is detailed or general, it is important. It helps you to organize your thoughts, meet objectives, coordinate materials, and be prepared for instruction. By planning properly, your teaching will be more effective.

LESSON PLAN IDEA #2: ESSENTIAL COMPONENTS AND CRITERIA OF A SUCCESSFUL LESSON

Aims and Objectives

1. Meaningful and appropriate to the levels of students

2. Elicited from students

3. Personalized in question form

4. Definite and expressed

5. Achieved and realized

6. Written on board and in student's notebook

7. Varied use of Bloom's Taxonomy (discussed later in the chapter)

Decide what your goals are in teaching this unit. In looking over the content that you plan to teach in a lesson, you must ask the question "What do I want the pupils to derive from the lesson that will be meaningful and worthwhile?" The aim that you decide upon will be the backbone of the lesson. All activities should point toward the achievement of that aim. Let the student derive the aim rather than having the teacher state it at the outset. This helps the students identify with the lesson and make it their own. Your motivation should be the vehicle for revealing the aim to the class. The objectives do not necessarily have to be formally stated. Rather, they are written explicitly in your plan book. The aim is a general statement based on your objectives. Some teachers prefer to inform students about both the aim and objectives. For sample objectives, see the Web site listing for Web Quest in Appendix B.

Motivation

1. Arouses interest

2. Sustains interest

3. Connects to aim of lesson

4. Challenges students

5. Relates to students' experiences

6. Easy transition to lesson

Motivation is a device to arouse student interest in the content to be taught, and also to reveal to the class the aim of the lesson. Effective motivations stimulate curiosity and utilize the experiences and the knowledge of the pupils. Some devices that can be used to motivate a lesson are challenging statements, personal experiences, cartoons, a problem, a chart, or anecdotes. Some call this stage *anticipatory sets.*

Questions

1. Well phrased and understood

2. Stimulate critical thinking

3. Well distributed among students in class

4. Check for understanding

Pitfalls in Questioning

1. Calling on a student first and then asking a question

2. Relying only on volunteers

3. Saying "tell me" not "tell us"

4. Framing multiple questions

Student Responses

1. Avoid choral responses.

2. Don't repeat student response.

3. Use praise, prompt (student answers incorrectly), and probe (student answers correctly but lacks depth) techniques.

Aside from developing your aim and learning objectives, your use of questions is the most critical part of your lesson. The success or failure of a lesson is largely determined by the questioning techniques employed, by the quality of the questions, and by the sequence in which the questions are asked. Questioning is a powerful teaching tool. Through questioning, you can develop student learning styles and habits, stimulate higher levels of thinking, foster new learning, and evaluate the progress of achievement. You actually can mold students' minds through the effective use of questions.

Unfortunately, we often do not make as effective use of questions as we could, and as we should. Research has shown that most teacher questions are on the lower levels of thinking, predominantly information and short answers, rather than on the higher levels, such as judgment, inference, application, analysis, and synthesis. This problem can be overcome by becoming familiar with the thinking hierarchy (such as Bloom's Taxonomy) and by generating questions that promote higher thinking.

Benjamin Bloom's taxonomy is one of the most important concepts in all of teaching. Basically, he asserts that learning occurs in a hierarchical manner, beginning with simple thinking processes and proceeding step by step through more complex processes. He classifies six major learning behaviors or ways of thinking, that translate into six types of questions you need to consider and use appropriately.

Bloom's Taxonomy
Knowledge
Comprehension
Application
Analysis
Synthesis
Evaluation

1. *Knowledge*—The lowest, most basic level of learning or thinking occurs when students are asked to recall or recognize bits of information. Key words here are *who, what, when, which, how many, name, identify, recall,* and so on. Examples include "Who discovered the Indian Ocean?" "What happened to Alice in the story?" "Where did her mother send her?" Students merely are asked to recall bits of information. At this stage, students may merely memorize information but may not comprehend what they have learned. I once had a fourth grader who had phenomenal decoding skills who could read every word in the *New York Times.* Everyone marveled at his ability to "read." He really couldn't read because he could not understand what he had read, which brings us to Bloom's second and higher level.

2. *Comprehension*—This next behavior or thinking level occurs when students can explain or paraphrase information. Asking students to explain in their own words what a concept means or give an example may indicate that students comprehend the information. Key words here are de*scribe, explain, use your own words, translate, interpret,* and so forth. Examples include "What do the words _____ mean?" "Explain what _____ means." Ask a student "What is a Lut?" He doesn't know, so you tell him "A Lut is a Zut." Now, you ask him again, "Okay, what is a Lut?" He responds, "It's a Zut." Though he has some knowledge—that is, that a Lut is a Zut—he may not understand what a Lut really is. Ask, "Okay, explain in your own words what is a Lut? Zut?" If he can explain correctly, you may assume he comprehends the information.

3. *Application*—This next higher level of thinking or behavior requires the student to use the information learned to solve a specific problem or apply it to a situation. Key words here are *solve, choose, apply,* and so on. Examples include "How might the *Roe v. Wade* decision affect human rights issues?" "How can you apply what we have learned to . . . ?" A student, for instance, may know a rule of grammar and may even understand the rule. However, can he or she apply the rule to a new situation or context; for example, using it correctly in an essay?

4. *Analysis*—This higher cognitive domain of learning expects students to take a situation apart and to understand the relationship between parts. For example, you may show your third-grade class a picture of three groups of animals and ask them which group does not belong. The student is required to analyze the various characteristics to arrive at an answer. Key words here are *analyze, show, how, distinguish,* and so on. Examples include "Who can distinguish between fact and opinion in the article we just read?" "Why did the balloon inflate?" "How does the use of similes convey an emotional impact to the reader?" "What is the difference between _____ and _____?"

5. *Synthesis*—At this higher level, students can creatively put elements or information together to form a new structure or idea. Key words here are *create, develop, devise, predict, invent,* and so on. Examples include "Given the elements of a lesson, you will develop an original lesson of your own, put together the carburetor, invent a machine that would make life easier."

6. *Evaluation*—This is the highest level according to Bloom. Too often, teachers ask students to make judgments about something without challenging them at the prior levels of thinking or behavior. Evaluation requires students to state their opinions, justify their points of view or answers. Key words here are *decide, judge, discuss, choose, recommend, give opinion, explain why, evaluate,* and so on. Examples include "Was the story good? Why or why not?" "Which technique would be better? Explain." "Who can tell the class what is wrong with . . . ?" This final level encourages critical reasoning and judgment.

Here's a little quiz for you. Identify the correct level of Bloom's Taxonomy in each of these objectives:

_____1. Given any art materials of your choice, you will create an oil painting using no more than four colors.

_____2. Given a number of objects that you have not previously seen, you will identify all those that are squares.

_____3. Given 20 new multiplication examples, you will solve 80 percent of them correctly.

_____4. Given eight poems written by European poets, you will determine the common theme.

_____5. From memory, list the eight planets in our solar system.

_____6. Given five master's theses, you will select the best research design.

Answers: 1. synthesis, 2. comprehension, 3. application, 4. analysis, 5. knowledge, 6. evaluation.

A mnemonic for recalling Bloom's Taxonomy is *Keep Calm At All Sports Events.*

However, another problem in questioning is frequently overlooked. The vast majority of questions asked in classrooms are by the teacher. Students ask few questions, other than for assistance or clarification. If we are to develop active minds, not just passive and reactive ones, we must encourage students to learn how to formulate effective questions, for it is through questions that productive thinking occurs. Pupils must learn to question so that they can be critical processors and consumers of information. This process should begin in elementary school and not be limited to the higher grades, for learning and thinking patterns begin at early ages and shape all learning thereafter.

Here are several techniques to involve students in questioning.

1. *Class Work/Homework Questions*—Have students make up questions for class work and or homework. For example, tell your students, "Make up five questions that would test whether someone had really understood the assigned readings. Make sure the answers are not in any one sentence." This exercise promotes thinking, as well as learning how to write questions. As a bonus, you can choose a few of the best questions to duplicate and give to the class.

2. *Journalist Style Questioning*—Invite a guest to class, but instead of having a presentation followed by "Are there any questions?" have students prepare questions in advance. Help students write questions that go beyond facts and lower cognition levels.

For example, students might prepare questions such as these for a visit by the school principal: "Why did you select education for your career?" "What's the toughest part of your job as principal?" "Imagine you had the resources and influence to do anything you wanted in this school. What would you do and why?"

3. *Questioning Through Games, Simulation, Role Playing*—An excellent way for students to learn questioning is through games, simulation, and role playing. In each of these activities, students are presented with a problem or situation in which they must ask questions to seek solutions.

For example, at a simple level, play games like "Changing Storybook History." Ask, "How could the gingerbread boy have outsmarted the fox?" "If you were Little Red Riding Hood, how would you have avoided the wolf?" For higher levels, simulations and role playing offer opportunity for mini-investigations. For example, the teacher presents the following problem to science class: "Over the past five years, there has been a dramatic increase in lung disease and asthmalike conditions in a particular city in the United States. Desiring to find the reasons for the increase and to correct the situation, city officials have called in a group of scientists to solve the problem. You are the scientists."

The team, or teams, might begin by posing questions that gain general information, such as where and what are the characteristics of the city, whether the problem has occurred elsewhere, and what are the symptoms of the ailing residents. The students should lay a data foundation from which they can draw conclusions. Or the students might begin by listing possible reasons for the problem (pollution, a change in the people's diets) and then ask questions to gather data that might confirm or deny the hypothesis.

4. *Student-Oriented Questions*—When a student is having difficulty making a point or is confused, ask that student to formulate a question. This technique helps the learner to identify the area of concern and obtain the needed help.

5. *Wait Time*—What would your reaction be if someone started firing questions at you at every two or three seconds? Such rapid questioning appears to be typical of teachers around the country. After asking a question, a teacher waits one second or less for a student to answer. Then the teacher typically repeats, rephrases, or gives one second or less for a student to answer. Once the student has responded, the teacher typically waits less than one second before commenting on the answer or asking another question. We need to think about reducing the number of questions and getting more pay-off per question.

In the pausing behavior of teachers, there are two important pause locations, called wait times. Wait time one is the pause following a teacher's question; whether students respond quickly or slowly, the teacher tries to wait. Wait time two is the pause after a student's response; the teacher tries to wait before commenting on the response or asking another question. When this second pause is cut short, all the student's amplifying, qualifying, and speculation is chopped off by teacher intervention. Perhaps this is one reason that students in fast interactive systems speak in fragmented sentences. A child needs more time to verbalize.

Some Poor Types of Questions

1. *Multiple*—"What started the war with Iraq and why did we get involved?"

2. *Chorus*—"Were we right?"

3. *Leading*—"Aren't the terrorists bad? Don't you agree?"

4. *Addressed to the teacher*—"Give *me* the answer." "Tell *me*." (Use *us* instead.)

5. *Yes/No*—"Did the girl go to the store?"

6. *Calling a student's name before the question*—"Jose, what's the answer?"

7. *Calling on nonvolunteers sometimes*—"OK, Ronaldo, you raised your hand. What's the answer?"

Procedure

1. List learning activities for the lesson.

2. Include pivotal (main) questions.

3. Include a brief sequential description of how the lesson will proceed.

See lesson plans later in the chapter for sample procedures or lesson development.

Teacher . . .

1. Reviews prior lesson or knowledge at outset

2. Stops to review after difficult material is presented

3. Provides a medial review (in middle of lesson)

4. Provides a summative review (at end of lesson)

Review . . .

1. Allows students to explain what they know

2. Allows teacher to check for understanding

In some lessons you might provide for a brief definite review that will help to clinch the concepts, skills, and understandings that had been taught in the previous lesson. Reviews may be conducted in various ways. You can pose a few thought-provoking and factual questions that ask for a summary of the previous lesson. You can pose a question that calls for a comparison or for an application. You can ask a student to present a summary of the previous lesson. After such a presentation, the other members of the class should be asked to make corrections and additions.

Lessons in General . . .

1. Are well paced

2. Are worthwhile

3. Are individualized

4. Have varied student activities

5. Have smooth transitions

6. Have medial and final summaries

7. Need follow-up

Tests . . .

1. Are appropriate to ability level

2. Are clearly worded

3. Have valid content

4. Have clear directions

5. Include sufficient time

6. Vary in format

See Chapter 7 for a more complete discussion of assessment that goes beyond testing.

Homework . . .

1. Grows out of the lesson

2. Is specific and well defined

3. Is varied—option driven

4. Is differentiated—allows for different abilities

5. Is explained and understood

Homework can be an important part of the student's process of learning. It can be an extension of a day's lesson, preparation for a new lesson, or the culminating activity for a unit of study. Homework assignments should be well thought out and relevant to the subject matter being taught. Here are some suggestions on this particular aspect of teaching.

1. Place the homework assignment on the chalkboard, indicating the date it is due. Students can then copy down this information and refer to it when needed.

2. Give the homework assignment during class when there is adequate time for explanation and student questions.

3. Vary the type of assignment.

4. When possible use the previous day's homework as the basis for a class discussion, for review purposes, or as a lead-in for the new lesson you are presenting.

5. Homework assignments should be realistic. Do students have enough knowledge to do the work assigned? Will they have the materials

needed at home to successfully complete the work? How long should it take to do the assignment?

6. Always collect the students' work the day it is due.

7. Grade the homework papers and return them to the students as soon as possible.

8. Notify parents if a student continually fails to do the assigned homework. Parents have a right to know if their son or daughter isn't doing the assigned work.

Good schools have a clear and consistent homework policy, and teachers of different subjects in these schools coordinate homework assignments in terms of length and difficulty. Homework must be marked, reviewed, and graded. Know that research indicates that homework given and reviewed appropriately can raise student achievement (Walber, Paschal, & Weinstein, 1985).

Homework Guidelines

1. Develop classroom homework in line with school policy.

2. Coordinate the amount and type of homework with other teachers.

3. Homework in early grades should not generally exceed 15 to 30 minutes, three times a week, and in middle grades 45 to 90 minutes, four times a week. In high school, the time should be broken down by subject/class because no teacher has a clue as to the amount of homework given in other classes.

4. Homework must be relevant, interesting, and appropriate to the ability level of the student.

5. Never use homework as a punishment.

6. Don't use homework to introduce new ideas or concepts below the high school level.

7. Homework should sometimes incorporate nontraditional sources such as television, newspapers, and the Internet.

8. Students should not be permitted to go home without fully understanding the homework (it's unfair to the students and it irritates parents).

9. Don't give homework unless you will grade, return, and review it with students.

10. Differentiate assignments.

11. Keep parents informed of homework policy and their expected role.

12. Develop procedures for collecting homework and for checking homework.

Evaluation

It is always wise to evaluate a lesson plan. (See Table 4.1.) It's especially important if the lesson plan fell short of your expectations the first time around. Effective evaluation can be accomplished by considering the following questions:

- Were my aims relevant and realistic?
- Was I well prepared?
- Was my presentation organized and clear?
- Was my presentation varied enough?
- Did my students understand what they were doing and why they were doing it?
- Were my questions well phrased in language the students could understand?
- Did the students respond properly to my questions?
- Did all the students listen to and take part in today's lesson?

Keep in mind the following *strengths* and *weaknesses* of some aspects of your lesson.

| |

Strength |

Weakness |
|---|---|---|
| MOTIVATION | Based on need or sustained interest | No real motivation
Overlong
Not related to
aim or lesson |
| AIM | Definite
Suitable
Clear
Achieved | Lacking
Not related to lesson
Poorly worded
Trivial |

	Strength	Weakness
DEVELOPMENT/ PROCEDURE	Well paced Sequential Varied approaches	Digressions Confusing Poor transitions Inadequate content Too abstract Summaries poor
QUESTIONS AND ANSWERS	Clear wording Good distribution Pivotal questions Stimulate critical thought	Confused wording Talking after question No wait time Reliance on volunteers Poor distribution One-word answers Repeating answers "Tell *me*"
OUTCOMES	Subject matter skills Concepts Attitudes Lesson learned	Not learned No check for learning Skills not mastered Lack of remediation or enrichment
HOMEWORK	Clear Appropriate Motivated Explained Individualized	Missing Inappropriate Vague or confusing Too long or too short

Table 4.1 What's wrong or right with each scenario? Check the appropriate column

	Strong	Weak	Recommendations
1. Teacher to pupils who chorus out the answer: "Boys and girls, you shouldn't call out that way. Charles, why shouldn't we call out our answers?"			

(Continued)

Table 4.1 (Continued)

	Strong	Weak	Recommendations
2. A teacher in an eighth-grade social studies class praises committee A for having just completed an excellent report on the Hindu religion in India. She was especially pleased to note that each member of the committee read the report in a loud, clear voice.			
3. *Teacher:* "John, can you point out the Erie Canal on the map?" John goes to the map in front of the chalkboard, but can't find the Erie Canal on the map. *Teacher:* "Can you help John, May?" May goes to the map and finds the Erie Canal. *Teacher:* "Class, is May right?"			
4. The reading teacher has organized four groups in her seventh-year corrective reading class. She starts instruction with the poorest group as they need her help the most.			
5. In the industrial arts room, two boys are reading *Popular Machines* in the corner of the room while the other boys are at their respective stations working on projects.			
6. The drill in the seventh-grade mathematics class consumes 10 minutes. All pupils work on the same example and answer the questions successfully.			
7. The language arts teacher says to the class, "Before we start, I'll tell you what to do. Read the story on page 8. Then answer the questions on pages 9 and 10. Write each word you don't know in your notebook. Now, get busy."			

	Strong	Weak	Recommendations
8. In a reading lesson, the teacher notes that some pupils are reading aloud. She comments: "I hear someone reading aloud. How should we be reading?" *Pupil:* "To ourselves. Only with our eyes." *Teacher:* "Why shouldn't we be reading aloud?" *Pupil:* "It disturbs our neighbors." *Teacher:* "I'll read this paragraph. First I'll read it silently (10 seconds elapse). Now, I'll read it aloud (she reads slowly). Now, which did I read more quickly?" *Chorus:* "The first time." *Teacher:* "Right. When you want to read to get information you read silently. In that way, you read faster. If you are reading to someone you would read aloud, but then you must read slowly or no one will understand you."			
9. The class is reading a passage silently. The teacher circulates around the room. *Teacher:* "If you need help, raise your hand. I'll come to you." No hands were raised. The class continued to work. Many pupils finished their work, took out other books, and read silently.			
10. In a social studies class: *Teacher:* "Howard, name the New England states." Student falters. *Teacher:* "George, let's see if you can do a better job than that."			

Some suggested sample answers (others may apply):

1. It's good to point out that choral responses do not allow teachers to assess who really understands the information.

2. Effective use of positive reinforcement is a good thing.

3. Several problems here. Don't call on student first and then ask a question. Other students will tune out. Avoid saying "Class, is Mary right?" Call on a particular student. Allow for wait time.

4. Nothing particularly wrong unless she always groups her class that way.

5. Depends on teacher's objectives. Is the teacher aware of what is occurring?

6. Does the teacher check for understanding? Do pupils always work on the same problem at the same time? Does the teacher differentiate her examples?

7. It's busywork. What is the educational purpose of this activity?

8. The teacher models desired behavior and stimulates student thinking.

9. Teacher circulates and students seem to know class routines and procedures.

10. No attempt to assist student and denigrates student.

Respond

Critique each of the following lesson plans using the criteria discussed and explained above. Indicate any strengths or weaknesses. See more detailed (much better) sample lessons at the end of this chapter.

Lesson #1: Grade 5, Inclusive, Science

Aim: To learn about fossils

Do Now: Read pages 123 to 187.

Motivation: Open books and read aloud.

Procedure: Discuss fossils, read story about fossils, have students ask questions, show film about fossils, answer questions on board.

Questions: How were fossils made? And so on.

Homework: Answer questions on handout sheet after reading pages 187 to 199 in science book.

Lesson #2: Grade 5, Gifted Class, Language Arts

Aim: To define persuasive writing and write a persuasive composition

Do Now: Should we have split session to ease school overcrowding?

Motivation: Refer to "Do Now" question and ask what a split session is. Would it solve overcrowding in our school? Why? Why not?

Procedure: How would you go about convincing someone that your opinion is the correct one? How would you write this in a composition?

Steps:

1. Read question carefully.

2. Plan out your opinion.

3. Make an outline.

4. Provide facts.

5. Choose a topic sentence.

6. Choose a summary sentence.

7. Write a first draft.

8. Proofread.

9. Write final draft.

Homework: Write the second draft of essay started in class. Include at least four reasons to support your opinion.

Evaluation: Check and review essays in class. Have children read to class.

Lesson #3: Grade 8, Below Average, Social Studies

Aim: To learn about the final battles of the American Revolution

Motivation: Direct students to page 65. Tell them that the picture shows George Cornwallis, the British commander, leading his army out of Yorktown after surrendering to George Washington. Explain that a band was playing a song called "The World Turned Upside Down." Ask, "Why do you think the British surrendered? What do you think Cornwallis was thinking about?" And so forth.

Development: Have students read pages 162 to 163. Ask, "What did the Americans do when the British began to take the war to the southern states? Who was Swamp Fox?" Have students describe the battles leading to the end of the war. Write what they say on board in list form. Ask further exploratory questions.

Summary: Have students list the reasons for the American victory as given on page 163.

Homework: Read pages 163 and 164.

Lesson #4: Grade 3, Average, Reading

Aim: To find the main idea

Motivation: Show pictures of interesting historical events and have class determine the main ideas of each picture.

Vocabulary: List ten new words on board and read aloud with the class.

Development:

1. Read out loud the first page of story to class.
2. Ask them to locate the main idea.
3. Ask another child to read next page and repeat procedure.
4. Have them answer main idea questions on a handout to give them— they may refer to story.
5. Read Sophistication Series pages 34 to 46.
6. Review homework.

Homework: Study handout on main idea.

Evaluation: Test on Monday on main idea.

Lesson #5: Grade 10, Average, English

Aim: To appreciate Shakespeare

Motivation: Read a passage from *Hamlet* and discuss why Shakespeare may be boring to students. Discuss some exciting elements about Shakespeare that students can appreciate and even enjoy.

Procedure:

1. Hand out excerpts from *Hamlet*.

2. Read selected portions with class.

3. Point out relevant parts.

4. Ask questions.

5. Provide worksheet.

Homework: Read Part I of *Hamlet* and answer questions.

Each of the previous lesson plans has deficiencies—primarily, no stated objectives, no attempt to differentiate instruction, and lack of detail. See the much better sample lesson plans that follow.

LESSON PLAN IDEA #3: SAMPLE LESSON PLANS

Sample Lesson #1

Diagnosis:

Subject: Social Studies	*Topic:* Geography	*Grade Level:* Third
Ability: Heterogeneous. 2 Asian students, 4 Latino students, Average ability. A total of 18 students.		
Time: 30 minutes	*Sequence:* Introduction to world continents	

Goal: Students will know the seven continents of the world by name and make a cultural/landmark association.

Objectives:

- Students will be able to identify the continents by their shape and size. (Knowledge)
- Students will be able to list and describe several different landmark or cultural habits to that continent. (Comprehension)
- Students will be able to compare and contrast the land mass of the countries by categorizing them from smallest to largest. (Analysis)

Aim: What is life like on another continent?

Prerequisite Knowledge: Students are already familiar with their own community and the city they live in. They are also aware of some New Jersey history and U.S. history.

Rationale: This lesson will emphasize the location and major attributes of the continents of the world. It will provide students with knowledge and understanding of the world and the place of North America within the world.

Standards: Ties lesson to state, city, or local standards.

Motivation: Who has ever traveled out of America? Does anyone have any family members that are from another country? Ireland? Poland? South America?

Materials: Globe, wall map of world

Do Now: Name three places outside of the United States.

Instructional Strategies: (Table 4.2)

Table 4.2

_X_whole group	_X_direct instruction	_X_small group
_X_cooperative learning	___review prior to test	___guided reading
___developmental lesson	___shared reading	___guided practice
___reciprocal teaching	___peer tutoring	___test sophistication
_X_skills development	_X_ individualized instruction	___read aloud
___paired reading	___review after test	___other

Procedure: Knowledge content, linguistic (based on Gardner's Multiple Intelligences)

1. Has anyone ever traveled outside of the United States? Is there anyone in the classroom who is from or has family from outside of the United States? Have map on board and globe available. First, we will look at the map and the globe and discuss how we already are familiar with these two maps and how they show the same areas.

2. Can anyone name for the class any of the continents? We will go over the definition of continent. Then I will write the seven continents on the board and have them repeat the names.

3. Can anyone in the class think of a tune or a song where we can use the names? If not, I will sing them my song (Music). We will use choral singing to remember the continents.

4. Okay, class, close your eyes. Imagine you are in a plane and we land in Asia. Before you open your eyes, think about what that part of the world might be like. Can you see the people? What kinds of foods might be eaten there? Okay, now open your eyes. Who can tell the class what they saw?

Comprehension/Knowledge: Linguistic

We will go over certain landmarks that the children might know. For example, kangaroos are a very familiar animal in Australia. Coffee is from parts of Africa and South America. Tea is plentiful in India and China.

Mathematical/Logical (based on Gardner's Multiple Intelligences):

By looking at this map, can anyone guess which continent is the largest? The smallest?

I will cut out several scaled shapes of the United States. I will ask the students to see how many United States can go into one continent (if time permits).

Class, which continent is the biggest in land mass? Which continent is the smallest?

Conclusion and Summary: We will review the seven continents first by singing our song. Then students will write a one-minute paper saying what they learned today and what interested them.

Homework: Write a paper on a day in the life of a child in a different continent. Use your imagination.

Evaluation: Have class write a one-minute paper saying what they learned and what has piqued their curiosity.

Sample Lesson #2

Diagnosis: Ninth of a 10-lesson U.S. history unit on World War II. The students are of heterogeneous ability. This lesson will last approximately 40 minutes and be divided into three segments: 12 minutes for lecture-discussion, 13 minutes for group activity, and 15 minutes for class debate.

Goal: This lesson will teach students the historical events leading up to Japan's surrender during World War II. It will also force them to criticize and assess their own opinions regarding the U.S. decision to use the atomic bomb.

Aim: How did World War II end in the Pacific Theater?

Objectives: Having listened to the brief lecture on the closing days of World War II in the Pacific Theater, and participating in the two group/class activities, students will be able to:

1. Understand the events that took place during this period (Knowledge)

2. Discuss the event on a factual and interpretive basis (Comprehension and Application)

3. Decide for themselves whether the atomic bomb should have been used as a facilitator to end the war (Evaluation)

Rationale: Aside from the general knowledge of learned history, this lesson will emphasize the social responsibilities mankind must uphold in a technologically advanced world he creates.

Vocabulary:

- *Fat Man*—The short, egg-shaped bomb exploded over Nagasaki
- *Little Boy*—The more slender missile-shaped bomb used at Hiroshima

Materials: Video projector, VCR, picture handouts, quote handouts

Motivation: Students will view a video of actual World War II footage concerning the events leading to the conclusion of the war.

Instructional Strategies: (Table 4.3)

Table 4.3

_X_whole group	_X_direct instruction	_X_small group
___cooperative learning	___review prior to test	___guided reading
___developmental lesson	___shared reading	___guided practice
___reciprocal teaching	___peer tutoring	___test sophistication
_X_skills development	_X_ individualized instruction	___read aloud
___paired reading	___review after test	___other

Procedure:

1. Class will be adjusted to foment discussion in a U shape.

2. Begin lecture on closing days of World War II:
   a. Germany has surrendered.
   b. FDR has died; succeeded by Truman.
   c. Potsdam meeting
   d. Successful test of A bomb
   e. Truman approves its use:
      i. Generals remind him of severe fighting/losses to date.
      ii. Forecast of prospective losses if U.S. invades rather than bombs.
      iii. Demonstration of bomb?
   f. Aug. 6—Hiroshima, 180,000 dead
   g. Aug. 8—USSR declares war on Japan.
   h. Aug. 9—Nagasaki, 70,000 dead
   i. Aug. 15–22—formal surrender/ceremony

3. Show pictures of devastated cities.

4. Ask pivotal questions: Should the bomb have been used? Should the second bomb have been used? What were the alternatives? Why do you think they were not chosen?

5. Divide class into three groups:
   One group probomb
   One group proinvasion
   One group status quo

6. Explain roles:
   Recorder—writes ideas down
   Manager—keeps everyone focused and ensures their understanding
   Monitor—makes sure all participate
   Brainstormers—responsible for conveying ideas

7. Allow groups to work for 10 minutes or so to come up with arguments supporting their "belief" and anticipate adversarial critiques.

8. As a class, each group will propose its ideas and defend them against constructive criticisms from opposing groups. Each group will have the opportunity to state its case and defend at least one criticism from each group.

9. Conclusion: A brief summary verbally explained by each group relating what they have learned.

Homework: Have students read last section on costs of war, human and monetary, in preparation for the next day's lesson.

Evaluation: In addition to the discussions during the lesson, the unit exam will have numerous short-answer and essay questions to test their knowledge on this unit.

Sample Lesson #3

Diagnosis: Second of two seventh-grade science lessons on the tropical rain forest biome. The class is of heterogeneous ability (inclusive setting) with 19 of 25 students on grade level, three above, and 3 below. The lesson will last approximately 30 minutes.

Goals: Students will learn about the tropical rain forest biome.

Objectives: Having read the featured handout on the importance of tropical rain forests and participating in class activities, students will be able to

1. Understand the importance of the world's rain forests (Knowledge)

2. Identify and discuss issues concerning the rain forests (Knowledge and Comprehension)

3. Role play the different positions on rain forest usage (Application)

4. Recognize and discuss contradictions (Comprehension)

Aim: Why are the rain forests important to all people?

Rationale: This lesson will emphasize the importance of rain forests to the world's population. It will reinforce the idea of interdependence among all people and make students more thoughtful about the use of the environment.

Vocabulary: Learned in previous lesson

Materials: Reading handouts, fact review sheet, homework sheet

Motivation: Display of rain forest products (bananas, cloves, brazil nuts). Mayan proverb written on chalkboard: "Who cuts the trees as he pleases cuts short his own life."

Do Now: Read handout "Why Rain Forests Are Important . . . " pages 142 and 143, and read Fact Review sheet:

- More than 5,096 of all living things on earth live in tropical rain forests.
- A form of leukemia common in children can be cured with a substance found in a rain forest plant called the rosy periwinkle.

Instructional Strategies: (Table 4.4)

Table 4.4

_X_whole group	_X_direct instruction	___small group
_X_cooperative learning	___review prior to test	___guided reading
___developmental lesson	___shared reading	___guided practice
_X_reciprocal teaching	_X_peer tutoring	___test sophistication
_X_skills development	___ individualized instruction	___read aloud
___paired reading	___review after test	___other

Procedure:

1. Write *Tropical Rain Forest* on the chalkboard. Ask students what they think of when they see these words (trees, vines, orchids, hot, wet, monkeys).

2. Ask pivotal question: How would the disappearance of the rain forest directly affect you? Alter precipitation, add to expanding desert lands, alter temperature, and so on.

3. Divide class in half. One side argues for clearing the rain forest, the other against.

4. Explain roles to the students.
   a. If you wanted to clear the rain forest, who might you be? (farmer, rancher)
   b. If you wanted to protect it? (environmentalist, scientist)

5. Ask students to think of arguments for their side.

6. Write answers in two columns on board.

7. Ask pivotal question: *Can all these opposing statements be true at the same time?*

8. Form students into groups of three or four and have them discuss ways to save the rain forests. Tell them to write down ways to use what they have learned for their homework assignment.

9. Review previous lesson
   a. Located near the equator
   b. Climate warm and humid
   c. Seasons differ only in amount of rainfall
   d. Three levels: canopy, understory and forest floor
   e. Provides habitat for plants and animals
   f. Scientists may discover new species—beneficial
   g. Helps regulate earth's climate

Homework: Write a science journal entry answering questions on the homework sheet. Use rain forest product chart on sheet and group discussion to help you.

1. What rain forest products can people collect without harming its plants?

2. What will happen to earth if people continue to destroy rain forests?

3. How do you think we can save the rain forests?

Evaluation: Check homework journal entries for concepts. Have children read ideas to class.

Sample lessons #4 and #5 are really superb plans (from two of my former students, reprinted with their permission). Notice some elements they add and the detail they present—truly impressive.

Sample Lesson #4

By Marissa Ankiewicz

Title of the Lesson: Animals of the Rain Forests Around the World!

Target Student Population: 3rd Grade, 24 students: 19 general education, 5 special education.

Objectives:

- Students will be able to tell where rain forests are located around the world. (Knowledge)
- Students will be able to compare and contrast the difference between what a rain forest is like and what a forest is like during class discussion. (Analysis)
- Students will produce an accurate description of their chosen rain forest animal by summarizing what the animal, eats, where it lives,

why it lives there, what are its characteristics, and any other important information about their animal. (Comprehension)

- Students will be able to demonstrate their knowledge of their chosen animal by sharing information with the class and teacher. (Application)

Concept/Main Idea/Aim of the Lesson: Introductory lesson to a unit.

Aim: What do I know about the rain forest and the animals that live there?

Students will be exploring the location of rain forests on the planet Earth and the animals that inhabit those rain forests. Students will have a chance to research one animal in a more thorough manner to gain deeper understanding of how that animal lives and acts in its natural habitat.

Learning Standards:

New York State Learning Standards

4.1 Living things are both similar to and different from each other and nonliving things.

4.2 Organisms maintain a dynamic equilibrium that sustains life.

4.6 Plants and animals depend on each other and their physical environment.

ACEI Standards

2.1 Reading, writing, and oral language

2.2 Science

2.4 Social studies

3.1 Integrating and applying knowledge for instruction

3.2 Adaptation to diverse students

3.4 Active engagement in learning

3.5 Communication to foster collaboration

4.0 Assessment for instruction

5.1 Professionalism growth, reflection, and evaluation

Teaching Strategies and Activities: During this lesson, the teacher will use whole-class instruction at the beginning of the class, incorporating interaction (students coming up to the map and pointing) and group discussion (student's will be sharing their animals from the list that they make based on their prior knowledge). Also partner/individual work (depending on the individuals' preference). They will use partner work after the Do Now to share and exchange answers! Following the movie, students will join in group discussion, discussing what they saw and making comparisons to things they can relate to (rain forest to the forests in New York and New Jersey). Also, they will be able to work in partners if they choose to during the activity following the lesson. During the activity, the teacher will walk around and work with students one on one or in small groups to help clear up any confusion and check for comprehension. At the end of the lesson, students will lead the discussion and share with each other things that they have learned. Students can interact and ask questions, therefore they will feed off of one another and learn from one another.

Lesson Introduction/Do Now: Students will begin the lesson by completing the activity that is written on the board and read aloud to the class.

- Do Now: What kind of animals do you think live in the rain forest? Make a list of all the animals that you can think of.
- Students will be given a couple of minutes to think and write down their answers in their notebooks. After a couple of minutes, students will turn to their neighbors and exchange any animals that their partner did not come up with, and discuss any animals that they are unsure of.

Learning Activities:

1. The teacher will begin by saying "Before we go over the Do Now, let's get a clear understanding of exactly where all the rain forests are located on our planet, Earth!" The teacher will then ask a few different students to come up to the map of the world and point to where they think some of the rain forests are located. After doing this, the teacher will turn on the overhead projector and show the students a transparency that highlights the areas where rain forests are located. Possibly a map similar to the one on the Web site at http://www.srl .caltech.edu/personnel/krubal/rainforest/Edit560s6/www/where.html could be printed out onto an overhead transparency.

2. The teacher will then proceed to go over the Do Now, but first allowing students to take a minute to add any other animals to their list that they think might live in the rain forests, now that they have seen a map of the rain forests' locations. Students will then be invited to raise their hands and share a few animals on their list with the class; the correct ones students can add to their lists in their notebooks, and they can cross off any incorrect animals. Now students will have a long list of animals that live in the rain forests already in their notebooks.

3. The class then will watch a 15–20 minute clip of the video "Tropical Rainforests," which was created by the Discovery Channel. After watching the video, students will discuss what they saw, including some animal survival techniques, different ways the animals get food, what the plants and environment looked like, and so on. The teacher will ask questions such as:

   a. Describe to me the colors/types of the insects and reptiles of the tropical rain forest.
   b. Can someone describe to me what some of the plants looked like? (e.g., bright green, vibrant colors, very lush)
   c. What are some of the sounds of the rain forest? (water, birds, animals making sounds, etc.)
   d. Is there any water in the rain forest? What kinds? (rivers, lagoons, etc.)
   e. What is different about the rain forests we saw in the movie and the forests that are around here and in New Jersey and New York?
   f. Tell me about some of the animals that you saw. What is different about the animals in the rain forest and the animals in forests near us? Do you think any of the same animals live in forests here and the rain forests that we saw today?

4. After the class discussion on rain forests, the teacher will explain their activity. The class will be creating a Rain Forest Animal Archive. Students will be asked to choose an animal from the rain forest that they saw today, or that is on the list that they made earlier, and research a little bit about that animal. They can use the books and encyclopedias that the teacher has pulled out for them to find information, or magazines like *National Geographic* that are in the classroom. They are also welcome to use the Internet and go to one of the Web sites from a list of science sites that are available to the students in the computer area. The teacher will have a handout for the students of the areas they should be researching the animals in. The handout would include the following:

   a. Please find a description of the size of the animal and any other physical characteristics that you can find, such as skin/fur color, tail/no tail, or padded feet, any information that would help us to better picture the animal.
   b. Find out what the animals' diet (everyday food, maybe plants, a specific type, or insects, rats etc.) consists of. If possible, how they get their food, hunting at night or in the day, and so on.
   c. Find out what continent(s) that animal lives on. (There are rain forests in Central America, South America, Africa, Australia, and Southeast Asia). Please include a picture of that continent and circle the area that the rain forest is located.

d. Find out anything you can about their characteristics. Do they take care of their young? Do they sleep during the day or at night? Do they travel in groups or alone? Do they play with each other? Any accurate, interesting facts that you can find would be great!

Once they find their information, they are to go to a computer and create a Word document about their animal. They should put the name of their animal at the top of the page, and include lots of pictures and vibrant colors! The students then will be asked to type the information about the research that they have found. The information shouldn't be too intricate so it shouldn't take long for them to type. The students will be asked to write their animal down on a sheet of paper in the front of the room; that way no one does the same animal. They are more than welcome to research reptiles or insects from the rain forest as well, instead of an animal. Some options of animals to choose from include the spider monkey, jaguar, hummingbirds, toucans, iguanas, poison arrow frog, electric eel, bandicoot, laughing kookaburra, monarch butterfly, tigers, tree shrews, moon rats, chimpanzee, gorilla, or the hippopotamus. These are just a few examples from the wide variety the students may choose from.

5. As students work, the teacher will circulate about the room helping any students that need some extra assistance, and encourage the students who are finishing up quickly to look for some more information about their animal—research a little deeper! Also, the teacher will make sure that the students are on task and not going on any mischievous Web sites or sites that don't contain accurate information. Once students finish up, they can print out their work twice so they can display it on the Rain Forest Animal Archive Bulletin Board, and also put a copy in their student portfolio.

Lesson Closure/Transition:

Closure: Once the class is finished, the students will come back together and share some of their information. Students are welcome to ask each other questions and pass around their sheets so they can see the pictures of their exotic animals!

Transition: Before moving onto the next subject, students will write down on a piece of paper one or two interesting facts that they learned about an animal of the rain forest and hand it to the teacher before they return to their seats for the next lesson.

Resources: Students first will be watching a DVD so that they can get a better visual of what the rain forest looks like.

Next the students have the option, depending on whether they are comfortable enough using the Internet, to research their animal online. (If not, they can use books, encyclopedias, and the like.)

Students then will go on a computer and use Microsoft Word to create their Rain Forest Animal Archive Fact Sheet, and when it is complete they will print it out so they can share it with the class. Then it will be placed onto the bulletin board to create an archive of information about rain forest animals.

Assessment: The teacher will know that the students are aware of where rain forests are located in the world by observing the students who come up to the map and point, and by checking the students archive sheets to see their picture of the continent and whether they correctly circled the area where the rain forests are located on that continent.

The teacher will be able to check for student understanding of the differences and similarities between rain forests and local forests during group discussion; this will be observed informally for now, and in a separate lesson will be looked at more in depth after more information has been shared.

The teacher will be able to see what students learned about their animal from the rain forest archive sheets that they turn in. They will be graded using the following rubric. A 6/6 would be the best grade possible. (6 = A, 5 = A–, 4 = B, 3 = B–, 2 = C, 1 = D, 0 = F)

Rubric for Rain Forest Animal Archive			
	Excellent (3)	Satisfactory (2)	Needs Improvement (1)
Content	Student has clear understanding of the rain forest animal and went above and beyond providing all of the information that was asked for.	Student provides most of the information that was asked for, with some details being provided.	Student gives minimum information about animal and did not do adequate research.
Visual	Student added great visuals and used lots of color and creativity. Student also incorporated picture of continent(s) animal lives on.	Student incorporated some pictures for visuals. Student also incorporated picture of continent(s) animal lives on.	Student added minimal pictures and did not incorporate picture of continent.

The teacher will be able to see what the student learned when they demonstrate their knowledge of rain forest animals through their archive sheet with the class. Also, when the teacher walks around and works with the students individually or in small groups. This assessment will be informal to make sure that the students do not have any confusion that needs clearing up.

References:

Col, J. (1996). *Enchanted Learning.* Retrieved February 12, 2008, from http://www.enchantedlearning.com/subjects/rainforest/animals/Sampling.shtml

Houghton Mifflin Company. (n.d.). *Make a habitat fact file.* Retrieved February 12, 2008, from http://www.eduplace.com/activity/3_4_act1.html

MT & PK Productions. (n.d.). *Where are the rainforests.* Retrieved February 11, 2008, from http://www.srl.caltech.edu/personnel/krubal/rainforest/Edit560s6/www/where.html

CEC Accommodations: For students who need a little extra help in the class-room, any of the following can be done to accommodate their needs. They can be paired with a student who is willing to help and explain things, someone who has patience and is good at explaining things as well. The teacher will take the time to explain the directions again to the student if necessary and make sure that the student is seated accordingly in the classroom. Students who require extra time to finish their project will be given that time at the end of the day or the next morning during their morning routine, any extra help will be given to the student in a one-on-one strategy. The students can then share their work with the class when they are finished and confident with their final product!

Here are Marissa's comments about her plan:

You are more than welcome to use the lesson plan that I wrote. That would be very exciting! However, I did get some of my ideas from a Web site—it's cited in my lesson plan. The following two links inspired me to come up with the lesson plan that I created. They just gave me the basic idea; they are not full lesson plans, but just provide ideas for teachers.

http://www.eduplace.com/activity/3_4_act1.html
http://www.eduplace.com/activity/amazon.html

Sample Lesson #5

By Lauren Pollock

Title of the Lesson: "What's Your Name?"

Target Student Population: Grade 1—Literacy

Objectives: Students will be able to . . .

- Recall (knowledge) their own names.
- Distinguish (comprehension) classmates from one another based on their names.
- Create (synthesis) a desktop name tag using Microsoft Word.
- Describe (evaluation) their desktop name tag design to the class.

Concept/Main Idea/Aim of the Lesson: The aim of the lesson is for the children to apply their literacy skills to create a desktop name tag—using Microsoft Word—that can be used throughout the year.

Learning Standards

New York City Literacy Standards

First Grade Reading Standard 1: Reading habits
- *Independent and assisted reading*—Students will be able to "read their own writing and sometimes the writing of their classmates" and "read functional messages they encounter in the classroom (for example: labels, signs, instructions)."

First Grade Reading Standard 2: Getting the meaning
- *Comprehension*—Students will be able to "describe in their own words what they gained from the text" and "answer comprehension questions similar to those for kindergartners."

First Grade Reading Standard 3: Print-Sound code
- *Phonemic awareness*—Students will be able to "separate the sounds by saying each sound aloud" and "blend separately spoken phonemes to make a meaningful word."

First Grade Writing Standard 2: Writing purposes and resulting genres
- *Getting things done: functional writing*—Students will be able to "claim, mark, or identify objects and places."

First Grade Writing Standard 3: Language use and conventions
- *Punctuation, capitalization, and other conventions*—Students will be able to "demonstrate interest and awareness by . . . capitalization of proper names."

ACEI Standards

ACEI Standard 1.0: Development, learning, and motivation

ACEI Standard 2.1: Reading, writing, and oral language

ACEI Standard 2.5: The arts

ACEI Standard 3.1: Integrating and applying knowledge for instruction

ACEI Standard 3.2: Adaptation to diverse students

ACEI Standard 3.3: Development of critical thinking and problem solving

ACEI Standard 3.4: Active engagement in learning

ACEI Standard 3.5: Communication to foster collaboration

ACEI Standard 4.0: Assessment for instruction

ACEI Standard 5.1: Professional growth, reflection, and evaluation

Teaching Strategies and Activities: This lesson will incorporate independent work (decoration of their desktop name tags, worksheet activity, etc.), along with group work (computer station activity), direct instruction (lesson on letters and how to spell their names), and numerous hands-on activities (creation and decoration of the name tags). The NYC Reading and Writing Standards will be applied to the lesson in all aspects, helping to develop and enhance the literacy skills of the first-grade students through the classroom activities, work, and games. *For example:* Writing Standard 2 would be applied in that children would be able to identify, or "claim" their desks as their own; ACEI Standard 2i would be applied in that connections would be made across numerous subjects, such as technology, English, and art in the lesson; Reading Standard 1—where students are able to identify words either independently or with assistance—would be applied through the name tags, once they are completed, and the children can connect spoken names with their written form. Each aspect of the lesson can be related back to at least one of the identified NYC and ACEI Standards.

Lesson Introduction/Do Now:

- Have the children stand around in a circle and put on the CD with the Richard Graham song "What's Your Name?" (http://www.genkienglish.net/namesong.htm)
- Go step by step and teach the children the lyrics and what to do at each part of the song.

Learning Activities:

- *Transition:* Have the students go back to their desks.
  o "Okay everyone, let's return to our seats."

- Have the Alphabet People out in the front of the room for all the students to see.
  - ○ "Using the Alphabet People, *(name of student),* come and find some of the letters that are in your name."
  - ○ Do this activity with a few students.
  - ○ *Give positive reinforcement and discuss the outcome of the activity:*
    - ✍ "Great job!"
    - ✍ "How did you know that that letter was in your name?"
    - ✍ "Class, what sound does the letter ___ make?"
- *Transition:* Have the students independently write in their Literacy notebooks how they think they spell their name.
  - ○ "Everyone, can you please take out your Literacy notebooks?"
  - ○ "Turn to a clean page and, at the top, please write your name for me."
  - ○ Give stickers to each student who makes an attempt for positive reinforcement.
- *Transition:* Explain the name tag activity to the students.
  - ○ "One table at a time, we are going to use the computer to make name tags for your desks. So when I call your group, come join me at the computer and we will make your name tags."
  - ○ "While you are waiting patiently at your seats, please color in the worksheet and write your name at the top where it says 'My Name is _____.' Can everyone see that?"
  - ○ Use a template for the name tags so that every name tag is the same size and shape (see Figure 4.1).
  - ○ Work with each group and allow for the students to help each other spell their names correctly.
    - ✍ "Sound it out. What letter makes the _____ sound?"
    - ✍ *Use positive reinforcement and appropriate techniques to help the children problem solve.*
    - ✍ *Make sure that the other children in the class remain focused on their worksheet and reprimand them if necessary.*
- *Transition:* Once everyone has made their name tag, print them out and have each student decorate their name tag as the teacher goes around the room and checks that the worksheet has been completed.
  - ○ "Everyone, take a seat while I hand out your name tags. Please decorate them with markers or crayons, or anything that you would like. I am putting some stickers at the front of the room if you want to use them."
  - ○ "I'm going to walk around the room as you decorate your name tags and check to see that you did your worksheet."
    - ✍ *Use the worksheet as an indicator as to whether they can spell their name better than before.*

o "When you are finished decorating your name tag, come over to me and I'll show you what we're going to do next."

✐ Show the children the laminating machine and how to seal their name tags with it.

✐ Explain the safety precautions and let them help if deemed appropriate.

o "Let's share our name tags with each other!"

✐ *For example:* "Sarah, why did you draw flowers on your name tag?" "Kevin, I like that you put a guitar on your name tag. Do you play guitar?"

✐ *Make them feel like their work is important and let them each express one thing they like about their name tag.*

o "Put your name tags on your desks and I will come around so that we can tape them down."

✐ *Not only are the name tags useful, but they serve a purpose in the classroom to help learn each other's names.*

Lesson Closure/Transition: "Name, Name, Goose!"

- "Before we have snack, let's play a game. Everyone come and sit in a circle on the floor, we're going to play 'Name, Name, Goose!'"
- "I'll go first . . . . I'm going to walk around in a circle and tap each of you on the head. If I say your name, you stay where you're sitting. But if I say 'Goose,' you get up and chase me around the circle! If I make it to your seat before you catch me, you're 'It!' If not, I have to do it again."
  o The point of the game is to get everyone familiar with each other's names, while having a fun activity to end the lesson with.
  o Once the game is over, send everyone back to their seats for snack.

Resources: The resources being used for this lesson are:

- CD player
- Genki English CD
- Alphabet People
- Computer
- Microsoft Word
- Printer
- Printer paper (thick matte)
- Markers, crayons, and so on
- Stickers
- Lamination machine

Assessment: The best way to assess whether learning took place is through observations and documentation, by looking at the work product (worksheets, desktop name tags, etc.) and through the "Name, Name, Goose!" game played at the end of the day. All of these things will help to prove that the students can say and at least attempt to spell their own names, can identify their classmates by their names, can use Microsoft Word to make a name tag, and can talk about why they designed their name tags the way that they did. By making and keeping copies of student work, progress can be assessed over time. Any future tests given on letters and spelling would be effective indicators as well.

References:

Association for Childhood Education International. (2007). *2007 ACEI-NCATE elementary education standards and supporting explanation.* Retrieved February 11, 2008, from http://www.acei.org/ACEIElementaryStandards SupportingExplanation.5.07.pdf

Graham, R. (1999/2008). *Genki English: What's your name?* Retrieved February 11, 2008, from http://www.genkienglish.net/namesong.htm

Mom's Network. (1997–2008). *Mom's Network Exchange.* Retrieved February 12, 2008, from http://www.momsnetwork.com/kids/coloring/boypajama.gif

New York City Department of Education. (2008). *First grade reading and writing standards.* Retrieved February 12, 2008, from http://schools.nyc.gov/offices/teachlearn/documents/Standards/literacy/First_Grade.pdf

Wardle, C. (1996–2007). *Christy's Clipart.* Retrieved February 12, 2008, from http://www.christysclipart.com

Figure 4.1

My name is _____

My name is _____

CEC Accommodations—If this lesson were to be taught in an inclusive classroom, accommodations would be made in any way, shape, and form that the child might require. *For example:* If the child were to need extra assistance in the area of writing, while the other students are working, the teacher, or perhaps a paraprofessional, could assist the child in honing writing skills. Or, if the child had motor skill issues and could not play the "Name, Name, Goose!" game, that child could be made the moderator, who could ensure that the other children played fair, or be assigned to make judgments on whether a person was tagged. While those are just several examples, the lesson can easily be adapted to suit the needs of any child.

Lauren's comments:

I feel honored that you wish to use my lesson plan! The actual lesson plan itself is my own creation. The only outside sources I used are noted in the resources section of the lesson, which include the images for my lesson's worksheets, as well as for the Genki English CD, which can be ordered through the Web site that is listed. But the layout of the lesson is purely original.

Again, I would like to say what an honor it is for you to put my lesson in your book! I look forward to the new edition, seeing as I own and have read the original.

CONCLUSION

Writing lesson plans is vitally important. Whether you are a 1st-, 5th-, or 15th-year teacher, planning lessons is necessary. Even if you have previously learned much about lesson planning, there is always more to learn. I hope you learned at least a few useful ideas about lesson planning and delivery of a lesson in this chapter. As lifelong learners and professionals, good teachers continually strive to achieve excellence and professional growth.

Follow-Up Questions/Activities

1. What sections of this chapter will serve to help you write and deliver better lessons?

2. Write a lesson using the components explained in this chapter.

3. Read the Lesson Plan for Current Events that follows (drawn from materials the author obtained while seeking certification as a principal in New York City in the 1970s, source unknown)

What's wrong with this lesson? Identify one strength and one weakness, giving evidence for why it is a weakness and including a recommendation for improvement. Consider the aim of the lesson, the questioning techniques, the assignments, and teacher behavior in general. Can you write the lesson plan the teacher should have developed?

Grade: 7

Ability: Average

Teacher: Mr. Jones

Lesson: Current Events

Mr. Jones, a well-respected seventh-grade teacher with seven years of teaching experience, will be discussing violence in society for his weekly talk about current events.

Mr. Jones: "What can you tell me about violence in society?"

[Calls on David, who has his hand raised.]

David: "It's a very serious subject."

Mr. Jones: "Yes, it is very serious, but what else can you tell me? What do you consider violent?"

[Calls on Alisa, who has her hand raised.]

Alisa: "Hitting someone would be violent."

Mr. Jones: "That's right, Alisa. What else can you tell me?"

Alisa: "How about rape?"

Mr. Jones: "Right?'

[Calls on Billy Bob, who has his hand raised.]

Billy Bob: "I guess most crimes are violent."

Mr. Jones: "No, Billy Bob, many crimes are not violent at all. What are some of the causes of violence?"

[Calls on Freddie, who has his hand raised.]

Freddie: "Violence on TV shows and in the movies."

Mr. Jones: "Right, TV shows and movies that contain violence. Who else can tell me something that may cause violence?"

[Calls on Skip, who has his hand raised.]

Mr. Jones: "Skip, what do you think?"

Skip: "Music"

Mr. Jones: "What do you mean, Skip?"

Skip: "Some music makes people violent"

Mr. Jones: "I guess you're right."

[Calls on Brian, who has his hand raised.]

Brian: "Video games also contain violence."

Mr. Jones: "Right, Brian, and that is a hot topic right now. A rating system on video games is in the process of being created."

Mr. Jones: "What would you do, if you or someone you know was attacked?"

[Calls on Jimmy, who has his hand up.]

Jimmy: "I would get them."

Mr. Jones: "What do you mean, Jimmy? You mean you would call the police and let them get them, right?"

Jimmy: "No, I would do whatever they did to me and do it back, but worse."

Mr. Jones: "That is why we have such a problem, because people want to get revenge instead of letting the police take care of things."

Jimmy: "I don't care. I would do whatever it took to get them back."

Mr. Jones: "Well, Jimmy, that's wrong and you would just get yourself in trouble. It would also be dangerous and somebody could get severely injured."

Jimmy: "Laws that say you have to get in trouble for doing something back to someone are stupid, and I don't care if I hurt the person that did something to me."

Eddie: [Without being called on.] "He's right. I would get the person back, too. Why shouldn't I? And laws that do not let me are stupid."

Mr. Jones: "Guys, you have the wrong idea. The best course of action would be to call the police and let them 'get' the person for you."

Eddie: [Without being called on again.] "No way. Cops are idiots and they would never get them. I would make sure I got them."

[At this point, the class is very noisy and Skip is yelling at Jimmy.]

Skip: "I still never got you back for breaking my CD player!"

Jimmy: "Shut up, Skip. I told you it was an accident."

Skip: "Don't tell me to shut up, and it wasn't an accident." [Jimmy then punches Skip in the face.]

[Mr. Jones separates the boys and sends them to the office. He instructs Eddie to escort them so they do not fight on the way. Skip can be heard yelling at Jimmy from down the hall.]

Mr. Jones: "This is a perfect example of why there is so much violence today. People insist on getting even. This entire incident could have been avoided if Skip would have listened to Jimmy when he told him that it was an accident."

Eric: "But it wasn't an accident. I saw him break it!"

Mr. Jones: "We better just end this discussion right now, before another fight breaks out."

Mr. Jones then assigns the homework.

The homework assignment is to write an essay on what steps can be taken to protect people from violent crimes and make the neighborhood safe.

ACTIVITY 5

Role play with a colleague the following scenario: Jerry, a precocious sixth grader tells you, in front of others in class, "I ain't doing your stupid homework." Let your colleague play the role of Jerry. Continue to role play for about a minute. Then ask your colleague to give you some feedback on how you dealt with the situation. Record findings below. What might you do differently next time? Okay, now try role playing again.

_____

_____

_____

_____

_____

_____

_____

_____

_____

_____

_____

_____

_____

_____

_____

_____

_____

_____

_____

_____

_____

_____

_____

Can I Effectively Manage My Classroom?

Do not train children to learning by force and harshness, but direct them to it by what amuses their minds, so that you may be better able to discover with accuracy the peculiar bent of the genius of each.

—Plato

Discipline problems are minimized when students are regularly engaged in meaningful activities geared to their interest and aptitudes.

—J. E. Brophy and T. Good

1. What is your greatest fear, if any, about dealing with student misbehavior?

2. Have you been adequately prepared to deal with serious misbehavior in the classroom?

3. Can you identify any classroom management theories or theorists that have helped you set up a discipline plan?

4. Do you have a well-thought-out discipline plan? Explain.

5. What do you want to know about classroom management?

Teaching is a challenging, complex art and science that demands not only knowledge and skill, but also empathy, caring, and commitment. Frequently frustrating and exhausting, good teaching encourages, inspires, and arouses that latent spark within each student. Still, teachers are confronted with difficult, seemingly insurmountable obstacles that can be puzzling and exasperating. Student misbehavior, for instance, may drive a teacher to the very limits of his or her endurance.

The principles and practices of effective discipline and classroom management are among the most important professional concerns that practicing educators confront daily. The public's attitude toward education, assessed by Gallup Polls sponsored by *Phi Delta Kappan,* indicate that discipline is one of the most intractable problems public schools must face. Further, teachers maintain that student misbehavior is perhaps the most troublesome and disconcerting problem they encounter in the classroom. The resultant frustration associated with student misbehavior not only increase levels of fatigue and stress, but also negatively impacts teacher performance.

Compounding the difficulties associated with classroom management and discipline is the fact that teachers are often ill prepared to deal with inappropriate student behavior. Ineffective suggestions such as "not to smile until Christmas" or that a well-planned lesson always will eliminate disruptive student behavior are out of step with current realities that confront classroom teachers.

There are no ready-made prescriptions to manage student behavior.

Unfortunately, there aren't ready-made prescriptions to manage student behavior, nor are there specific techniques that apply to all classroom situations. Despite the assertions of some who attempt to promote their particular "discipline system," no "one best system" of classroom management exists. An effective teacher utilizes an array of sound strategies to meet specific problems in particular situations in the classroom.

My purpose in this chapter will be to

1. Outline some practical strategies for dealing with classroom misbehavior

2. Assist you in developing your own system of discipline based on your unique needs and circumstances (see the sample later in this chapter titled "My Personal System of Discipline")

CAUTIONARY NOTE: Many schools employ building rules and/or discipline programs. Find out if your school does so and make sure to incorporate them into your system or rules.

Before introducing some key terms as a prerequisite for developing your own discipline plan, examine some of your preferences about student behavior.

The following reflective activity might stimulate thought about some personal needs that inevitably will be manifested in your discipline plan.

Reflect

What is your preferred teaching style? Do you prefer students to sit in rows and quietly pay attention to your lesson? Do you mind if students interrupt with questions? Do you structure lessons around group activities during which students work with each other on projects? Can you tolerate the inevitable noise that may result? Describe your preferred teaching style or styles. Also describe what you consider to be desirable student behavior. Finally, describe the relationship between your teaching style, student behavior, and how students learn best.

_____
_____
_____
_____
_____
_____

Share your responses with a colleague and see how your reflective comments above influence the discipline plan you develop later in this chapter.

CLASSROOM MANAGEMENT
IDEA #1: BASIC TERMS AND ELEMENTS

Let's define some terms and review some key information. Note that information here is gleaned from Charles (2001). See Appendix A for the best resources on the topic.

Behavior—all the physical and mental acts people perform. For example, a hiccup, neither good nor bad, is a human act.

There are various levels of misbehavior.

Misbehavior—the label given to any behavior that is considered inappropriate in a given context or situation. That hiccup, for instance, when performed intentionally in midst of a reading lesson may be considered misbehavior.

Discipline—steps taken to cause students to behave acceptably

Classroom Management—the process by which discipline strategies are implemented

Rules—guidelines that inform students how to act in class (e.g., please walk in class)

Procedures—deal with a specific activity and how to do it (e.g., how you expect students to line up for lunch)

Five Levels of Misbehavior—(In Declining Level of Severity)

1. *Aggression*—the most severe form of misbehavior, including physical or verbal attacks by students

2. *Immorality*—acts such as cheating, lying, and stealing

3. *Defiance of Authority*—when students refuse to comply with regulations

4. *Class Disruptions*—perhaps the most common form of misbehavior; acts including calling out, getting out of seat without permission, and general fooling around

5. *Goofing Off*—included in this category are those students who, for example, don't participate, daydream, and don't complete assignments

Three Stages of Discipline

1. *Preventive Discipline*—refers to those steps a teacher may take to preclude misbehavior from occurring in the first place

2. *Supportive Discipline*—refers to those steps a teacher may take to encourage student behavior during the first signs of misbehavior

3. *Corrective Discipline*—refers to those steps a teacher may take to restore order once misbehavior occurs

Six Elements to Consider About Classrooms

1. *Multidimensionality*—many events and acts occurring (i.e., the classroom is complex, not a simple, environment)

2. *Simultaneity*—many things happening at same time (i.e., teachers must remain cognizant and think quickly)

3. *Immediacy*—rapid pace at which events occur (i.e., events occur at an unbelievably fast pace)

4. *Unpredictability*—difficult to always know for sure what may occur (i.e., you are dealing with human beings, not inert raw materials, and therefore it's difficult to predict behavior)

5. *Publicness*—teach on stage (i.e., teachers are role models and must always remain aware of the effect they have on their students)

6. *History*—class develops a culture of experience and norms that provide the basis for future interactions (i.e., each class is different and assumes a "personality" of its own)

CLASSROOM MANAGEMENT IDEA #2: DEVELOPING YOUR PERSONAL SYSTEM OF DISCIPLINE

A plethora of effective strategies and techniques for maintaining classroom management are available to assist teachers in positively redirecting student misbehavior. Rather than developing a list of *do's and don'ts*—which have ephemeral benefits, to say the least, and more important, don't address your specific needs for maintaining classroom control. This chapter can assist you in developing your own system of discipline.

Student misbehavior, at some level, is inevitable. However, effective classroom managers are proactive, not reactive. They take effective steps to minimize occurrences of misbehavior. Preventive measures indicate a teacher's awareness that misbehavior might occur and establish guidelines for appropriate classroom behavior.

Still, misbehavior will occur in the best of classrooms. That's why supportive measures are necessary to quell disturbances at the outset. Corrective guidelines are necessary when preventive and supportive steps are inadequately implemented or ineffective with more severely disruptive students.

Developing a discipline system or plan that incorporates each of these three stages of discipline is essential to effective classroom management. Let's discuss some of the basic components of each stage and practical recommendations for their implementation.

Preventive Discipline

This is really the planning stage. It includes all the steps you'll take to establish a positive classroom environment conducive to student learning. Your effectiveness as a classroom manager depends on your ability to thoughtfully develop a plan that anticipates misbehavior and establishes guidelines for appropriate behavior.

Incorporating the three stages of discipline is essential to effective classroom management!

1. Preventative
2. Supportive
3. Corrective

1. *Develop a stimulating and worthwhile lesson*—Although a well-planned lesson alone is not an assurance that misbehavior never will occur, it's certainly advantageous in motivating and encouraging student participation. Incorporate a wide array of teaching strategies such as discussion groups, oral reports, role playing, cooperative learning, and peer tutoring. Intentionally deliver instruction in a variety of ways to meet the diverse learning-style needs of your students. Here are some effective teaching strategies matched to each of three learning style preferences:

> *Visual Preference*—For those who learn best by seeing, use pictures, films, charts, flash cards, computers, and transparencies.

> *Auditory Preference*—For those who learn best through verbal instructions, use lecture, oral directions, records, peer tutoring, mnemonic devices, and song.

> *Kinesthetic Preference*—For those who learn best by doing, use manipulatives, 3-D material, debate, projects, pantomime, interactive videos, physical movement, and plays.

2. *Organize your physical environment*—Your seating plan can affect student interaction. Regardless of your physical setup (e.g., rows, groups, horseshoe, pairs), make sure all seats are positioned to ensure visibility and allow you to gain proximity to any student as quickly as possible. Ensure that your room is uncluttered and that learning centers, sinks, clothing areas, and entrances are accessible. Though I personally like a nicely decorated room, too many classrooms are overly decorated and some students may be easily distracted.

3. *Develop five rules and procedures for appropriate behavior*—Rules establish clear expectations for student behavior. Rules let the students know what performance and behaviors you deem acceptable. Develop five rules for acceptable classroom behavior that you'll review the very first day of class and reinforce throughout the year. You can have your students add a rule or two that they feel should be included. Guidelines for establishing rules include the following:

> *State rules in a positive way* (e.g., "Please walk in the classroom" instead of "Don't run.").

> *State rules clearly* (e.g., "Listen in class" is too ambiguous; "Look at the person who is speaking to you" is clearer and conveys the behavior expected).

> *Make certain rules are consistent with school rules.*

Plan on common procedures you intend to review with your class (e.g., lineup procedures, what to do if students miss an assignment, and procedures for walking into the classroom after lunch).

Research indicates that effective managers spend time teaching rules and procedures. Don't worry that instructional time will be initially lost. Teaching and reinforcing rules and procedures are times well spent and may do much toward preventing inappropriate behavior.

4. *Use positive reinforcement, or "Catch 'em bein' good"*—Everyone wants encouragement and recognition. Effective teachers use varied and frequent reinforcement for acceptable behavior. As often as possible use some of these reinforcers:

> *Social Reinforcers*—Use verbal acknowledgments such as "I appreciate your hard work," "Keep it up," "Wow, I'm impressed," "Excellent." As a classroom teacher for 16 years, I always kept a list of 100 different expressions I could use. After a while, my students couldn't wait to hear which one they would receive! Use nonverbal reinforcers such as a smile, pat on the back, or a handshake. Reinforce every student at least once a day.
>
> *Graphic Reinforcers*—Use marks, checks, stars, happy faces, and the like.
>
> *Activities*—Acknowledge students who comply with rules and regulations. Don't wait until they misbehave for them to receive your attention. Allow the student to assume monitorial duties, sit near a friend, have free time, read a special book, have extra time at the learning center, or care for the class pet.
>
> *Tangible Reinforcers*—Use a token reward system in which students can earn coupons, for instance, to obtain prizes. They can earn points to receive a special positive phone call from you to their parents!

5. *Who's the boss?*—You are the authority in the classroom. Develop high standards for performance and expectations for behavior. Be fair and consistent when implementing your discipline plan.

Supportive Discipline

Any experienced teacher realizes that the best plan can't deter all misbehavior from occurring. Misbehavior is inevitable. Notice what happens in the following scenario.

Jose throws a crumpled paper from his seat into the garbage pail. Teacher doesn't respond. A moment later Maria throws a paper. Teacher doesn't react. Then Ronald throws a paper.

Teacher: "Stop that, Ronald."

When a teacher ignores a breach of a class rule, others are likely to follow suit. In the case above, when the teacher finally did reprimand a student, it was too late. Ronald's complaint may be "Why didn't you yell at Jose or Maria?" This may escalate into a verbal argument between teacher and student. In addition, Maria and Jose may be upset with Ronald for implicating them.

When you notice a student breaking a class rule, don't ignore the behavior, but rather "nip it in the bud" by employing one of many types of supportive discipline techniques. Your personal discipline system should include numerous supportive strategies (see the sample later in this chapter titled "My Personal System of Discipline"). If you're a relatively new teacher, I suggest you keep these techniques written on small index cards for easy reference. These are some of the techniques that can be used to support discipline:

With-it-ness—Jacob Kounin (1977) maintained that teachers who were aware of what was happening in their classrooms were less likely to have problems escalate. For instance, you're working at the board with one student and notice Manuel throwing paper from his seat. You say, "Manuel, that's your first warning." You're "with-it." You've communicated to the entire class that you're aware of what's happening and have put Manuel on notice. Being "with-it" will nip problems in the bud when they first occur.

Send signals—When you see Ira misbehaving, communicate your dissatisfaction with a nonverbal signal such as a frown, stare, or wave of the hand.

Use physical proximity—When you either anticipate a problem or see one initially developing, walk over to Denise as nonchalantly as possible and stand near her.

Corrective Discipline

Despite your best efforts to prevent student misbehavior and support discipline, there will be times when more stern or corrective measures are necessary. Don't hesitate to use these corrective measures. They communicate that you care and are willing to insist on proper classroom behavior.

According to Charles (2001), "[Y]our corrective techniques should be neither intimidating nor harshly punitive, but instead only what is necessary to stop the misbehavior and redirect it positively" (p. 31). Consider the following corrective techniques:

Be assertive—Lee Canter's (1989) model has gained popularity among some educators because it trains teachers to act more assertively. Canter's distinction between three different response styles is instructive:

1. *Nonassertive Style*—"For the fifth time, won't you please stop throwing that paper?"

2. *Hostile Style*—"If you throw that paper one more time I'll kick you out of here, stupid!"

3. *Assertive Style*—"I want you to stop throwing that paper and get back to solving those problems."

Assertive responses are effective corrective measures because they make your expectations known clearly and in a businesslike manner. Assertive teachers are ready to back up their response with action.

Invoke consequences for misbehavior—When you reviewed your class rules, students should have been apprised of the possible consequences for noncompliance. Therefore, when Ernest refuses to stop throwing paper you might say, "Ernest, you're refusing to work so you'll have to complete your assignment during recess." In developing your own system, you should note the nature and severity of each consequence tied to a specific type of misbehavior. These guidelines should be publicized and reviewed periodically.

Contracting—I have personally found this corrective measure very effective. Don't confront a student, if possible, in the midst of acting out in class. If the student must be removed (e.g., time-out), then do so. Try to meet with the student as soon after an incident as possible to develop a cooperative contract for appropriate behavior. This should involve an actual written document (usually effective in elementary or middle schools) in which an agreement between teacher and student is reached regarding rewards for good behavior and consequences for inappropriate behavior. Effective contracts should

- Be mutually agreed upon, not teacher-imposed
- Be realistic and short term
- Be specific (e.g., "Work on math problems for 30 minutes a day over the next week" is better than "Study hard")
- Specify how long the contract will be in effect
- Specify rewards
- Be signed by student, teacher, principal, and parent

Time-out—Time-out is a disciplinary strategy in which a student is removed from a situation and physically placed in a designated time-out area. Time-out is particularly effective when the student's misbehavior is precipitated by peer pressure. Though effective for younger children, time-out areas located outside your classroom are more effective with older students (plan time-out areas with your dean or assistant principal). Keep in mind these four steps when implementing time-out:

1. Designate a time-out area that is isolated to sight and sound as much as possible. The area should be undecorated and as disinteresting as possible.

2. Student must remain idle without work or amusement to occupy the time.

3. Establish a specific time for the punishment to last (e.g., five minutes). I used to place a stopwatch at the desk so that the student could self-monitor.

4. Follow-up. When a student returns to his or her seat make sure you say a few words about your expectations about future behavior. If you must briefly meet with the student after class, then do so.

Recollection

As I reread the suggestions above for preventive, supportive, and corrective discipline, I was reminded of a former student for whom none of the above-mentioned strategies worked.

Shaheim was a student in my fourth-grade class in the South Bronx, New York, during my second year of teaching. Shaheim was a clever miscreant. My day was made, I'm sorry to admit, when I took attendance and Shaheim did not respond because he was absent. Oh, what a day that was. Unfortunately, there weren't many days that Shaheim was absent. He appeared to love school, or shall I say loved to make my day a horror. He would do anything and everything to get under my skin. His senseless tapping of the pencil on his desk, despite my protestations, and his throwing papers around the room annoyed me to no end. Hardly a day passed without Shaheim getting into a physical fight, harassing a fellow student, or arguing with a teacher or fellow student. I was at my wits end. I tried everything I learned in college. Positive reinforcement didn't work, nor did time-out. Private consultations with him were short-lived and his parents were no help. In fact, they looked to me to "solve" his problems. Visits to the assistant principal's office provided momentary respites, but before too long Shaheim was back in class. I referred him to guidance and even suggested he be tested for learning disabilities or something. Reports came back that he was fine and "normal." Never once, by the way, did they observe his behavior while in class. To make a long story a bit shorter, Shaheim made it through fourth grade but I barely did. One of the lessons I learned during that second year of teaching was that even one disruptive, unruly student can really disturb a class. "It only takes one" is a very true aphorism chanted and acknowledged by teachers. Still, I was glad the year was over and really hoped that Shaheim would mature enough in the following years so that his future teachers would have it easier than I did.

Six years passed and during my lunch period one day I had a visitor who wanted to meet with me. I looked up at this tall, lanky well-dressed young man. Was this Shaheim? Indeed, it was. He introduced himself and declared, "I came back, Mr. Glanz, just to see you because I am now halfway through high school and I'm doing really well thanks to you." "Thanks to me?" I retorted. Shaheim made my day when he was absent. I yelled at him and threw him out of my class any chance I could. I did everything I could to no avail. In fact, I wish I could relive those early years of teaching. I made so many mistakes. Especially in the way I dealt with students like Shaheim. I now know better how to more positively work with students like Shaheim. In those days I'm sorry to admit, I resorted to anything to "get him to behave." I'm not particularly proud of the sarcastic, belittling remarks I would make in a vain attempt to pacify students like Shaheim. So when he declared that he wanted to thank me, I felt like apologizing to him! Also, I thought, "If he is praising me as his best teacher, could you imagine the other teachers he had?" I listened.

"Mr. Glanz, yes, thanks to you. Sure you were rough with me, but I deserved it. Others threw me out and gave up. You never gave up. I remember the talks we had during lunchtime or after school. You never gave up on me. You cared." I was stunned. I was touched beyond words. A few moments passed in small talk and then he shook my hand. As I am now writing about this incident, I can feel his warm, generous, and firm handshake. I never saw Shaheim again. I hope he's reading this book. I want to thank him because he made my day that day. He affected me so deeply that I recall the incident in order to try to inspire you to realize that we, indeed, make a difference, even when we think we may not.

What are your recollections of any Shaheims you might have taught or tried to teach?

_____

_____

_____

_____

_____

_____

Seven Steps to Developing a Personalized Discipline System

1. *What are your needs?* The first step in developing a discipline system is to prioritize your needs for classroom management. Make a list of those conditions essential for your ideal classroom (e.g., students should have assigned seats, work quietly, respect fellow classmates and teacher, and hand work in on time).

2. *What are your rules and procedures?* Develop a list of acceptable behaviors, culled from your needs list, that you want to teach and reinforce.

3. *What are the consequences for compliance and noncompliance?* Compose a list of positive and negative consequences tied to each rule and procedure.

4. *What strategies will you employ?* List specific strategies you feel comfortable implementing in each of the three stages of discipline: preventive, supportive, and corrective.

5. *How will you implement your plan?* Plan to teach your system through discussions, role playing, and practice sessions. Review and reinforce your plan throughout the year.

Develop Your Own System of Discipline

You'll need to

List essential conditions

List rules and procedures

List consequences

Plan strategies

Plan implementation

Test

Modify and expand your plan as need arises

---

6. *How will you test your plan?* Start putting your system into action. Be fair and consistent, yet flexible. Modify your plan as needed.

7. *If problems arise, as they most certainly will, should you give up?* Never! All students can learn self-control. All students want acceptance and recognition. Your system can satisfy their needs for social acceptance. Always seek to expand the repertoire of strategies in your plan. Consistency is the heart to carrying out any discipline strategy or plan. Seek assistance and guidance from others. If you believe all children can learn, then believe that all children can become sincere, courteous, responsible, and disciplined.

CONCLUSION

Do experienced teachers need a plan? Regardless of experience, all teachers need to plan strategies for dealing with nonconformity to classroom rules and procedures. Your personalized plan should be reviewed periodically and matched to the unique needs of your current class. Not every technique will work with every student or class. There aren't quick-fix recipes to easily implement. Some students definitely will need special referrals. Nevertheless, develop your plan, share ideas with colleagues, and continue to find ways to help your students reach their full potential. See the sample discipline plan that follows. Hopefully it will guide you in developing your own. Then, assess your ability to effectively manage your classroom by completing the Respond activity that follows the sample plan.

CLASSROOM MANAGEMENT
IDEA #3: A SAMPLE DISCIPLINE PLAN

My Personal System of Discipline

by Rachel Schwab

I teach a first-grade boys' mainstream class. My curriculum includes reading, writing, math, social studies, and science. My students usually are not used to the rules and behaviors that are expected in a first-grade classroom. Rules, procedures, and reinforcers (especially negative ones), are a new experience for them.

Therefore, I must be careful to present and explain my rules, positive consequences, and negative consequences in a clear, easy to understand, and precise manner.

Personal Belief Statement

One of my main goals as a teacher is *to make a difference in the life a child.* I aim to accomplish this, first, by getting to know each child well, as the whole person that they are. I also aim to create a positive and warm atmosphere in my classroom, in which every child is encouraged to reach his full potential, knowing that I believe in him. I do my best to maintain a "fun" and interesting atmosphere as well, so that my students' early experience in learning will be one of fun and enjoyment. To this end, I show my students love and respect, yet at the same time set specific limits, so that my students' self-esteem grows while they learn responsible behavior.

These smaller goals are meant to fulfill my belief in making a difference in the life of a child, by helping their year in first grade be one of accomplishment and growth in a pleasant atmosphere. In this way, their first experience in "real" school is a positive one.

My Needs

One of my most basic needs is a well-managed classroom, where students know what is expected of them, the room is orderly, and routines are set with room for flexibility when necessary.

Another personal need is for each child to feel that he gets what he needs, academically, emotionally, so that he can grow in knowledge, self-esteem, and responsibility.

It bothers me when my students are mean to each other or laugh at one another; therefore I do not allow these behaviors in my classroom. This includes teaching my students to act respectfully toward one another and to show caring for each other, both of which are important social skills.

Within the set routines, it is important for there to be a lively, warm and positive atmosphere in my classroom, so that my students can develop a lifelong love of learning.

My Rules

1. Follow directions.

2. Raise your hand before you speak.

3. Work quietly in your seat without disturbing others.

4. Be kind and polite to each other.

5. Speak with respect.

I selected these rules because they focus on two of my major concerns: (1) maintaining order in the classroom and (2) promoting a positive classroom atmosphere with warmth and respect. If these conditions are not met, the potential for learning cannot be fulfilled.

The first rule is important during independent work, group work, and during transition times, to promote good classroom management.

The second and third rules help maintain a calm, pleasant environment in a classroom. Of course there must be some flexibility within these rules, such as during discussions and specific activities.

The third, fourth, and fifth rules are particularly helpful in maintaining an atmosphere of caring and respect and a positive environment. Caring, trust, and respect must be present between students as well as between the teacher and her students.

Rule four also encourages good social skills, which are important skills in a first-grade classroom.

I have separate rules for when the students work in cooperative groups. Since the nature of the setup is so different, my expectations when students work together differ from those when they are working independently or when I am teaching them.

Cooperative Group Rules

1. Take turns talking quietly.

2. Listen to each other's ideas.

3. Praise each other's ideas.

4. Help each other when asked.

5. Stay together until everyone is done.

6. Talk about how you worked well together and how you can improve.

So as not to overwhelm my students with so many rules, I do not present all the rules to my class the first week of school. Cooperative group rules are first presented and modeled when we begin working in groups.

Before posting the rules, I read them to my students and we discuss them and why they are so important in a classroom setting. We also role play them to make sure that the students understand them.

I find that having rules for the various ways that we learn helps create an orderly classroom and a pleasant learning environment. Children like to know procedures and what is expected of them. The time spent teaching rules is always regained when a classroom can be managed well because of the rules and procedures that are in place.

Positive Consequences

1. Catch them being good—use verbal praise. Not only do children themselves respond to the praise they are given, it also causes a positive ripple effect. The other students also want to be recognized, so they imitate the behavior that was praised.

2. Students who behave well can get a positive note, a "happygram," sent home at the end of the day. I also make positive phone calls home, and I find that parents are thrilled to receive them.

3. My students love helping me, or being chosen to be my monitor. Students who follow the rules and behave are chosen to be monitors for various tasks.

4. Children earn the right to be first in line for library or recess by behaving appropriately.

5. For extra special recognition, I have a child take a note to the principal, detailing his good behavior.

6. Depending on the class and the time of year, I have some type of reinforcement system set up, either individual or row charts, or classwide contests. In these ways, the children can accumulate a predetermined number of stickers to reach a larger reward. The rewards vary from tangible prizes to extra recess, planned trips, or miniparties. I also have small rewards that I give out randomly. In this way, the children get the incentives they need without constantly "working for a prize."

Negative Consequences

(In increasing order of severity)

1. Eye contact—the student knows that I am aware of what she is doing, yet she has a chance to correct her behavior before it becomes an issue.

2. Warning—the child receives a verbal warning about the inappropriate behavior.

3. The child works away from the group for five minutes. I do not increase the amount of time spent working away from the group. I usually find that due to their age, it either works the first time or the child continues to act up, and a longer period of time only serves as a greater distraction to others.

4. Lose two minutes of recess. I do not take recess away completely, since children need that time to move around and be part of social interaction. I do find that losing two minutes of recess is very effective and still allows them some time to take part in recess activities.

5. Call parents.

6. *Severe clause:* Go to the principal.

My rules, positive consequences, and negative consequences are sent home to the parents as our classroom discipline plan. The parents discuss it with their children, sign it, and return it to me. This way, they know how I run my classroom and can better understand anything that might happen.

Preventive Discipline

1. My students and I discuss the rules at the beginning of the year. We review the rules and the necessity for them during the year. The class understands what is expected of them.

2. I plan the use of my classroom space to maximize visibility and proximity—and use these techniques.

3. "With-it-ness"—when students realize that you know what's going on and that you won't put up with it, they don't try to test you as much. Also, if you exude self-confidence and an air of authority, students respond appropriately.

4. When my lessons are well planned, organized, interesting, and creative, students are less likely to misbehave since they are interested and actively participate.

5. Rewards from my list of positive consequences reinforce positive behavior and serve as an incentive for others as well.

Supportive Discipline

1. Establish eye contact with the student.

2. Use of nonverbal signals—shaking head, hand signals, and so on.

3. Use proximity control/touch.

4. Use verbal warnings.

5. Discuss relevant rules and firmly demand appropriate behavior (includes the broken-record technique).

6. Use rewards from my list of positive consequences.

Corrective Discipline

1. Firmly demand specific behavior.

2. Implement negative consequences (previously listed), based on the severity of the behavior.

Closing Statement

This plan will be the foundation of my personal system of discipline. The system gives me a way of addressing my classroom needs. It corresponds with my philosophy toward children and teaching. However, classes differ from year to year, so I need to be aware that not all methods will work every year. I also believe that it is important to remain flexible, since students vary greatly from one another because each child is an individual with specific needs. This is not in conflict with remaining consistent. Consistency is one of the most important details of any system of discipline. Students can understand what is expected of them and know the inherent consequences both positive and negative. However, there always will be students with special needs who demand greater understanding. Because of this, a certain amount of flexibility for rules and consequences must be anticipated. Sometimes students need individual behavior plans, charts, or systems. I have found that students understand and respect this concept, as long as they feel their needs are being addressed and they get what they need. They can accept that fair is not always equal since everyone has individual needs.

I feel that being aware of my needs in the classroom, as well as being aware of my beliefs in dealing with children, can help me become a reflective practitioner, a teacher who thinks about what I am doing in the classroom and what I hope to accomplish. This, together with knowledge, ideas of positive consequences and negative consequences, and an understanding of my students, hopefully will assist me in reaching my goal of making a difference in the life of a child.

Respond

Rubric for Assessing Classroom Management

Directions: Assess how effective a classroom manager you are. Circle the Performance Dimension for each of the eight categories

| | Performance Dimension | | | |
	Distinguished	Proficient	Emerging	Unsatisfactory
Monitoring Seat Work	Teacher very well aware of what is occurring in the classroom; appears to have "eyes in back of head"; able to do several tasks simultaneously; defines rules of what's expected from students during seat work; offers social praise to those who are working; able to immediately "nip in the bud" a child who may seem off-task; able to "overlap" and do two things at the same time; spends just the right amount of time with each child; monitors seat work very well.	Teacher aware of what is occurring in classroom; uses effective verbal and nonverbal communicative techniques to monitor student behavior; gives praise most of the time and reprimands those students who do not follow class rules; spends a bit too much time with each child; help provided as needed; uses eye contact and scans the room every few minutes; attentive to monitoring seat work.	Teacher scans room occasionally; somewhat aware of what students are doing; misses some off-task behavior; stays near desk or concentrates attention on one half of room; aware when arguments occur and separates students; tries to implement monitoring strategies, albeit inconsistently.	Teacher works extensively with one group while ignoring others; unaware of off-task students; fails to reinforce those on-task; employs ineffective supportive disciplinary techniques to off-task students; unaware of what students are doing; does not monitor students effectively.
Transitions	Actions of the students are seamless; students wholly responsible for their actions and teacher overlaps; teacher seldom	Teacher has a set schedule posted in a prominent place in classroom; students aware of when to	Teacher may give instructions during transition; instructions vague; verbal	No well-defined set of procedures for transitions; students unsure how to proceed; teacher

| | Performance Dimension | | | |
	Distinguished	Proficient	Emerging	Unsatisfactory
	behind desk during transitions; teacher walks among students and incorporates proximity control; visual and audio reminders are apparent; little or no loss of instructional time; motivational devices displayed so students are encouraged to move and get ready quickly; teacher masterfully facilitates transitions.	expect changes; students can respond to instructions efficiently most of the time; procedures for transitions are reviewed weekly and practiced so that when actual transitions occur little instructional time is lost; students are reinforced for good transitions; teacher models desired behaviors to students; teacher aware of the importance of transition and implements strategies that facilitate smooth transitions.	praise may be given to students complying with the routine; teacher may put transitional times on the board; delays between activities are no more than five minutes; teacher prepares materials, but spends too much time setting up; teacher aware of the importance of transition but has difficulty in facilitation.	remains in fixed position rather than circulates; long delays before start of activities; teacher unprepared for next activity and takes time putting belongings away or taking out material for next subject; teacher has little idea of the importance of transition.
Classroom Setup	Furniture arranged for easy movement by both teacher and students;	Teacher has access to every student; every student has a way of	Classroom visibility impaired, but there is a constant	Furniture arranged in a way that is unsafe or

(Continued)

(Continued)

	Performance Dimension			
	Distinguished	Proficient	Emerging	Unsatisfactory
	all students have access to each other and to necessary materials, even during special activities; teacher can see all the students at all times; students can see teacher and board at all times; classroom neatly arranged; materials organized and labeled; materials in an appropriate location in close proximity to working area of students; each student has designated area for personal belongings that is both organized and accessible; use of space in the classroom maximized.	retrieving necessary materials; classroom neat and organized; classroom safe and aisles are clear; teacher aware of the importance of classroom setup.	rearrangement of desks and other furniture in an effort to ensure that all students can see teacher and board; classroom generally untidy; students have a general area to keep their belongings; classroom generally safe except for clutter and occasional obstacles; seating arrangement not always followed.	impedes accessibility of both teacher and students; teacher has a hard time getting through desks and cubbies when trying to reach a student who needs help; materials stored in areas where both teacher and students cannot access them easily; not every student visible to the teacher and vice versa; room poorly decorated; classroom untidy and disorganized; seating arrangement rigid.
Classroom Atmosphere	Students supported by teacher; students motivated to participate and eager to achieve; students share	Students generally participate and seem comfortable; teacher seems satisfied and	Some students comfortable but others seem tense; students are not comfortable	Students hesitate to answer and seem tense and anxious; teacher seems frustrated

| | Performance Dimension | | | |
	Distinguished	Proficient	Emerging	Unsatisfactory
	information and risk giving their opinions voluntarily; teacher welcomes students enthusiastically in the morning; teacher gives lots of specific praise; teacher encourages constantly; students feel that class is safe and fun; students appear to trust the teacher; atmosphere open and students can share anything appropriate with teacher and class.	pleased with the class and her teaching; teacher uses positive reinforcement most of the time; teacher generally consistent with discipline procedures; teacher cares about the students' well-being; atmosphere appears warm and open.	with offering their own opinions; teacher smiles less as the day progresses and is often moody; teacher compliments and criticizes; teacher gets frustrated with weaker students; teacher uses inconsistent discipline procedures; teacher shows warmth and care inconsistently; teacher tries to control anger; classroom atmosphere not ideal for learning.	and tired; teacher barks instructions and uses lots of criticism and sarcasm; teacher often threatens to punish students; teacher inconsistent in discipline procedures; teacher appears disinterested and uncaring.
Response to Student Misbehavior	Teacher consistent in dealing with misbehavior; develops a positive approach to classroom management; remains calm and does not overreact;	Teacher alert and usually aware of misbehaviors; responds to misbehaviors with verbal interventions that are private so as not to embarrass	Teacher generally aware of misconduct but unsure what to do; responds verbally to a misbehavior but doesn't use other	Teacher unaware of what is transpiring most of the time; often intervenes physically to misbehavior; screams and sometimes

(Continued)

(Continued)

	Performance Dimension			
	Distinguished	Proficient	Emerging	Unsatisfactory
	clearly states academic and social expectations; elicits rules and procedures from students; reacts immediately and positively to misbehavior; firm, fair, and caring; develops a systematic approach to classroom management.	student; responses to misbehavior appropriate but inconsistent; addresses the misbehavior, not the character of the student; develops established rules and procedures; teacher uses logical consequences; responds to early signs of misbehavior.	strategies; takes misbehavior personally; inconsistent in discipline strategies; eager to remove students who misbehave; eager to learn positive strategies but has difficulty implementing them.	threatens students with punishment; punishments are unreasonable or inappropriate; teacher uses humiliation or sarcasm to get the students to listen; ineffective in dealing with misbehavior.
Reinforcement	Teacher provides constant and consistent reinforcement for positive behavior; all students are acknowledged and reinforced positively; students have developed, with teacher's assistance, intrinsic motivation; teacher develops systematic approach to reinforcement;	Teacher consistently incorporates reinforcement strategies; acknowledges most of the students in class every day; uses names of students most of the time; provides tangible rewards as soon as appropriate behavior observed;	Teacher occasionally uses reinforcement, though inconsistently; praises students superficially; reinforces only some students but ignores most others; lacks training and experience in applying reinforcement.	Teacher infrequently uses positive reinforcement techniques; lacks a systematic approach to reinforcement; infrequent use of tangible or nontangible reinforcers; seems uncomfortable or reluctant to use reinforcement.

| | Performance Dimension | | | |
	Distinguished	Proficient	Emerging	Unsatisfactory
	reinforcement genuine, appropriate, and well distributed.	sends notes home about good behavior; realizes the importance of reinforcement.		
Rules and Procedures	Rules and procedures are collaboratively established, posted, reviewed, practiced, monitored, and reinforced for all class matters.	Rules established and reviewed by teacher; students know what is expected of them; consequences established and evenly distributed; students obey rules, even though they may not thoroughly understand them; rules stated positively; develops consistent rules and procedures.	Too many rules for students to remember; rules are not posted to remind students; unrealistic or unreasonable consequences; rules not elicited and reviewed; rules not vigorously enforced; procedures not well defined; teacher is eager but lacks training and experience.	No set routine— different every day; few set rules; no set consequences; too much freedom; children do not know what is expected of them; rules are stated negatively; no set procedures during transition time, and so forth.
Lesson Presentation	Lessons well planned, interesting, and meaningful; teacher incorporates multifaceted approaches and	Teacher plans lessons; goals and objectives stated; material organized; students encouraged to	Teacher somewhat familiar with content/ subject; planning evident but has difficulty with delivery;	Teacher unfamiliar with content/ subject; lesson planning inadequate; lessons

(Continued)

(Continued)

Performance Dimension			
Distinguished	Proficient	Emerging	Unsatisfactory
methods to teaching; teacher uses technology; projects voice and modulates at appropriate times; excellent pacing and wait time; sensitive to learning styles and multiple intelligences; lesson, although very structured with an introduction, body, conclusion, medial summaries, and reinforcing activities, is also innovative; students' level of understanding monitored well; clearly, a master teacher.	participate; teacher projects voice and has good pacing; teacher uses visual aids; lesson has a clear beginning, middle, and end; incorporates medial summaries; teacher communicates lesson well.	objectives of lesson are at times unclear; pacing and delivery problems evident; students not encouraged to participate; poor wait time; inability to project or use voice effectively; eager but needs additional training and experience.	unsuitable for level of class; lecturing occurs most of the time; teacher speaks in monotone; teacher's explanations are vague; students appear uninterested and off-task; teacher relies heavily on textbook; needs training and experience with lesson plan development and presentation.

Follow-Up Questions/Activities

Based on the information in this chapter, develop your own system of discipline.

My Personal System of Discipline

1. Grade and instructional levels

2. Subject

3. Social realities

4. A personal belief statement

5. My classroom rules (list at least five rules and discuss briefly how you would implement them)

6. Positive consequences (list)

7. Negative consequences (list)

8. My preventive discipline measures (list)

9. My supportive discipline measures (list)

10. My corrective discipline measures (list)

11. Closing statement

What useful information about managing your classroom did you learn in this chapter?

List ten suggestions you would offer to a fellow beginning teacher about handling student misbehavior.

_____

_____

_____

_____

_____

_____

_____

_____

_____

_____

_____

_____

_____

_____

_____

_____

_____

_____

_____

_____

ACTIVITY 6

In Google or your favorite search engine, type in *cognitive learning strategies*. You'll find a lot of material. Record your findings below and then share your findings with a colleague.

_____

_____

_____

_____

_____

_____

_____

_____

_____

_____

_____

_____

_____

_____

_____

_____

_____

_____

_____

_____

_____

_____

_____

_____

_____

How Can I Help My Students Learn?

It's not what is poured into a student, but what is planted.

—Linda Conway

When I first began teaching, I visited with a former teacher who I respected greatly. I asked him for some advice. He responded without hesitation, "A good teacher must love his students." "Love?" I queried. "Yes, love. When you come to care about each student as your very own child, then you'll become a great teacher."

—Jeffrey Glanz

Focus Questions

1. What factors affect student learning?
2. How can you help your students learn?
3. Do you really believe that what you do in the classroom makes a difference in student achievement? Explain.
4. What did your teachers do to help you learn?
5. How does cooperative learning promote student achievement?
6. Can you think of one very important element of good pedagogy often neglected by teachers and schools that directly impacts learning? Read on.

Many factors affect student learning. In the space provided below, list as many such factors as you can.

_____

_____

_____

_____

_____

Did you include any of these?

- Organized, safe, and well-run school
- Strong, professional administrative leadership
- Active and positive parental involvement
- Sufficient federal, state, and local funding

These and other *external* factors, while important and perhaps essential, do not have an immediate and direct impact on student achievement. If you've learned anything thus far in *Teaching 101,* it's that you, the teacher, are the most critical element in the classroom. An experienced, credentialed teacher who possesses specialized content and pedagogical knowledge, instructional skills, and positive dispositions directly affects student learning more than any other factor (Darling-Hammond, 2003). Did your list above include any of these factors related specifically to what a teacher does in the classroom?

- Utilizes varied teaching strategies, including direct teaching, discussion, Socratic dialogue, and cooperative learning (see discussion later in chapter)
- Sets high expectations
- Establishes a consistent classroom management and discipline plan
- Engages students in well-planned, meaningful lessons
- Stimulates critical thinking
- Communicates complex ideas simply
- Checks for understanding
- Employs strategies to keep students successfully on-task
- Responds well to individual learning differences
- Differentiates instruction so that low and high achievers' needs are met
- Uses culturally relevant pedagogy
- Offers appropriate, genuine praise and reinforcement
- Challenges students with thought-provoking activities
- Assesses student learning on a consistent basis
- Cares for the students

Though all of these factors collectively are important to promote student achievement, I wonder how many of you listed *study skill instruction* as one important factor for promoting student learning. Teaching your students how to study, including listening, note-taking, and test-taking skills, goes a long way toward helping them succeed in school. An often neglected aspect of learning is teaching students the essential skills for academic survival, such as how to study, memorize, take notes and tests, and generally succeed in school. This chapter is devoted, in large part, to introducing you to some of the key elements in an area of study officially known as cognitive learning strategy instruction (Pressley & Woloshyn, 1995). The strategies in this chapter, drawn from extensive research in the field, are relatively simple to learn and are very effective in promoting student learning. Cognitive learning strategy, more simply known as study skill instruction, is premised on these key ideas:

> Cognitive learning strategy is study skill instruction.
>
> Teach students how to think and process information.
>
> Integrate study skills instruction into lessons.
>
> Plan.
>
> Have the right attitude.
>
> Use strategies.

- Our most important task as teachers is to ultimately promote student learning. Caring for students and even posing the right questions are important only to the degree to which students learn. Certainly, learning is more than scoring high marks on standardized reading tests. We need to broaden the way we assess student learning; more about that in Chapter 7.
- We, as teachers, have a powerful influence on student learning. Effective teachers do not lift their hands in defeat, proclaiming, "Well, what more can I do if Jerry doesn't get support from his parents and if I am continually harangued by administrators." Effective teachers have a high sense of self-efficacy; that is, we feel and know that we make a difference, and we don't give up.
- We promote learning not only with rich, content-based instruction utilizing sound pedagogy, but we take an active role in fostering learning by teaching students how to think and process the information they learn.
- Students can learn almost anything as long as they have the necessary study skill strategies. Once students have practiced and developed these skills, they can apply them to any learning situation.

I have written this chapter to introduce you to this important area that impacts student learning, and I will provide several practical suggestions and strategies. The strategies included are based on sound theory and research in cognitive learning. While there are countless "how to study" books on the market, this chapter is unique in that I have translated cognitive learning theories into a simpler format. I have not included every possible skill that can assist in learning, nor have I treated these strategies comprehensively (that's for a separate book; actually, there are several good ones on the market, see Appendix A for suggestions). I have only chosen, however, research-proven techniques that I have personally used with countless students in order to introduce you to these ideas. You may want to extend your understanding by consulting some of the reference works cited. Our goal as teachers is to make learning the skills easy and fun.

Very important: Spend time in class teaching your students the ideas below. Introduce the study skills as a unit of activity at the beginning and reinforce them throughout the year or semester. In fact, research indicates that when teachers actually refer to and teach these study skills as they teach lessons, student achievement rises dramatically (Mangrum, Iannuzzi, & Strichart, 1998).

Reflect

Although you may concur that study skills instruction is important, how, you might ask, does a teacher find the time to teach study skills in an already overcrowded curriculum? What are some ways you can incorporate these study skills in your class? One hint: Rather than think of cognitive strategy instruction as a separate curriculum area, how might you integrate such study in your teaching without really missing the proverbial "beat"? Jot some ideas down and then read the suggestion below. I'm sure you'll come up with other ways as well.

_____

_____

_____

_____

_____

Okay, here's one way to easily integrate study skill instruction into a lesson. Suppose you are teaching your students a science unit on erosion and you explain that weathering, a process that breaks down rocks, is aided by running water, ice, rain, plants, animals, and chemicals. You might assist student memory of the material by teaching them a quick and easy mnemonic strategy (refer to mnemonics later in this chapter) by asking, for instance: "Okay, these six forces help break down rocks, how might we remember them easily?" Perhaps, give them an opportunity to develop ways, or say, "Why not use the first letters of the words, such as in RIP RAC?" "So, when I ask you on the test what the six ways that weathering can break down rocks are, you'll say RIP RAC and explain that R is running water; I is ice; P is plants; R is rain; A is animals; and C is chemicals." Providing in-class time to develop these learning strategies may indeed take up some class time, but I assure you the time will be well spent. Good teachers don't expect students to already have these skills. Good teachers actively teach the skills and incorporate them into their lessons. Although these study skills are particularly helpful for students with formally assessed learning disabilities, they are useful for all students, even for you and me.

Experience has taught me that all people can become successful learners. All that's needed is a plan, the right attitude, and study skill strategies.

The remainder of this chapter is divided into five sections:

1. Simple Strategies for the Early Grades

Study skill instruction should begin early on in a student's education. The strategies listed below are simple yet powerful to get students to develop good study habits.

2. Strategies on How to Improve Note-Taking Skills

Success in school depends on how well your students can take notes. Since much instruction in schools is communicated in a traditional manner— that is, through lecture—note-taking skills are essential to success.

Many research studies demonstrate the importance of listening skills as a prerequisite to effective note taking. Listening is the foundation of all language skills as well. Success depends on how well students listen in class. The better listeners they are, the better notes they will take during class.

Students can indeed learn to become effective listeners and note takers. Guide them through the steps that follow. The more strategies they adopt, the better listeners and note takers they'll become.

3. Simple Strategies on How to Improve Study Skills

Obviously, success in school depends, to a large degree, on how well students study. Notice I didn't write *how hard they study*. Too many students think that studying long and hard is the best way to study. Not true. Why study hard when they should study *smart*?

By learning and incorporating various study skill strategies, they will become more efficient and better learners. If they are D- or C-level students, these skills certainly will help them do much, much better. Surprisingly, even if they are B or A students, they'll benefit with the use of these study techniques because they'll become more efficient learners. They may, in fact, reduce their study time by at least a third and still get those As! I'm sure they'll appreciate that extra time, too.

Follow each strategy outlined below using the same format used above for listening and note taking. The more strategies your students adopt, the better at studying they'll become. With enhanced studying skills, they're on their way to that A.

4. *Simple Strategies for Reading Material From a Chapter or Book*

Students need guidance on gleaning material as they read. Often we tell students to read pages so and so without giving them strategies to cull relevant information. Research in study skills demonstrates that when teachers offer guidance to students as they learn and read, student comprehension and achievement increases.

As you introduce these aforementioned ideas to students, have them complete the following by checking those that apply.

I use this strategy all the time._____

I sometimes use this strategy. _____

I will try this strategy. _____

This strategy works. _____

This strategy doesn't work. _____

This strategy works sometimes. _____

5. *Cooperative Learning*

Discussion of cooperative learning, though mentioned earlier in the book, is explained here in more detail because it has been proven to be one of the most valuable ways to promote student learning (Slavin, 1994). Research indicates that teachers who incorporate cooperative learning strategies promote student achievement. Cooperative learning is an especially useful strategy when employing cognitive strategy (study skills) instruction because many students learn best in cooperative groups. Cooperative grouping to promote study is particularly effective.

Some strategies in the following section require explanation, while others are self-explanatory.

HELPING MY STUDENTS IDEA #1: SIMPLE STRATEGIES FOR THE EARLY GRADES

Strategy #1: Listen

Play listening games with students. Repeat a few words and have students repeat them. Award points, give out stars, and so on. Have students listen to songs on tape and have them repeat (sing) them.

Strategy #2: Thinking About Thinking and Learning

Ask students a simple question like "What do you want to do now?" As they answer, stop and encourage them to think about how they decided to answer the question. Encourage them to become aware of how they think, how they solve problems, and how they learn. Starting this metacognitive process early on will yield academic benefits years later.

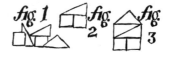

Strategy #3: Taking Directions

Play games such as Simon Says. Select a student to play teacher. Have the child give directions to others. Discuss with class why following directions is important. Role play how to follow directions.

Strategy #4: Breathe

Teach young students how to effectively deal with stress. Encourage them to talk about their concerns. Teach them simple breathing exercises.

Reflection

Share with a colleague how you would use any or all of the preceding ideas.

HELPING MY STUDENTS IDEA #2: SIMPLE STRATEGIES ON HOW TO IMPROVE LEARNING

Strategy #1: Being Prepared

Ask students, "What does being prepared mean to you?" Elicit that being prepared means getting ready before they come to school. Being prepared includes having extra sharpened pencils; working pens, highlighters, and/or markers; notebooks or loose-leafs with blank sheets for writing; textbooks; and any other materials needed. Have them make a list of what they need and have them check everything the evening before school.

Getting to school on time is a form of preparation as well. Also, remind them to come to school with the right attitude—ready to learn! On an index card, have them write the following sentence and urge them to keep it handy: *"I'm ready and willing to learn and I will learn!"* Repeating the sentence every morning for the next ten school days and then once a week until the end of the school year is suggested. Obviously, depending on the age and grade level of your students, you will have to modify this approach. But do tell your older students that *affirmations* are very powerful instruments of success for adults.

Therefore, being prepared means

1. *Bringing materials*—Having the proper supplies will prepare them for note taking.

2. *Arriving on time*—Arriving on time is important because they'll likely hear the instructor review the lesson objective and overview.

3. *Having a positive attitude*—Self-affirmations, like "I'm ready and willing to learn and I will learn," are powerful and effective strategies because they affect one's subconscious in a positive way. With the proper attitude, students are more likely to succeed.

Strategy #2: Sit in the Front Row

Remind students to get to class early, especially the first day of class, to get a seat in the front row. Encourage them to sit in the middle of the row. Sitting near the entrance or a window will be distracting. If the teacher later asks them to move to the back, they should respectfully insist on sitting at the front, saying simply "I learn best when I'm near the teacher!" Advantages of this approach include the following:

- Sitting in the front allows them to hear the teacher, even whispers or low intonations.
- Those who are seated at the front get the "goodies" first. For instance, handouts or special props are handed to those sitting nearest the instructor. The handouts may run out before those seated in the back get them.
- The teacher naturally will see those students seated in the front. He or she will interact with them, verbally and otherwise, far more than those students seated in the rear.
- There is also a psychological benefit to sitting up front. The teacher will consider them more involved and interested in class, and that certainly can't hurt their chances of getting a better grade.
- Students are more likely to pay attention and take better notes when they are seated near the instructor.

Strategy #3: Be an Active Listener: Look Attentive and Alert

Encourage students to look at the teacher and use good eye contact. Model behavior for students during your teaching. Give them examples by role playing inactive listeners versus active ones.

Strategy #4: Don't Sit Next to Talkers and Troublemakers

Explain why doing so may keep students off-task.

Strategy #5: With the Teacher's Permission, Use a Tape Recorder for Difficult, Content-Laden Lessons

Would you allow a student to record a session? For some students this technique is a superb way to ensure that they at least get the information. That way they can play back the tape at home to record missing notes.

Strategy #6: Ask Questions and Ask Teacher to Repeat

Encourage students to ask questions. Inform the class that you are willing to repeat and further explain any idea mentioned in class.

Strategy #7: Don't Write Down
Every Word; Use Key or Main Words

Explain to students that they should not try to write everything down. They should record main ideas. Give them a mock lecture and have them record notes. Then, divide class into groups for them to compare notes. Compare your notes with a classmate to determine the extent to which you took adequate notes. Though this is a time-consuming activity, research again indicates that when teachers take the time to teach students how to study, or in this case to take notes, student achievement increases.

Strategy #8: Listen, Then Put the Teacher's Ideas
Into Your Own Words (Paraphrase)

Teach students to paraphrase. Model an activity for them and have them practice with your guidance and correction.

Strategy #9: Use Abbreviations/Symbols

Teach students to devise their own symbols for commonly used words. Let them use pictures to help as well. Provide examples.

Strategy #10: With the Permission of a Good Friend,
Make Photocopies of Her or His Notes

Encourage students to exchange notes and to photocopy them as well.

Strategy #11: Know What
Notes to Take and When

Explain to students to record the following:

- Key information written or highlighted on board
- Any questions the teacher asks and spends time getting class to answer
- Points stressed by teacher (teacher cues)—"Now, boys and girls, this is very important . . . "

Strategy #12: Write Legibly (Rewrite Notes)

Rewriting notes is time consuming, but one of the very best strategies for retention of information. Train students to do so right after class or at home that evening.

Strategy #13: Label or Date Notes

This simple suggestion helps organizes notes.

Strategy #14: Use Outlines

Model sample outlines, such as

I. Main Idea

    A. Supporting detail
    B. Supporting detail
       i. subdetail
      ii. subdetail

Strategy #15: Don't Miss the First and Last Minutes of Class!

Explain to class that that's when overviews and reviews occur—the most important parts of the lesson.

Strategy #16: Remember, FACT

F = focus
A = ask yourself questions
C = connect main ideas with each other
T = try to picture what the speaker is saying

Strategy #17: General Guidelines

Encourage students to

- Focus on sentences, not words
- Try to get general meaning
- Not jump to conclusions based on expectations rather than what's actually being said
- While listening, ask questions about what the speaker is saying, then try to answer questions
- Try to "picture" what they are hearing in their mind's eye
- Regularly summarize what the speaker has said
- Listen first, judge later
- Take notes to remember

Reflection

Share with a colleague how you would use any or all of the pre-ceding ideas.

HELPING MY STUDENTS
IDEA #3: SIMPLE STRATEGIES
ON HOW TO IMPROVE STUDY SKILLS

Strategy #1: Study Smart

Explain to students that there is no need to study hard and long. Tell them to "study smart—use the right tools." Much study time is wasted when students review what they already know—what they know they know. They should spend time studying only areas of difficulty. Many of them use a yellow highlighter to identify important topics or ideas. After a while, they look back and everything in the chapter is highlighted! Encourage them to highlight only material they don't understand or know well. That way, they'll spend the time studying those areas that are difficult for them. This approach to studying can cut their study time in half.

Additionally, tell them to be prepared for study by

- Bringing home their books/materials
- Setting aside a specific location and time for study
- Spending between 15 to 45 minutes studying at one time, then taking a break (5 to 15 minutes) before resuming
- Having a positive attitude

Strategy #2: Rewrite Notes Using
3 × 5 Index Cards for Easy, Quick Review

Rewriting notes aids review. Use of index cards allows students to carry them and study almost anywhere.

Strategy #3: Tape Record Your Notes
and Chapter Content and Play It Back

Listening to a lesson on tape is a wonderful strategy for auditory learners.

Strategy #4: Study in Short Bursts

Tell students not to study for prolonged periods of time; say no more than 20 minutes at a time (varies with grade level). Four periods of study like that are much better than one prolonged study period.

Strategy #5: Study Five Minutes Each Night Reviewing the Day's Lessons

The same concept applies.

Strategy #6: Avoid Cramming

Students will tell you, "It sure works for me." Well, if they are straight A students, fine. If not . . .

Strategy #7: Overstudy Areas of Difficulty

Research indicates that overstudying is good when one does so selectively.

Strategy #8: Meditate/Breathe/Listen to Music

Before and during study.

Strategy #9: Make Your Own Written Exam Questions

Students like to play teacher no matter what the grade level.

Strategy #10: When Studying a Book Chapter, Convert Headings and Subheadings Into Questions and Answer Them

Strategy #11: Form Study Groups

Form groups in person, over the phone, or via e-mail.

Strategy #12: Set Up a Special Study Space

Study in a comfortable setting, bright light, favorite chair, and so on.

Strategy #13: Study and Review Notes Soon After Class—Write an Outline

Strategy #14: Review Notes Out Loud and Ask Yourself Questions!

Use the mirror and role play the teacher.

Strategy #15: Study in Morning/Night—Use Your Own Biological Clock

Strategy #16: Eat Before or After Study—Not During

Unless you ace your exams by studying during study periods.

Strategy #17: Ask for Help

Ask a teacher, friend, parent/adult, or previous students.

Strategy #18: Use Mnemonics: Memory

Use Acronyms

- Use first letters; for example, *PGA* for Professional Golf Association.
- Make up your own.
- They are helpful for spelling (e.g., "Emily's Mom Broke A Red Rocker As She Sat" for *embarrass*).

Use Rhyming

- Use established rhymes (e.g., "30 days hath September, April, June, and November; all the rest have 31, except February").
- Make up your own rhymes.

Use Linking

Linking can be used. For example, to remember parts of a flower: "Mr. Stigma shot a pink anther with a pistil while Miss Sepal fixed the stem of her bicycle petal." Or, for remembering parts of the eye—pupil, cornea, lens, iris, retina: "Iris watched a pupil through the lens of her Red Tin telescope eating corn-ea on the cob."

Use Key Words

Make up and memorize your own key words (sometimes called *pegs*). Use them to associate new information.

My key word	Words to memorize	How I associate
1. won	pin	I won a pin
2. pair	sunglasses	a pair of ___
3. tree	monkey	___ up a tree

My key word	Words to memorize	How I associate
4. star	movie	movie star
5. foot	pencil	a 5-foot-long ___
6. pack	squirrel	6-pack of ___
7. 7-up	hat	hat full of 7-up
8. ate	cat	ate a ___
9. iron	trumpet	shaped like a ___
10. tent	pizza	tent made of___

Try the *body peg*. Identify 10 spots on your body to place information; for example, on each foot (2), on each hand (2), on your lap (1), on your chest (1), on each shoulder (2), on your face (1), and on the top of your head (1). That should equal 10 spots (you can even use locations in your home and have up to 50 locations!). Now, place some information on each peg. Let's say I'm outside and have no pen to record information. Simply place the new information on each peg. You remember you have to call your mom and your best friend. Shrink their heads and place them mentally and visually on each foot. Hear them say, "Call me when you get home." Later, you remember that you have to take out the meat from the freezer. So, imagine a piece of meat on your lap. And so on . . . . Now, when you arrive home and ask yourself, "What am I supposed to do?" Look, at your feet. What do you see? Of course, your mom and best friend. Now, what's on your lap? It's fun and it works.

Remember this mnemonic: *CAR*. Whatever you need and want to remember, make it **C**olorful, **A**ction-oriented, and **R**idiculous. When you have to memorize anything, make it as colorful as possible, make it move, say up and down, and imagine it doing something ridiculous. For instance, I have difficulty sometimes remembering names of people I first meet. Let's say I am introduced to a woman named Jane. As I shake her hand and say hello, I imagine her hair in deep purple with globs of jam flowing down it. Now, that is certainly colorful, action-oriented, and ridiculous. When I see her next, I envision that image and say, "Hi Jam, oh I mean Jane?!" Ha.

Try this one. Your parent or spouse tells you to pick up the following grocery items on the way home from work: Milk, loaf of bread, ketchup, and napkins. No need to write the info down. Simply mentally record the items using CAR in one of your pegs. Now, earlier I mentioned the body peg and the home peg. You can also have the hood-of-the-automobile peg. Place the items on the hood of your car so that when you get into it on the way home all you have to do is to look at your peg, the hood of the car. What do you see? Of course, white napkins all over sprinkled with red ketchup, and in the center is a container of milk with a loaf of bread balancing in see saw fashion. Now that's certainly ridiculous, colorful, and action-oriented. You'll surely remember the groceries and, thus, avoid an argument with your spouse or parent!

Use Rote Memorization

As long as you rehearse, the good, old-fashioned ways sometimes ain't bad.

Reflection

Share with a colleague how you would use any or all of the preceding ideas.

HELPING MY STUDENTS IDEA #4: SIMPLE STRATEGIES ON HOW TO READ MATERIAL FROM A CHAPTER OR BOOK

Strategy #1: SQ4R

Teach your students this popular technique: SQ4R (Survey, Question, Read, Reflect, Recite, and Review).

1. *Survey*—get an idea of general organization and topics by skimming headings, subheadings, charts, and highlight words

2. *Question*—turn headings into questions

3. *Read*—the material, to answer the questions

4. *Reflect*—on the material and relate it to previous knowledge or information

5. *Recite*—the information by asking or answering questions

6. *Review*—the material then reread it; ask questions; complete practice exercises

Strategy #2: Don't Use a Highlighter

Students often highlight everything. When they are ready to study they are overwhelmed by the "sea of yellow." Instead, teach them to place check marks in margins next to information they feel they need to review. If they insist on highlighting, then teach them to highlight only parts they are unsure of; they should not highlight parts they know.

Strategy #3: Make Notes on 3 × 5 Index Cards
Strategy #4: Write Questions as You Read
Strategy #5: Write an Outline

After each major section or chapter, take a piece of paper and outline in your own words the main ideas.

Strategy #6: Read Aloud or Sing Portions

Just make sure students are alone.

Reflection

Share with a colleague how you would use any or all of the preceding ideas.

HELPING MY STUDENTS IDEA #5: COOPERATIVE LEARNING

In a chapter devoted to helping students learn, discussion of cooperative learning is imperative because it is such a powerful instrument to promote achievement, as well as an invaluable means to reinforce study skill instruction. Students study more effectively, for instance, when placed in well-functioning cooperative learning groups.

What Is Cooperative Learning?

Definition

According to Robert Slavin (1994), "cooperative learning refers to a set of instructional methods in which students work in small mixed ability learning groups . . . . The students in each group are responsible not only for learning the material being taught in class, but for helping their group mates learn" (p. 5).

What It Is Not

It's not enough just to place students in random groups, especially without specific guidelines or with minimal training.

Benefits

- Higher student achievement
- Increased self-esteem
- Greater enjoyment of school
- Decreased absenteeism
- Greater motivation to learn
- Respect for students with different backgrounds

Formation of Groups

Teachers can place students in appropriate groups based on academic and/or social considerations. Groups generally should be formed using the acronym SEA; that is, evenly based on **S**ex (gender), **E**thnicity, and **A**bility. A random placement technique often employed is the count off; for example, students count off 1, 2, 3, 1, 2, 3, and so forth. All *ones* go in one group, *twos* in another, and so on.

Elements of Learning

Use the acronym PIGS FACE.

Positive Interdependence—The success of the group depends on the success of each member. Therefore, it's vital that each member participates. How can you ensure that each member actively engages in the particular activity? Give, for instance, only one worksheet per group. This technique requires each member to look on with other group members. If you give out a sheet to each member, each would probably work alone, thus defeating your purpose.

Individual Accountability—Each student is responsible for learning the material, completing assignments, and so on. Teachers hold each group member responsible for learning. In cooperative learning, one person cannot sit back and let others do the work. Teachers can ensure accountability by giving each member a test, oral questions, and so on. Typically, each member is expected to sign the worksheet to indicate that he or she participated and learned the material.

Group Processing—Group members reflect on how well they worked together or whether they have accomplished their task. Teachers have groups rate their work at the end of an activity. Teachers also provide feedback to each group.

Social Skills—The interpersonal and communication skills necessary for effective group instruction. One of the most critical elements is that students must be taught the social skills necessary to work in groups. Teachers spend significant time reviewing rules and procedures and incorporating role plays to ensure compliance.

FACE-to-Face Interaction—Students interact with one another in close proximity. What can you do as a teacher to facilitate face-to-face interaction?

Roles

For students: Each group member must be assigned a specific and distinct role, such as reader, recorder, monitor, captain, encourager, spell checker, and so on. What impact does assigning each student a role have on group functioning and output?

For teacher: Determines group size; assigns students to groups; arranges classroom; determines academic and social tasks; makes expectations for group work clear; monitors, observes, and walks around; intervenes as needed; provides feedback; evaluates each member and group.

Basic Types of Groups

Think-Pair-Share—just turn to your neighbor . . .

Focus Triads—working in small groups of three on specific short-term tasks

Reading Groups—group answers several comprehension-type questions together

Jigsaw—each member assigned a different part to research and, like a jigsaw puzzle, comes together at the end

Table 6.1 Comparing Cooperative Learning With Traditional (Competitive) Grouping

Cooperative Learning	Traditional Group
Group members depend on each other	Group members compete with one another
Mixed abilities	Homogeneous
Leadership roles are shared	One leader
Social skills taught	Social skills assumed or ignored
Teacher observes and interacts	Teacher not involved much
Group members assess their effectiveness	No group processing

Can you think of other differences?

Other Factors to Consider

Group size—varies depending on purpose

Physical arrangement of room

Duration of grouping

Selection of group members

Rotation of groups

What do you do when a group completes a task during a period and the rest of the class is still working? Plan activities from learning centers, silent reading, individualized instruction, and so on. Have brainteasers on the board; for example: What seven-letter word doesn't contain any of the five vowels? Or, what word contains three consecutive pairs of letters in it?

Answers: rhythms, bookkeeper

Sample Lesson Planning Format

Decisions: Subject, Topic:

Group Size: __2 __3 __4 __5

Assignment to Groups: ___teacher assigned ___heterogeneous by ability randomly ___self-selected ___other

Room Arrangement: ___small cluster of groups ___round tables with chairs ___three desks together T-shaped ___other

Materials: ___one set per group ___one set per person ___other roles? (specify)

Social Skills, Specify Social Objectives of Lesson:

Lesson:

Instructional Objectives:

Positive Interdependence: ___one paper per group ___each member gets same reward ___one set of material to share ___each member has a special job ___assign roles ___team logo, name, song, etc. ___each person has only part of information (jigsaw) ___other

Individual Accountability: ___signatures ___individual quiz ___ test random testing or quizzing ___individual homework ___other

Expected Behaviors: ___listening ___encouraging others ___moving quickly and orderly ____staying in group ___taking turns ___listening ___praising one another ___checking for understanding ___sharing ideas ___asking for assistance ___paraphrasing ___summarizing ___challenging ___other

Monitoring:

Feedback:

Group Processing:

> **Reflection**
>
> Share with a colleague how you would use any or all of the preceding ideas.

CONCLUSION

In an attempt to answer the question "How can I help my students learn?" this chapter introduced the importance of study skill instruction, including cooperative learning. Research indicates that teachers who actively teach study skills help students significantly, not only academically, but emotionally as well. Students equipped with study skills have the confidence to succeed in school and, most important, in life. I'd like to end this chapter by highlighting another answer to the chapter's question. Above all else, it seems to me, communicating to your students that they can succeed, indeed, that you expect them to, is imperative.

I think you need to remain aware of the extensive literature on the *self-fulfilling prophecy*. The term as first coined by Robert Merton (1948). Later on Rosenthal and Jacobson (1968) in *Pygmalion in the Classroom* related Merton's theory to classrooms. Essentially, the principle goes something like this: If you expect someone to behave a certain way and treat them accordingly, then the person likely will fulfill your expectations; thus, your prophecy for them is fulfilled. The word *Pygmalion* comes from Greek mythology. Pygmalion was a sculptor who carved an ivory statue of the perfect woman. While doing so, he fell in love with his creation and longed for it to become real. Aphrodite, the goddess of love, feeling sorry for Pygmalion, allowed the statue to come to life. The sculptor's wish was fulfilled. The more modern version of the effect was the theme of George Bernard Shaw's play *Pygmalion* and the musical *My Fair Lady*. A crude, unrefined flower girl is transformed into a confident and charming lady. In the end, Eliza Doolittle proclaims, "The difference between a flower lady and a princess is not how she acts, but how she is treated." This is the essence of the self-fulfilling prophecy.

How does the self-fulfilling prophecy actually work? The first step involves a teacher who forms a negative expectation about a student. Negative expectations may arise from a bias toward a student's ethnic group, gender, social class, and so on. Sometimes, the expectations stem from the student's behavior. For instance, if Alfredo has a history of being referred to the dean's office, the new teacher, having heard or read about Alfredo's indiscretions, may react by expecting the student to get into trouble. Once a teacher expects a certain behavior, the teacher acts in a differential manner. In Alfredo's case, the teacher, upon meeting the student for the first time, may state, "I heard about you; now, you better not cause me any trouble." Alfredo may be unfairly targeted by the teacher for misbehavior. Even if another student acts in a similar way, the teacher may ignore the misbehavior but rather focus on Alfredo based on what she heard about his past.

Recollection

I recall that a fellow teacher once told me the humorous story that follows to illustrate the essence and power of the self-fulfilling prophecy. It's probably not true, but you'll get the point.

There was an eighth-grade class that had five teachers quit within a three-week period. The principal was at her wit's end. How can she find a suitable teacher for these seemingly incorrigible youngsters? Whenever she hired a teacher, that teacher would invariably resign within a matter of days. The class was simply "dumb and uncontrollable."

She placed an advertisement in the local paper hoping to "sucker"—I mean convince—some teacher to assume this position. Luckily, a young gentleman appeared at her office apparently interested in the job. The principal hurriedly interviewed him and offered him the position. (Of course, she conveniently neglected to inform him what he was in for!)

A week passed and no word from class 8–303. Two weeks. The principal was dumbfounded. Why had this young, inexperienced educator not resigned. Three weeks, yet no word.

> *One morning the freshman teacher was passing the principal's office. The principal could not resist. She reached out and yanked his sleeve, asking him to step in her office. As he entered, she closed the door and asked him to have a seat. He complied.*
>
> *"I must admit, I thought you'd have quit by now."*
>
> *"Quit?!" wondered the new teacher. "Why should I have quit?"*
>
> *"Well, you must know by now how difficult your class is?" replied the principal.*
>
> *"The class is just fine," the teacher rejoined.*
>
> *"Just fine? You have a group of undisciplined and dim-witted kids. You must know that."*
>
> *"I know nothing of the sort. These kids are doing quite well. I don't know what you mean. You must have the class confused with some other class."*
>
> *"I certainly have the right class. Did you know that five teachers quit before you assumed the job? They quit because they couldn't handle the class."*
>
> *"Well, I find that hard to believe. The class I have is a group of hard-working, intelligent youngsters. Don't you remember you escorted me into the class that first day? You then handed me the class roster. On that roster was noted each child's IQ score beside each name: John-114; Mary-124; Jose-140; Louise-119; Trevor-139, and so on. These kids are smart!"*
>
> *"Smart?" queried the dubious principal. "That roster listed their locker numbers, not their IQs!"*

One of the classic studies that addresses how teachers convey expectations was conducted by Ray Rist (1970) titled "Student Social Class and Teacher Expectations: The Self-Fulfilling Prophecy in Ghetto Education." Teachers may convey low expectations in many ways, including direct verbal communications (e.g., "You'll never succeed"), indirect means (e.g., assigning menial tasks, providing low-grade curriculum materials, or giving these students little time to respond to teacher questions), among others. I encourage you to read Rist's study because his findings have been replicated and are just as relevant today as they were in 1970.

Robert Tauber (1997) comprehensively and clearly reviews the research into self-fulfilling prophecy. He provides the following testimonial:

> A student who came to our school from another district was labeled as a discipline problem. His records were filled with discipline letters. The child's parent felt that her child's behavior deteriorated because

he was living up to what the teacher expected of him. Right or wrong, I kept this young man's records from the teacher for his first 6 weeks in our district. He was assigned to a teacher with outstanding classroom organization and control. The teacher clearly related her academic and behavioral expectations for the boy. The boy apparently believed he was to behave in a certain manner, and he fulfilled these expectations. The teacher was surprised to find out that the child had a severe discipline problem in his prior school, and she disregarded the reports in the boy's file. (p. 124)

While the study of the self-fulfilling prophecy is intriguing and among the most interesting of educational topics, suffice it to say here that if you want your students to learn, perhaps the single greatest factor that may determine their success is understanding this self-fulfilling prophecy, how it works, and how it affects your behavior in the classroom. Maintain high expectations for all your students, regardless of their backgrounds or what others report about them. Avoid labeling students, for "labeling is disabling."

A quick story is in order. This story I heard Lee Canter relate. One day, he said,

I received a call from the district office that I was to expect a new admit to enter my school. I was warned to "watch out" because she apparently had a "rough and tough look." I got all worried. My grade levels had just achieved a degree of stability after three months of turmoil. Now it was early December, and to receive a new admit at this stage was, to put it plainly, a pain. My worst fears were confirmed when I saw her as she walked into the main office. She wore tattered clothing, her hair was strewn about, and she had this tattoo on her arm, partly concealed by her shirt. I could make out several words, however: *Born to . . . .* Oh no, I thought to myself. I know what that says *Born to kill.* I became abrupt with her and asked her for evidence that she in fact lived in our district. I wasn't very friendly toward her and I must have communicated my lack of enthusiasm for her presence because she responded in kind. To make a long story short, I placed her in a sixth-grade classroom. Though she had trouble adjusting at first, she turned out okay. In fact, she was a rather sweet girl once you got to know her. She had had a rather difficult life. She had no parents and was moved around from home to home. She craved to be loved and wanted. I felt very guilty after I discovered that her tattoo fully read *Born to be loved.*

Teacher educators face an awesome challenge in preparing future educators to teach in a multicultural, multiethnic, and multiracial school environment.

Extraordinary demands have been placed on teacher educators to prepare informed, dynamic professionals who have the requisite knowledge, skills, and dispositions to affect learning positively. Knowledge involves competence in content areas, and the ability to articulate philosophies, attitudes, and beliefs that guide instructional decision making. Skillful teachers use a variety of instructional strategies, match curricular content with individual needs of students, and provide opportunities for active learning. These professionals also have dispositions or mind-sets that radiate dedication, enthusiasm, empathy, resourcefulness, and imagination.

Expecting students to succeed is one such important disposition. Teachers who communicate high and affirming expectations to their students help them become self-confident, successful learners. Conversely, communicating negative expectations often produces disinterested and disaffected students. The literature is unequivocal; teachers' expectations of student performance is a major determinant for academic success and social adjustment to school and classroom life.

What we expect, all too often, is exactly what we get. Nowhere is this more true than in education, where teachers' expectations of students are crucial. As a teacher educator, I realize that teachers must be made aware of the self-fulfilling prophecy and how it functions within the classroom. The self-fulfilling prophecy functions whether or not we are aware of it. Becoming aware of how we tend to expect certain students to fail or not succeed more than others is crucial. Communicating positive expectations for all students, regardless of gender, age, ethnicity, social class, and so on, is a primary professional responsibility for all of us.

Follow-Up Questions/Activities

1. Describe how you would incorporate study skills instruction in your class.

2. What additional information do you need to know and how do you plan on obtaining the information?

3. Take one of the strategies previously mentioned and teach it to someone else not in your class, perhaps a family member. Did it work? Explain.

4. Share information in this chapter with a colleague.

5. How else can you help your students to learn?

ACTIVITY 7

1. Share with a colleague an experience you've had as a student in which the exam administered was unfair. Describe what made it unfair and what you'd have done differently if you were the teacher.

_____

_____

_____

_____

_____

_____

_____

_____

_____

_____

2. Conduct a Web search and describe the difference between formative and summative assessment.

_____

_____

_____

_____

_____

_____

_____

_____

_____

_____

_____

How Should I Assess and Grade My Students?

The aim of assessment is primarily to educate and improve student performance, not merely to audit it.

—Grant Wiggins

If you want to determine if students can write, have them write something. If you want to determine if students can operate a machine, have them operate a machine. If you want to determine if students can conduct an experiment, have them conduct an experiment. In short, if you want to determine if they can perform a task, have them perform the task.

—Norman E. Gronlund

Focus Questions

1. How will you determine whether students in your classroom have learned the material?

2. What is the relationship among measurement, evaluation, and assessment?

3. What is the relationship among performance assessment, alternative assessment, and authentic assessment?

4. What is portfolio assessment?

5. What do you want to learn about assessment?

6. Do you know how to obtain an electronic grade book?

When I began teaching, the only methods I used to determine student achievement were teacher-made tests, primarily, and results from standardized achievement tests. Traditional assessment and evaluations consisted of multiple-choice questions, true or false, matching, fill-ins, and so on. Recently, these test formats have received severe criticism (Popham, 2002). It's true that such narrow views of assessment do not really capture all facets of student learning. Relying on these traditional forms of assessment does not consider the full range of student work and achievement. Professional educators today view student achievement in a much more comprehensive way that accurately reflects the varied learning styles and achievements of students.

> **Reflect**
>
> What forms of assessment were you exposed to as a student in college during teacher preparation? How do teachers in your school currently assess students? How do you plan on doing so?
>
> _____
>
> _____
>
> _____
>
> _____

ASSESSMENT IDEA #1: ASSESSMENT BASICS

What's wrong with traditional assessment? The problem is not the traditional testing format itself, but the misuse of the format. We have taken a perfectly good tool and used it for the wrong purpose. A hammer is great for driving nails; it's poor for cutting wood. Multiple-choice tests are very good for comparing to norms and standards, but they are not very good for measuring integration of skills, providing continuous feedback during the school year, and evaluating particular areas such as creativity and performing arts ability.

In addition to misusing this format, the scores of traditional assessment affect major decisions such as class placements, promotion, and funding. Moreover, the results do not show well enough how instruction can be improved. It's as if curriculum, evaluation, and teaching methods are three separate areas with very little connection. To overcome these deficiencies, teachers must find the right tools for the right jobs. Certainly, no single test method is the cure for all evaluation needs. Multiple-choice and true-false tests serve their purposes, and so do essays, group projects, and the like. By using each effectively, you can take advantage of their strengths.

How should you assess and grade your students? The same way you would want to be assessed and graded. You would want someone to consider the varied ways you learn and not to rely on one or two assessment instruments or tests to determine your grade or readiness for learning. Remember taking a standardized test and how a teacher, administrator, or admission's office might have come to an erroneous conclusion about your readiness for learning based on a single assessment? If you're like me, you would resent such a generalization and categorization of your abilities. My guess is that if you're like me, you'd want to be assessed based on a variety of criteria or assessment instruments that draw a clearer picture of your abilities. That's what holistic assessment is all about: relying on data from a variety of sources to inform some sort of decision.

Recollection

I recall that as a high school student I was a hard worker. I was not brilliant; subject knowledge did not come easy for me, but I always did well in school (an A student). To achieve high grades I worked and studied very hard and long. I attended class regularly, did the assigned homework, participated eagerly in class, and studied for all exams. Teachers thought highly of me and my potential to succeed.

All that changed rather abruptly, as I recall, after my English teacher saw my score on what was then called the Iowa Achievement Test. I don't know if the test even still exists, but in those days, the 1960s, they were very popular and were used a great deal. The principal explained to my parents the purpose of the test was to determine the "potential for academic success" of students. "Jeffrey," exclaimed my English teacher in private to me, "I would have thought you'd score much higher." Her look of extreme disappointment and surprise shocked me. "Maybe," I thought to myself, "I am dumb . . . . I will not succeed." I can tell you with certainty

(Continued)

(Continued)

that my English teacher and several others treated me much differently after reviewing my Iowa score. No longer was I their favorite. I was called upon in class with less frequency. It took me years later to realize how caught up they were with the presumed predictive value of that Iowa test and probably standardized tests in general. We now realize, at least many of us, that to stigmatize students unfairly based on a single score from a standardized test is misdirected. Had teachers at my high school understood the holistic way we should assess student performance, they would have used and valued alternate forms of assessment to realize that I might have had a bit more potential than my score on that Iowa test indicated.

Have you ever been stigmatized by a standardized test? Explain.

The theme of this chapter is that classroom assessment and grading should rely on a variety of sources to make an informed decision about student achievement or potential for learning. The best way, in my view, for a teacher to make a decision about student learning is to collect data from a variety of sources and to encourage students to develop portfolios that demonstrate their achievement. This chapter introduces you to assessment via the use of portfolio assessment as an ideal, holistic way to accurately assess student learning. First, let's define several terms.

- **Assessment** refers to the process by which a teacher gathers data to determine student achievement in order to provide constructive feedback to improve learning success.
- **Measurement** relies on quantitative data from traditional tests to specify student success in a particular subject (e.g., an 80 percent on a spelling test).
- **Assessment instrument** refers to any device used to collect data about student achievement, such as a teacher-made test, essay exam, oral presentation, standardized test, and so on.
- **Evaluation** refers to the decision made about student achievement or potential for learning.
- **Grade** refers to the numerical designation given to summarize a student's achievement in a given test or subject.
- **Traditional assessment** refers to the common ways teachers gather information to measure learning that rely exclusively on paper-and-pencil tests, including teacher-made tests and standardized achievement tests.

- **Performance assessments** require students to demonstrate their achievement by actually performing a task (e.g., writing a composition or essay).
- **Alternative assessments** include data from a variety of sources that go beyond traditional paper-and-pencil testing (e.g., oral presentations).
- **Authentic assessments** require students to demonstrate understanding by performing an activity that resembles a real-life situation (e.g., if you wanted to assess the extent to which a student can dribble a basketball you would have the student actually demonstrate dribbling as opposed to asking her to write an essay on dribbling).
- **Holistic assessment** considers traditional forms of assessment along with alternative means to obtain a complete and accurate picture of student learning.
- **Rubric** is a set of scoring guidelines (criteria) for evaluating student work. A rubric specifies standards of performance from minimal to outstanding. See sample rubric for assessing classroom management in Chapter 5.
- **Portfolio assessment** is a vehicle or framework by which a teacher and/or a student collects and presents evidence of student achievement. A student's portfolio, then, will include evidence of learning in a variety of ways. Assessment, therefore, does not rely solely, for example, on paper-and-pencil traditional testing to determine student learning. Alternate forms of assessment (including authentic and performance-based assessments) are encouraged (e.g., essays, oral presentations, artwork, musical performances, videos).

This chapter highlights portfolio assessment as an ideal way to collect evidence of student learning. Portfolio assessment is a form of holistic assessment that includes traditional and alternative forms of assessment. A portfolio would include performance and authentic assessments, where relevant. The portfolio is a vehicle to evaluate student learning so that a teacher might more accurately arrive at a final grade. The chapter focuses mainly on suggestions for setting up a system of portfolio assessment. I also highlight suggestions for constructing teacher-made tests (true-false, completion, multiple-choice, matching, and essay questions), developing rubrics, and grading students.

In order to reflect upon your own knowledge of assessment and related areas, take the self-test instrument that follows in Form 7.1 and read the accompanying explanations highlighting some fundamental assessment principles that form a foundation for the remainder of the chapter.

Form 7.1 RESPOND

RESPOND				
SA = Strongly Agree ("For the most part. yes") A = Agree ("Yes, but . . . ") D = Disagree ("No. but . . . ") SD = Strongly Disagree ("For the most part. no")	SA	A	D	SD
1. Teachers need to know about assessment because they need to monitor students' progress.				
2. Effective instruction requires that we expand our concern to a teaching-learning-assessment process, with assessment as a basic part of the instructional program.				
3. Paper-and-pencil testing must be replaced with more realistic and meaningful performance assessments.				
4. Teachers should be skilled in choosing assessment methods appropriate for instructional decisions.				
5. Teachers need to know how valid and reliable a test is.				

An analysis of your responses can be found in the next subsection of this chapter.

ASSESSMENT IDEA #2: SOME FUNDAMENTAL PRINCIPLES OF ASSESSMENT

Teachers indeed need to know about assessment because they need to monitor students' progress. Assessment as a process whereby a teacher gathers data from a variety of sources to help determine the extent of student learning is critical. Without it, a teacher would not know that after a lesson a particular student was experiencing learning difficulty. Teachers, however, need to know about assessment for other reasons. Teachers need to be able to diagnose a student's strengths and weaknesses. If Edward isn't comprehending while reading, then you'll have to make some instructional adjustments. Conversely, if Edward already knows how to multiply fractions then preassessing his knowledge would save instructional time. A third reason why teachers need to know about assessment is to assign grades properly. Popham (2002) concisely explains, "The best way to assign grades properly is to collect evidence of a student's accomplishments so that the teacher will have access to ample information before deciding whether to dish out an A, B, C, D, or F to a student" (p. 9). A fourth reason teachers need to assess student progress is to determine the effectiveness of their own instructional program. In other words, how will you know whether you are successfully promoting learning unless you pretest students prior to teaching a unit and then posttest them to determine student learning? Results from this pretest/posttest design will indicate whether you need to make some instructional alterations. Finally, current pressures reflected in high-stakes testing make it imperative that teachers become knowledgeable in assessment. *High-stakes testing* refers to the use of tests to make decisions that strongly impact students, teachers, and schools. Various states, for example, have employed state-delivered tests to determine which students will be granted high school diplomas. High-stakes test results also are used by several states to make promotional decisions. High-stakes tests are also used to make judgments about teacher and school performance. Many schools around the nation, for instance, have been labeled as "failing" based on results of standardized tests (Kubiszyn & Borich, 2003). Consequently, teachers are expected more than ever to be conversant in educational testing procedures. As Kubiszyn and Borish state, "With increasing public pressure for accountability, it does not appear likely that the average teacher will be able to get ahead or even get by without a good working knowledge of test and assessment practice" (p. 16).

The relationship between instruction and assessment is vital. Instructional planning must include assessment planning. As the teacher begins instruction, student readiness for learning must be assessed in order to provide an instructional program relevant to the learner's needs. Pretests of basic skills, arithmetic, or biology will contribute to a rich instructional program by providing the teacher with information to help remedy deficiencies, place students in appropriate learning groups, or use the results as a baseline for future assessments. Though the role of assessment in preplanning is crucial, equally important is its role during instruction. As students are progressing through the curriculum unit, good teachers use tests to monitor student progress. These formative assessments are "typically designed to measure the extent to which students have mastered the learning outcomes of a rather limited segment of instruction, such as a unit or a textbook chapter" (Gronlund, 2003, p. 6). Diagnosing and remedying student learning problems along the way are key to any successful instructional program. Finally, at the end of instruction, summative assessments are undertaken to determine the extent to which students have mastered the learning outcomes and to determine what grade the teacher should assign.

Paper-and-pencil testing should not be replaced with more realistic and meaningful performance assessments. Rather, teachers should consider all forms of assessment to determine student achievement. Teachers should determine which assessment instrument is most appropriate for a particular instructional situation. At times, paper-and-pencil testing is a more practical and accurate measure than an oral presentation. As in the case of portfolio assessment (see below), teachers use a variety of assessment instruments to determine student achievement.

Teachers should indeed be skilled in choosing assessment methods appropriate for instructional decisions, as was mentioned above. How should teachers do so? They should match the specific objective with the assessment instrument or procedure as in, for instance, "Objective: Student will be able to interpret pictographs. Assessment Procedure: Student writes explanation at end of lesson (minute paper) and student answers worksheet questions related to pictograph interpretation with at least two out of three correct." If the teacher stated that she would wait to see results of a teacher-made test given, perhaps, two weeks later, or a score on a standardized test, then she would have selected two inappropriate assessment methods in order to make an immediate instructional decision about a student's ability to interpret a pictograph. Obviously, this example is simple. Teachers have to match objectives with assessment procedures on an ongoing basis in all units of instruction. But teachers need other standards for teacher competence in student assessment (*Standards for Teacher Competence in Educational Assessment of Students,* 1990; as cited in Gronlund, 2003). Below you will find the standard, a brief explanation, and a practical suggestion for implementation.

Teachers should be skilled in developing assessment methods appropriate for instructional decisions. When teachers use external assessment instruments (e.g., citywide standardized reading test), they should use the results as part of their overall assessment approach to come to some sort of decision about student learning. One practical suggestion for implementing this standard would be for the teacher to identify the subject or specific skill being assessed (e.g., reading comprehension). Then, the teacher should list the various data to be used to arrive at a final report card grade in reading comprehension. The teacher may choose the following list of assessment methods in determining the grade: (a) average of grades on teacher-made tests; (b) responses to questions in in-class reading assignments and activities; (c) average of grades on homework assignments related to reading comprehension; (d) grade given on student-developed portfolio demonstrating reading comprehension; and (e) score obtained on reading comprehension on the citywide standardized test in reading. The teacher would actually organize this list in a form (see Form 7.2) and record a desired weight for each assessment method.

Form 7.2 Using Prespecified Standards to Interpret Data for Student X on "Reading Comprehension"

Assessment Method	Standard Desired	Weight	Final Grade
Teacher-made tests	A = 90% B = 80% etc.	30%	
In-class reading	Satisfactory rating on rubric	25%	
Homework	A = 90% B = 80% etc.	5%	
Portfolio section	Satisfactory rating on rubric	25%	
Citywide test	Grade-equivalent score (on-grade level, etc.)	15%	

Teachers should be skilled in administering, scoring, and interpreting the results of both externally produced and teacher-produced assessment methods. Teachers must not only be able to select appropriate assessment methods, they must also be able to apply them properly. One practical suggestion for implementing this standard would be for the teacher to become familiar with, for instance, standardized achievement tests. Widely used in schools, these tests are primarily norm-referenced tests in that they compare student performance to the performance of a representative sample of students in a norm group (e.g., a group of seventh graders at the national, regional, or state level). Administration of these tests follows a prescribed simple format. Scoring of these tests is beyond the purview of teachers. Interpreting the scores, however, is within a teacher's purview, although greatly influenced by the interpretations of school administrators and school board members who are, in turn, influenced by public perception. Nevertheless, the teacher should become familiar with two of the most common ways scores are compared: percentile ranks (e.g., a student who scores at the 70th percentile scores higher than 70 percent of students who took the exam) and grade-equivalent scores (e.g., a third-grade student who scores a 3.5 in reading, according to the test results, is in the fifth month on the third-grade level. If another student scores a 6.4, it doesn't mean that the student is reading at the sixth grade and four month level; it does indicate that the student is reading very well for his grade level). Though books on assessment explain in detail the meaning of standard scores, standard deviations, z scores, T-scores, and so on, these scores are infrequently used in comparison to the two previously mentioned ones and are, in my estimation, not essential knowledge for classroom teachers.

Teachers should be skilled in using assessment results when making decisions about individual students, planning teaching, developing curriculum, and school improvement. Teachers must play a vital role when participating in decision making at each of these levels. Administrators must include teachers in such decision-making activities. One practical suggestion for implementing this standard is for schools (i.e., principals) to develop ongoing and meaningful professional development for teachers in these areas and to involve teachers in decision-making processes (e.g., school-based decision teams handling curriculum development and school improvement). Teachers should advocate for such participation.

Teachers should be skilled in developing valid pupil grading procedures that use pupil assessments. For example, teachers must understand and appreciate the significance of grading as an essential part of professional practice. Grading procedures should be made known to students in advance of learning. After all, don't you want to know in your graduate course how you will be graded? Grades should be assigned based on the extent to which instructional objectives have been achieved. In determining a grade, will attendance and participation count? If so, how much? One practical suggestion for implementing this standard is for teachers to discuss with students during the first day of instruction how student performance will be graded. The class requirements that follow describe the grading procedure I use with my college students.

Class Requirements:
The course requirements are as follows:

1. Book Review (20%)
Student will select a book on a topic that has been approved by the professor. A brief book review is to be written (two to five pages). Review must include a title page, summary, implications, and recommendation. Review should be divided into three labeled sections: summary, implications, and recommendation. Evaluation criteria are

Content: Is reviewer knowledgeable of content and related critical issues?

Citation: Is book cited in APA form?

Coherence: Is paper well organized and are ideas developed clearly? Are implications reflectively developed?

Conciseness: Are summary, implications, and recommendation relevant, yet concise?

Control: Does writing style reflect good technical control.

2. Critical Issues Paper (20%)

Student will select an issue or perspective and write a well-reasoned essay in three to five pages. Evaluation criteria are

Content: Knowledge base, relevance, and significance

Coherence: Organization

Clarity: Readability

Control: Writing style

Analysis: Reflective insights

3. Research Paper (20%)

Student will collect three articles on a preselected, approved topic. The research paper will include summary and implications sections. Evaluation criteria are

Content

Format

Citation

Control

4. Discussion Groups (20%)

Students will select a theme to report on to class. Class discussions will ensue. Evaluation criteria are

Content

Presentation Style

Poise

Sufficient Discussion Time

Response to Audience Questions

5. Final Examination (20%)

Student will be administered an examination based on class lectures and relevant readings. Course grade will be computed by averaging scores on the above-mentioned assignments. Numerical equivalents for grades are

90+	average = A
88–89	average = A–
88–87	average = B+
80–84	average = B
70–79	average = C

Incompletes are offered at half reduction of grade. Extra credit assignments (with the prior approval of professor) can raise a grade by half, as long as assignment is handed in by last class session.

6. Attendance and Participation in Class Are Important

Up to 3 points can be added to the student's average for attendance and participation, as follows:

Attendance points (0–3)

0–1 absence = 3 points

2 absences = 2 points

3 absences = 1 point

4 absences = 0 points

5 or more = failure

(Note: 2 tardies = 1 absence)

Participation points (0–3)

Very active and coherent participation = 3 points

Active and coherent participation = 2 points

Occasional, yet coherent participation = 1 point

Little, if any, participation = 0 points

You can ask the professor at the end of the course how man points you earned. Attendance and participation points will be totaled and divided by 2, resulting in the points added to your average to determine your final course grade.

Teachers should be skilled in communicating assessment results to students, parents, other lay audiences, and other educators. Teachers should publicize their assessment plan not only to their students but also to parents and school officials. Publicizing the plan will avert misunderstandings and possible misuses of results. One practical suggestion for implementing this standard is for teachers to first share their assessment plan with the building supervisors to solicit their input and approval. Teachers should then write a detailed letter to parents explaining the assessment plan. Teachers should use conferences with parents as additional opportunities to open lines of communication and parent involvement. Such practices will, at the very least, minimize parent complaints (e.g., "Why and how did my child receive *that* grade?").

Teachers should be skilled in recognizing unethical, illegal, and otherwise inappropriate assessment methods and uses of assessment information. Teachers should justly administer their assessment plan so that all students are treated and evaluated fairly. Teachers should behave ethically by avoiding cheating or illegally providing students, for instance, with answers or information that would give them advantages on a particular test. Teachers should not teach-to-the-test nor be caught up in the pressures, usually placed on them by administrators, to ensure student achievement at all costs. We've all heard horror stories of teachers providing students with actual test questions in advance or actually changing answers on exams. One practical suggestion for implementing this standard is for teachers to assign grades that accurately reflect student achievement. The following six guidelines for effective and fair grading (drawn, in part, from Gronlund, 2003) are important.

1. Inform students, parents, and administrators at the beginning of instruction what grading procedures will be used, as explained previously.

2. Base grades on student achievement, and achievement only. Extraneous factors such as misbehavior and tardiness should be dealt with separately from grading. If you, for instance, detract points from a student's exam because she misbehaved in class, then you lessen the impact of the achievement test. No longer does the score indicate achievement in science, for example.

3. Base grades on a wide variety of valid assessment data. As intimated earlier, sole reliance on paper-and-pencil tests is unfair because they assess only a narrow range of abilities. Alternative forms of assessments should be employed (e.g., evaluations of oral presentations, projects, laboratory work, recitals).

4. Ensure that students do not cheat. Many studies demonstrate that most students have cheated at one time or another. My guess is that most teachers would claim that no cheating ever goes on in their class because they are vigilant about student cheating. My guess is also that many of these teachers are unaware of the prevalence of cheating in their classrooms. Teachers can discourage cheating by changing the exam format and questions asked during each administration. Students may have copies of previous examinations, and if the teacher does not change the items, some students (those who have the previous exams) have an unfair advantage. I know of one teacher who claims she collects the exam booklets, therefore "none of my students could possibly have the exam." Consequently, she rarely, if ever, altered the exam format or questions. We later discovered that copies of her exam were distributed on a Web site. Teachers cannot effectively grade if cheating is not kept in check.

5. For essay-type exams have students write their names on the back of the exam booklet to avoid the dangers of negative or positive teacher expectations. If Mario is a stellar student and you know that you are reading Mario's paper, you naturally will tend to expect Mario to do well on the essay. Conversely, if Donald is a low-achieving student, you might tend to grade it accordingly. Grading exams without knowing whose paper you're grading might avert the influence of teacher expectations that might affect grading.

6. Don't give undue added weight to standardized achievement tests, especially when they radically contradict in-class or schoolwide assessments. Some students simply don't perform well on high-stakes tests. Though these tests should not be ignored, consider student performance over time on these tests rather than relying on a single score in a given year. Try to diagnose a student's weakness area on these exams and provide proper instructional support to improve achievement. Moreover, consider the range of assessment instruments holistically in determining a final grade in a particular subject.

Teachers indeed need to know the validity and reliability of a test. According to Gronlund (2003, p. 201), "The two most important questions to ask about a test or other assessment procedure are: (a) To what extent will the interpretation of the results be appropriate, meaningful, and useful? (that's validity), and (b) To what extent will the results be free from errors? (that's reliability)."

Validity

Validity refers to the extent to which a test, survey, or some other instrument measures what it is intended to measure. If I wanted to assess your knowledge of some aspect of educational research, I could administer a test. If the pretest was comprised of mathematical questions only, then the test would *not* be valid, as it did not measure your knowledge of research but rather your ability to compute and solve mathematical problems. For a test to be valid, it must, in simple language, test what it's supposed to test.

The four general types of validity are *concurrent, construct, content,* and *predictive.* Descriptions of each type of validity are not necessary since most classroom teachers are unlikely to ever need to use all four types of validity.

Perhaps the only exception would be use of *content* validity. When administering a test to assess your knowledge of research, I would undertake a content analysis of the curriculum or knowledge base of educational research, as I intend to teach it. The test items would be compared to the *content* base to ascertain that the questions on the test reflect the content.

Have you ever taken a test in which you said, "We never covered this stuff"? If you were to administer, for example, a test to a group of 12th graders based on Chapter 10 in their social studies textbook, you would check for content validity after writing the test to see whether answers to each question can be found in the chapter. If each question is, in fact, derived from the content of Chapter 10, then your test may be said to have content validity. By the way, determining content validity for standardized tests involves more sophisticated procedures.

Two other types of validity, although not thought of highly by many experts in the field, are useful for classroom teachers: *consensual* and *face* validity.

Consensual validity would be ascertained by asking people who will not be administered the test or survey (e.g., a colleague or a student in another class) whether the questions selected for inclusion are appropriate given the purpose of the assessment. Reviewers of these test or survey items may indicate ambiguously worded items, for instance, thus causing you to revise the items. Once an instrument is shown to several individuals and corrections made, the survey or test is said to have achieved consensual validity.

Face validity would be ascertained by asking participants or subjects to share their views about how valid a test or survey appears. Ever take an examination that was fair because it accurately reflected the content of the course? Such an exam might have high face validity. The converse could, of course, also be true if the content of the course didn't match the questions asked on the exam.

Reliability

Reliability refers to the degree to which an instrument yields consistent results under repeated administrations. When you hear the term *reliability*, you should immediately think of *consistency*. Usually, if you wanted to know whether a particular instrument was reliable, you would consult the test maker's manual. Reliability, whether reported by a manual or computed on one's own, is reported in terms of a correlation coefficient. The closer the coefficient of correlation, which is expressed in hundredths, comes to +1.00, the higher the reliability factor. Thus, for instance, a reliability coefficient of .80 would indicate that the instrument (e.g., a test) is reliable. Remember that no test is ever 100 percent reliable.

Common reliability tests include

1. *Test-retest method,* in which the same test is repeated over a period of time. Two test administrations are required. Correlations are taken between the two sets of test results. The resultant correlation coefficient is the index of reliability. Note that correlations can be inflated if the time interval between tests is short. Why do you think this is so?

2. *Parallel (or equivalent) forms method* (similar to the previous method) in which you retest the same group with an equivalent form of the test. This method requires two administrations (Form A of the test administered, for instance, in September, and then Form B administered to the same group in March). The two sets of scores are correlated as they were in the test-retest method.

3. *Split-half method,* in which the test is split into two parts (or halves), such as odd-numbered items and even-numbered items. The test is administered to the same group. Two sets of scores are obtained for each person: a score based on the odd-numbered items and a score based on the even-numbered items. These two sets of scores are correlated to obtain a reliability coefficient. Note that the longer the test, the more reliable the test will be. Why do you think this is so?

4. *KR-21* (Kuder-Richardson formula), used to measure the consistency of an instrument in which all items have the same characteristic or degree of difficulty. Tests that include diverse items or varied levels of difficulty should be subjected to split-half reliability assessments.

5. *Interrater reliability* (also known as *internal reliability*), which involves comparing ratings or rankings given by independent observers. The more similar the rankings, the higher the reliability. Interrater reliability, therefore, refers to the percentage of agreement among independent observers. Teachers use this form of reliability in grading standardized writing tests. Three teachers rate a given essay separately and an average score is then computed. In this way, no single rating is given preference. This is sometimes referred to as holistic scoring.

Reliability is enhanced by use of multiple data sources. In other words, the more assessment instruments you use, the more reliable your grade for a student will be in a given subject. Why do you think this is so?

Discussion of validity and reliability leads us to consider the construction of classroom tests, which are the traditional and main ways teachers assess student learning. The information that follows outlines guidelines for general test construction and preparing objective test items, including true-false, completion, multiple-choice, matching, and essay questions. The bulleted items are meant to serve as general guidelines rather than detailed prescriptions for use in test construction. It's likely you were introduced to these ideas in a graduate course on measurement and evaluation, or will receive some professional development or coaching as a new teacher in your school. If your experience is like mine, then you'll have to fill in the gaps on your own. Hopefully, these guidelines, drawn from the work of MacDonald and Healy (1999), are useful.

ASSESSMENT IDEA #3: CONSTRUCTING CLASSROOM TESTS

General Guidelines for Test Construction

The following are general guidelines to keep in mind as you approach the work of test construction.

- Have some questions that are easy enough for every student in the class to answer correctly. Begin with the least difficult question so all students will get a good start and will be encouraged to go on to the questions that follow.
- Make test items reflect instructional aims and the content taught. Test teaching objectives in proportion to their importance. If the test overemphasizes, under emphasizes, or omits representative portions of learned content, it will lose validity.
- Watch the vocabulary level of test items. To be valid, your test should measure the content students have learned, not reading ability (unless previously stated).
- Make it easy for students to demonstrate what they have learned. Do not allow writing ability, or speed in test taking to be a factor in student success. Everyone should have a chance to do well on the test.
- Make sure test directions are entirely clear to students. Ensure that students don't miss an item because they misunderstood the details for answering it.
- Place all items of the same type together so students are not confused.
- Include several test items for each objective. This will give students ample opportunity to demonstrate competence, thus avoiding the possibility that a chance error could give a false assessment of ability.
- Include all the information and material students need to complete each item. When you have to provide missing information or when students find it necessary to stop working to seek clarifications, the reliability of the test is affected.
- When one of your purposes is to determine differences in students' achievement, do not allow choices in the questions to be answered. You must use exactly the same measuring instrument for everyone, otherwise you jeopardize validity.
- Make more items than you will use. Select only the best items, then rework them as necessary to make the test reflect your best professional effort. The final product off the duplicating or copy machine should be neat, grammatically perfect, and clear.

Choosing and Preparing Objective Test Items

The preceding guidelines for constructing tests in general apply specifically to the development of objective tests. Among the most common varieties of objective test items are true-false, completion, multiple-choice, and matching questions.

True-False Questions

In this familiar type of objective test item, students are given statements they are to judge for accuracy. This kind of test can be useful for finding out if students can discriminate fact from opinion and valid from invalid generalizations. To rule out guessing (which would affect the reliability of the test item), students need to be called on to justify their answers with a sentence telling why they answered one way rather than another. On the surface, a true-false test seems simple to construct, but to produce true-false items that are free from ambiguity or false leads is usually a challenge. By taking the following precautions, however, you can avoid some of the main snags in making good true-false tests.

- Avoid broad generalizations. Words like *always* and *never* can serve as clues that statements are false.
- Attempt to keep a balance between true (T) and false (F) statements.
- Avoid using negative statements as items when possible. If you do use a negative construction, be sure the key word is underlined or capitalized to call attention to it (e.g., not, NEVER).
- Use clear language for questions. Textbook wording is likely to test memory rather than understanding.

True-false tests have the following major advantages.

- Items can be scored easily.
- Directions for true-false items are easy for students to understand.
- A good number of items can be answered in a short time.
- They are good for initiating discussions and for pretesting.
- They are a quick way to test for simple factual knowledge.

These are their main weaknesses:

- It's difficult to avoid ambiguous items because a statement is seldom entirely true or entirely false.
- Unless students are required to give reasons for their answers, student performance is subject to guessing and chance effects, thus affecting test validity.
- True-false tests tend to encourage memorization and guessing.

Completion Questions ("Gap-Fillers")

These are statements with important words or phrases left out that are to be written in by the test taker. These items are useful in testing whether students actually know something because they require the student to supply information that's not visible in the test. The following ideas should be helpful to you in developing completion questions.

- Be sure students know what is expected in terms of length and detail in their answers.
- Word the item so only one correct answer is possible. "Michelangelo was a famous _____" would be a poor question of this type because a number of answers would be equally correct (among them *Italian, male, painter*).
- Supply enough context in the statement to give the item meaning. The following is an example of an item with an inadequate ratio of words provided to words omitted: "The _____ protects _____, liberty, and _____."
- Avoid grammatical clues such as a blank following the letter a, which indicates that the missing word(s) would begin with a consonant.
- Design questions so only significant words are omitted. A poor example would be, "Washington_____ the Delaware to defeat the Hessians."
- Use a direct question if possible, and avoid textbook language.

The main advantages of completion items include:

- They are easy to construct and relatively easy to mark.
- They allow a rapid survey of information over a large area of content.
- Students find it difficult to guess right answers.
- They are useful when recall is all that is required.

Their central weaknesses are:

- It is difficult to construct items for which there is only one correct answer.
- When used exclusively, or excessively, completion items tend to encourage memorized learning of isolated facts rather than understanding.

Multiple-Choice Questions

These are the most commonly used form of objective test items, and they can be used in all subject areas. A multiple-choice item contains two major components, its stem and its alternative answers. The stem may be phrased as a question or a simple statement: "Most automobiles are propelled by." Of the alternative responses, one is the correct answer and the others are the distractors, so called because they are intended to mislead students who are not certain of the correct answer. In this case, the alternative responses might be

a. A steam engine
b. An electric storage battery
c. An internal combustion engine
d. A solar cell

Multiple-choice questions are relatively versatile types of test items because, depending on the complexity of the item, they can assess recognition of information that has been memorized, as well as some kinds of higher-level thinking. To produce good items requires considerable skill and attention to detail. The following guidelines apply to the development of multiple-choice tests.

- The stem of the question should be clear and contained separately from the possible answers. If the stem is in the form of an incomplete statement, it should provide enough meaning so students will not have to read the answers to understand the question.
- At least four responses should be provided. This will decrease the likelihood of guessing correctly and increase the validity of the item by requiring students to be more discriminating.
- Questions that call for "best answers" are more useful for measuring higher thought processes than those that call for correct answers.
- Make all the responses plausible, and when testing at higher levels, increase the similarity in the choices under each item in order to better test the powers of discrimination.
- If you can, avoid the use of negatively stated items. These tend to be somewhat more ambiguous than positively stated items.
- Distribute the order of correct answers randomly and equally, avoiding any discernible pattern, such as favoring first or last choices.
- Each item should test isolated information that gives no clues to other items in the test.
- Make the wording simple and clear. The language should be clear enough for even the poorest readers.

These are the primary virtues of multiple-choice items:

- A wide range of subject matter can be tested in a short time.
- They can be administered and scored quite rapidly.

- Items can be written to test for relatively fine discriminations in students' knowledge in a number of subject areas.
- They can be used to test both simple memory and higher mental processes.

The most significant disadvantages of multiple-choice tests are:

- Good items are difficult and time-consuming to write.
- Like all structured response items, they do not require students to provide information in their own words.
- They normally require a level of concentration and discrimination on the part of the test taker that may make them inappropriate for use with younger learners.
- Mechanical scoring of items requiring complex thinking provides no basis for checking the thought processes of students.
- It's never possible to be sure that the student identified the right answer for the right reason; that is, knows the right answer (as opposed to getting it by guesswork or for the wrong reason).
- They encourage a view of learning that plays down thinking and rewards recognizing or guessing.
- They encourage a process of learning in which students read by "biting," concentrating on identifying discrete pieces of information of the kind that turn up in tests, rather than on "texting," reading for meaning.
- The use of distractors to mislead students puts the teacher in the position of being seen by his or her students as trying to trick them into making a mistake.

Matching Questions

Matching items are a convenient means of testing for correct associations between related classes of information, such as names and dates, people and events, authors and books, terms and definitions, laws and illustrations, and the like. They are well suited to testing who, what, where, and when, but not to measuring understanding as distinct from mere memory.

In constructing these items, two lists are drawn up and the test taker must match an item in the first list with the one in the second list to which the relationship is closest. The following are suggestions for constructing good matching items:

- Include no more than 10 to 12 items to be identified or matched.
- There should be more items in the *answers* column than in the *questions* column. If the numbers are equal, students will be helped to make correct choices at the end through a process of elimination.

- All items in each column should be in the same general category. For example, events and their dates should not be mixed with events and the names of historical characters.
- Directions should clearly state what the basis for matching is. The directions should specify if choices may be used more than once.

The main advantages of matching questions:

- Their compactness allows you to test a good deal of factual information in a short period of time.
- They are particularly appropriate for surveying knowledge of definitions, events, personalities, and so forth.
- They are easy to score.

The most prominent weaknesses of matching items are:

- They cannot check the understanding of concepts or the ability to organize and apply knowledge.
- It's difficult to avoid giving clues that tend to reduce validity.
- The format requires the use of single words or very brief phrases.

Essay Questions

Essay tests require the learner to supply an unprompted, extended written response to a stated question or problem. They are appropriate for measuring ability to select and organize ideas, writing abilities, and problem-solving skills requiring originality. The student must create an answer from memory or imagination, so these items are capable of testing a higher level of knowledge than most objective tests. Essay tests are widely used, particularly by high school teachers, though they are often criticized for their subjective nature. The following are guidelines to be used in writing essay questions.

- Make the wording of the question as clear and explicit as possible. It should precisely define the direction and limits of the desired response. It is important that all students interpret each question in the same way.
- Include some items that expressly call for a paragraph response, requiring shorter answers, rather than a very few questions requiring long answers. This allows a better sampling of subject-matter knowledge and encourages more precise responses.

- Decide whether or not to include grammar and sentence structure in your evaluation of answers. You may wish to give two marks, one for the substance of the answers and the other, less crucial, grade for form and writing style. Be sure to announce to the class the basis on which you will be grading their answers before they begin the exam, and leave time to answer their questions.
- Provide students with guidance on how to use their time in answering the items. Suggest approximate time limits and answer lengths for each question, so students will distribute their time appropriately.
- Write the question while planning the unit of instruction rather than near the conclusion of the unit. This will help you to focus more clearly on the objectives of the unit as you are constructing the test.
- In general, do not allow students a choice on essay items unless there are different objectives for different students in the course. All students must take the same test if you are to have a sound basis for comparing scores.
- In general, do not ask questions that only sample a student's opinion or attitude without having the student justify the answer in terms of the cognitive content of the course.
- Have a colleague critique the test as a means of eliminating ambiguity and possible misinterpretations.

Essay questions have the following main strengths as evaluative instruments:

- They can measure more than the ability to remember information.
- They encourage students to learn how to organize their own ideas and express them effectively.
- Students tend to use better study habits when preparing for essay tests.
- They permit teachers to comment directly on the reasoning processes of individual students.
- A teacher need only write a few items for a test.
- Guesswork is largely ruled out.

Essay tests are subject to these drawbacks:

- Answers may be scored differently by different teachers or by the same teacher at different times.
- They are usually very time-consuming to grade.

- Only a relatively few questions on limited areas of knowledge can be responded to in a given period of time.
- Students who write slowly may be unable to complete the test even though they may possess adequate knowledge.

Source: From *A Handbook for Beginning Teachers,* 2nd ed. by MacDonald & Healy. Copyright © 1999 by Pearson Education. Reprinted by permission of the publisher.

ASSESSMENT IDEA #4: USING PORTFOLIO ASSESSMENT

Portfolios are used with increasing frequency by classroom teachers as a means of assessment. According to Gronlund (2003, p. 157), a portfolio "is a collection of student work that has been selected and organized to show student learning progress" (developmental portfolio) or to show samples of student's best work (showcase portfolio). Portfolios are arranged by the student, with the guidance of the teacher, to demonstrate learning over time in each content area. Although students should be allowed to demonstrate their achievement in any reasonable way in the portfolio, the portfolio should also include assessment instruments that the teacher deems appropriate and important. For example, students may want to include writing samples, computer reports, and diary entries to demonstrate effective use of English grammar. The teacher would also want the student to include scores in English grammar as measured by teacher-made tests and standardized achievement tests. A portfolio would include student self-assessment, peer-assessment, and teacher-assessment data.

Grading occurs as a result of examining the contents of a portfolio. Students must document achievement of each curriculum goal and/or learning objective specified by the teacher. Portfolios are advocated in this chapter as an ideal way to assess student's learning because they encourage holistic assessment and thus provide sufficient and varied information to demonstrate student achievement. Portfolio use mitigates the use of one form of assessment over another or to the exclusion of another. Portfolios have a number of other advantages, including encouragement of student reflection about learning and meeting learning outcomes, engagement of student in instruction and assessment, and increasing collaboration between student and teacher in the teaching-learning process.

You should be aware that portfolio assessment is more time-consuming than traditional assessment and much harder to standardize. Portfolios can focus on specific subjects or on activities that integrate several areas. A few examples include

- Self-evaluation through an "All About Me" portfolio in which students choose items through which they can express themselves, such as to their likes, dislikes, hobbies, personality, and family

- Written literacy portfolios, with such works as timed-writing samples, best notes, log and journal entries, essays, critiques, and short stories
- Creative expression, such as art, music, dance, and photography
- Math portfolios with such items as diagrams of problem solving and steps, written descriptions of math investigations, and responses to openended questions and problems
- Projects, such as science and social studies investigations
- Videotapes and written analysis of progress for physical skills such as gym, swimming, and dance

Portfolio Assessment Guidelines

The following suggestions for setting up, maintaining, and evaluating a portfolio are recommended.

- Introduce portfolio assessment on the first day of class. Explain in detail the purposes and uses of the portfolio. Try to show students a sample portfolio (it'll be easier to do this after your first year of teaching). Review all aspects of the portfolio (see below).
- Organize the portfolio by including a table of contents, an introduction, a list of learning outcomes addressed by subject or topic, a notation referring to district standards addressed, and a short reflection on each artifact included to indicate why the artifact was chosen and how it demonstrates learning.
- Include only artifacts and evidence related specifically to each learning outcome or objective. You cannot include every piece of evidence in a portfolio. The portfolio would become too cumbersome. Selection of artifacts are determined by both the teacher and student. For each entry (e.g., work samples, test scores, drawings, projects, multimedia), the student should explain why the entry was selected and what it demonstrates.
- Make certain students assume responsibility for portfolio maintenance. Reinforce the notion that grades will be determined solely on the evaluation of the portfolio (see evaluative criteria later). Obviously, in the early grades, teachers will maintain each portfolio with student participation to every extent possible.
- Schedule portfolio conferences with each student at least once a month. Ultimately, you are responsible for overseeing the portfolio process. A period or portion of the day can be devoted to portfolio inspections, or whatever else you'd like to call it.
- Involve parents, where appropriate and feasible, in the portfolio process. Reviewing portfolios, for instance, during parent-teacher conferences is suggested.
- Evaluate each portfolio. Preparing and evaluating a portfolio should be the joint responsibility of teacher and student. Teachers should, to

every extent possible, involve the student in the evaluative process. Portfolio evaluation should consider these factors:

1. Standards must be established ahead of time.

2. Standards should be very clear and specific.

3. Criteria should be related to learning goals.

4. Decide if the score should be based on performance against a standard, on a student's growth over time, or both.

5. Use a checklist rather than writing in the portfolio for feedback.

6. Develop a rubric for scoring portfolios.

I am a strong advocate of scoring rubrics. Form 7.3 is a sample rubric to assess a portfolio.

You can quantify evaluative results for the rubric. There are six items, each with a 5-point scale. Therefore, a score of 30 would be the highest score. Although you would develop a specific grade for each content area highlighted in the portfolio (e.g., math, science, or reading), you could assign a grade to the portfolio itself, as in the following example:

Form 7.3   Portfolio Rubric

Directions to Evaluators: Place an X on the continuum that reflects your evaluation of each of the following portfolio aspects. Use the comments section to provide feedback regarding your assessment.				
1. Introduction to Portfolio				
1	*2*	*3*	*4*	*5*
Little information about purpose and organization of portfolio			Significant information about purpose and organization of portfolio	
Comments:				
2. Evidence Cited				
1	*2*	*3*	*4*	*5*
Little evidence provided and not varied enough			Significant evidence and from varied sources	
Comments:				

3. Documentation/Choice of Artifacts				
1	2	3	4	5
Limited artifacts that do not provide substantial evidence in support of performance standards or categories			Variety of artifacts that provide irrefutable evidence in support of performance standards or categories	
Comments:				
4. Reflective Entries/Explanations				
1	2	3	4	5
Unclear narratives; lacking insight, critical thinking, and problem solving; little evidence of commitment			Clear narratives revealing significant insight, critical thinking, problem solving, and commitment to growth and learning	
Comments:				
5. Writing Mechanics				
1	2	3	4	5
Poorly written narratives, containing errors in grammar, spelling, and punctuation			Clearly written narratives with complete and correct grammar, spelling, and punctuation	
Comments:				
6. Organization and Appearance of Portfolio				
1	2	3	4	5
Unprofessional appearance; poorly organized			Neat, professional appearance; logically organized	
Comments:				

Portfolio Total Score

25–30 = Outstanding = A

20–25 = Good = B

15–20 = Satisfactory = C

10–15 = Needs revision = D

< 10 = Unsatisfactory = F

Score: _____

Rubrics are very important tools to evaluate student progress. The best Web site on rubrics is Rubrics 4 Teachers (http://www.rubrics4teachers.com/). Other good sites, such as Rubrics.com, can be accessed from this Web site as well.

Grading

A grade is awarded as a result of the evaluative process. You have accumulated data on student performance from a variety of perspectives. You've used a portfolio to document student progress. You can use a traditional grade book to record your grades or an electronic grade book, which is becoming increasingly popular in this country. Schools or districts may have a grade book they prefer. If you are free to select one on your own, I'd recommend one from these sources: http://www.classmategrading.com/ or http://www.teacherease.com/home.aspx.

The more essential question is "How will you now determine a student's grade?" Earlier in the chapter, in Form 7.2, I explained that you should list each assessment method, specify a success standard, weight each assessment method, and then determine the grade. As I also mentioned earlier, students should be apprised in advance of the criteria used in determining grades.

Some very good and general common sense tips on grading can be found in *Tools for Teaching* by Barbara Gross Davis (see http://teaching.berkeley .edu/bgd/grading.html). Here are some guidelines, paraphrased from Davis:

- Grade on what students have learned—the content. If, in the grading, you take points off for lateness, absence, or misbehavior, are you then grading them on what they have learned? Deal with absences and misbehavior in another way; let your grades reflect what students know about the subject you are teaching.
- Grade in a criterion-referenced way as opposed to a norm-referenced way. Norm-referenced grading compares students, usually along a bell-curve; thus, students compete for grades. Rather, establish criteria for achievement at various levels (e.g., A, A–, B+, B, etc.) and grade according to the extent to which each student achieves mastery of the criteria you have established.
- Awarding grades can raise anxiety levels in students. Grades are certainly important. Think when you were a student and how anxious you felt about tests and grading. What can you do to lessen anxiety levels in students? Here are some easy ways: (a) Don't keep talking about grades. (b) Don't post "best grades" on a classroom bulletin

board. (c) Acknowledge all students for trying to achieve. (d) Talk about learning for learning's sake. What other ideas might you have?

- Use formative assessments and don't merely rely on summative assessments. Provide students continuous, meaningful feedback every day. Research demonstrates that formative assessments increase student motivation levels and achievement.

CONCLUSION

Teaching 101 would not be complete without attention to the important relationship between instruction and assessment. Someone once advised me to "always keep the end in mind." Though that's good advice in general, it certainly makes sense in teaching as it relates to assessment. How can anyone become an effective teacher without attending to the way we view assessment of student progress and to the way we intend to grade our students? Our important responsibility is to ensure that our students develop the requisite knowledge, skills, and dispositions that will serve them well in school and in life. Holistic assessment, as advocated in this chapter, is the fairest way I know to determine the extent to which we meet this responsibility.

Follow-Up Questions/Activities

1. Interview an experienced teacher and ask how he or she awards grades.

2. How will or do you use portfolio assessment in your class?

3. Which ideas about assessment in this chapter were new to you and which do you think are most useful?

4. Construct a short-answer test based on the criteria cited in this chapter.

5. Develop a portfolio assessment system, along with grading criteria, and share it with your principal for her or his reaction.

6. Checkout the PowerPoints titled "Assessment OF Learning & Assessment FOR Learning," "Effective Feedback," and "Constructing Classroom Tests" at this Web site: www.yu.edu/faculty/glanz. Click on PowerPoints and scroll down to the last three listed. Review each one, all related to assessment, and make a list of new ideas about assessments that are of interest to you. I am certain you'll find the PowerPoints info-packed.

7. Collect some tests from those you've written, from other colleagues, or even from college courses you or others have taken. Based on the criteria discussed in this chapter, critique these tests. What suggestions for improvement would you make?

ACTIVITY 8

1. Define curriculum. Read the chapter, then decide how you might want to alter your definition.

_____

_____

_____

_____

_____

_____

_____

_____

_____

_____

_____

2. Visit a school. Then describe the curriculum in the school, including textbooks used, special programs implemented, philosophy, and so forth.

_____

_____

_____

_____

_____

_____

_____

_____

_____

_____

_____

_____

_____

_____

How Can I Best Incorporate State and District Curriculum Standards?

Curriculum development is a dynamic, interactive, and complex process that serves as the foundation for good teaching practice.

—Jeffrey Glanz

A school's curriculum refers to the expectations for student learning embodied in the school's learning objectives, programs, and course offerings, and translates the state or district content standards into a sequenced series of statements about what students will learn through their school experiences.

—Charlotte Danielson

Focus Questions

1. What comes to mind when you think of the word *standards*?

2. When was the last time you referred to the *scope and sequence* in your curriculum area(s)?

3. How can you teach to the standards and still make learning relevant and enjoyable?

4. How do you, if at all, address your state or local standards? Is professional development provided to assist you?

5. What do you want or need to know about implementing or aligning standards in your lessons?

Continued dissatisfaction with the public schools has prompted still greater attention to the need for national, state, and local standards (O'Day, 2002). The debate about standards (see, e.g., Smith, Fuhrman, & O'Day, 1994), as far as classroom teachers are concerned, is moot. As a classroom teacher, under most circumstances, you are not in a position to determine the viability or suitability of a particular standard. This is not to say that teachers should not weigh in on the debate. In fact, teacher unions play a critical role in the politics of establishing standards. Moreover, teachers serving on school-based curriculum development teams may have an impact on the way standards are structured and presented. The fact remains, though, that the beginning classroom teacher is charged with the responsibility of ensuring that established national, state, or local standards are adhered to and addressed. Accepting various standards is part of your professional work, even though, for the most part, they have been imposed on you by external bodies.

Accepting various standards is part of your professional work, even though, for the most part, they have been imposed on you by an external force.

As a teacher you should become acquainted with the standards you are expected to implement. For purposes of describing the teacher's role, I will refer to the establishment of local district standards, though the discussion is equally relevant to state or national standards. Presumably your district, via the principal or assistant principal, has reviewed the curriculum standards you are expected to adopt. Hopefully, in-depth professional development to inform you of standards and expectations for implementing them has been provided. You have likely been informed of the various *benchmarks* established for your grade level. A benchmark is a more specific component of a standard, as in the following example:

English Language Standard: Analyzes Western and non-Western creative fiction

Benchmark, Grades 9–12: Compares and contrasts the writing styles and plot development of William Shakespeare and Edgar Allan Poe with Homer and John Milton.

In this example, you may develop a unit on Western and non-Western creative fiction, but you will be expected to demonstrate that students can, among other benchmarks, compare and contrast the pieces of literature mentioned above. Lessons you design should indicate and demonstrate that you are attempting to assist students in accomplishing this objective.

Reflect

State, local, or district standards are sometimes based on national standards. For this reflective activity, you'll first need to download the national standards in each of the disciplines noted below, in order to consider two questions: (1) How do these standards compare with standards established by your school or district? (2) To what extent are you meeting or not meeting these national standards?

English: http://www.ncte.org/standards/

Mathematics: http://nctm.org/standards/

Science: http://www.nsta.org/publications/nses.aspx

Social Studies/History: http://www.socialstudies.org/standards/

_____

_____

_____

_____

In this chapter, I will provide a concise overview of curriculum development as you plan for instruction. Implementing standards is meaningful only within a sound and firmly grounded curricular program. You should, therefore, have some understanding of curriculum. As a teacher, you are expected to design curricula and plan instruction based on knowledge of the subject matter, student needs, and community and curriculum goals (including state and local performance standards). I will provide eight

Curriculum is based on knowledge of

Subject matter
Student needs
Community
Curriculum goals

steps to developing a curriculum on your own curriculum. The chapter concludes with suggestions for implementing and teaching to the numerous statewide and local standards-based reforms while at the same time developing creative, interdisciplinary lessons.

STANDARDS IDEA #1: WHAT IS CURRICULUM DEVELOPMENT?

Discussion of standards in isolation of an analysis of curriculum development, albeit brief, is not fruitful. Curriculum development is a dynamic, interactive, and complex process that serves as the foundation for good teaching practice. Teachers, as instructional leaders in their own right, must be actively involved in curriculum development. Such involvement is even more critical today because of national, state, and local attention to standards. Teachers, as mentioned earlier, are pressured to respond to the national movement toward standards-based education, including high-stakes testing, by raising student academic achievement.

What is curriculum? Before we can address this question, three more fundamental questions must be framed. What is education? Why is obtaining one so important? What are the purposes of an education? Curriculum cannot be studied in isolation of these fundamental questions. Ask a few people "Why do we need to be educated?" You might receive responses such as to learn practical skills, for intellectual fulfillment, to make money, to appreciate democracy, and to respect other cultures. An educated person seeks the following four notions, which form four basic purposes of education.

1. *Self-Realization*—Included in this broad category are ideas such as striving for intellectual growth, pursuing aesthetic interests, personal development, character building, and enhancing self-worth.

2. *Human Relationships*—Included in this broad category are ideas such as developing friendships, respecting others, fostering cooperation, developing ethical and moral reasoning, and promoting democracy.

3. *Economic Efficiency*—Included in this broad category are ideas such as work, career, money, and becoming an educated consumer.

4. *Civic Responsibility*—Included in this broad category are ideas such as seeking social justice, advocating tolerance for others, promoting world peace, respecting law and order, and fulfilling obligations to government.

Education is conceived as the deliberate, systematic, and sustained effort to transmit the knowledge, skills, and values that a society deems worthy. Schooling represents a small part in one's overall education. Life indeed educates. You may walk down the street one morning and meet a friend who "educates" you about a specific matter. Museums, television, family, religious institutions, theater, library, salespeople, and prisons educate. Schools certainly play a vital role in education. Three purposes can be identified:

1. Helping children acquire knowledge and skills

2. Transmitting ideas and values of society

3. Preparing children to live creative, humane, and sensitive lives

These purposes of education and schooling are meant to stimulate your own ideas. Other educators may select different definitions and aspects to accentuate when speaking about education and schooling. The point, however, is that when we as educators attempt to translate these broad purposes in schools into a program that offers intellectual and educational substance we enter the purview of curriculum. The curriculum field is devoted to the study and examination of the decisions that go into determining what gets taught. Hence, curriculum theorists deal with the following issues and concerns: epistemological ("What knowledge is most worthwhile?"), political ("Who controls this knowledge?"), economic ("How is this knowledge linked to power and goods and services?"), technical ("How should this knowledge be made accessible to all students?"), and ethical ("Is this knowledge morally sound?"). As a teacher, you may address these theoretical concerns from an academic perspective, but, when you work on a daily basis, you and your supervisors are most concerned with translating the broad or specific curriculum goals (standards) into practical lessons and units of instruction.

Of Definitions

William Schubert (1993) notes that the term *curriculum* is shrouded in definitional controversy. A discussion of this controversy, its history, and implications goes beyond the purposes of this chapter. Suffice it to say, that curriculum has been variously defined. Some common definitions include (see Beach & Reinhartz, 2000)

- All planned and unplanned learning experiences in a school
- All that is planned and directed by teachers to achieve educational goals

- Planned and guided learning experiences and intended learning out-comes, formulated through the systematic reconstruction of knowl-edge and experience, under the auspices of the school, for the learner's continuous and willful growth in personal—social competence
- Plans for guiding teaching and learning
- A work plan that includes both the content and the strategies for teach-ing and learning
- Includes careful planning, with the ultimate goal of increasing student achievement and is not only the written plan or construct but also the content, learning experiences, and results

What does *curriculum* mean to you? Many educators take curriculum for granted. It's sometimes and regrettably synonymous with the textbook. For many teachers curriculum is prescribed by district, city, or state agencies and presented as prepackaged mandates. Over the past several years, with great emphasis on high-stakes testing and standards-based education, educators at the school level have felt that they have had little control over what gets taught. Your principal and assistant principal can play important leadership roles here in con-veying to you that mandated curricula do not necessarily stifle creativity and curriculum innovation. You can be guided by a particular standard or benchmark but still be free to create meaningful learning experiences for your students that promote achievement.

You can be guided by a particular standard or benchmark but still be free to create meaningful learning experiences for your students.

One of the most helpful curriculum development models for teachers to easily implement is the one developed by Ralph Tyler (1949). His model is practical in the sense that teachers must establish curriculum goals that can then be translated into instructional objectives. Through curriculum develop-ment, teachers identify learning activities to provide students with meaningful learning experiences.

Widely known as the Tyler Rationale, this useful model identifies four steps in curriculum development:

1. What educational purposes should the school seek to attain?
2. What educational experiences can be provided that are likely to attain these purposes?
3. How can these educational experiences be effectively organized?
4. How can we determine whether these purposes are being attained?

According to Tyler, general goals must be stated in behavioral terms or objectives so that teachers can assess the extent of student learning.

Reflect

How might the Tyler Rationale help you develop curriculum? Be specific, giving examples.

_____

_____

_____

_____

Three criticisms have been leveled at Tyler's model. First, learning that is merely identified with observed changes in behavior is limited in the sense that while some kinds of learning are likely to be manifested in observable behavior, many other kinds are not. Sometimes change may not occur immediately but may blossom months after a particular unit is taught. Long-term development of intellectual patterns of thought are not considered in the Tyler model.

A second problem arises when teachers precisely identify learning objectives in advance of instruction. Progressives like John Dewey, for instance, saw objectives as arising out of activity, giving that activity a richer, deeper meaning. Objectives, according to this criticism, do and should not always precede activity.

A third criticism of the Tyler Rationale arises from a simplistic view of evaluation or assessment. A unit of instruction, according to the Tyler model, is successful when measured outcomes match prespecified objectives. Sometimes the most important outcomes may not have been anticipated. Therefore, simply measuring outcomes aligned with prespecified objectives may miss significant student learning outcomes.

Notwithstanding these criticisms, teachers can use the Tyler model, keeping in mind its limitations, to help them identify learning outcomes, develop learning strategies, and establish criteria for assessment.

Other models of curriculum development that should be looked at closely and considered as viable options are Paideia (Greek meaning education/ instruction to one's true nature) and Understanding by Design (UbD).

The Paideia design, developed in 1982 by philosopher and educator, Mortimer Adler (1998) and his colleagues known as the Paideia Group, consisted of three categories of instruction that together would enable students to acquire content knowledge and develop critical-thinking and problem-solving skills. The categories of instruction are didactic teaching (instruction led by teacher), coaching (one-on-one guidance from teacher), and Socratic seminars (small group discussions led by teacher). This design places emphasis on reading, writing, listening, speaking, and critical-thinking skills through a liberal arts curriculum. It also includes fine arts, athletics, and music that tie in with the liberal arts curriculum. Adler believes that coaching and seminars enable students to explore, develop thinking skills, and apply their knowledge in real life.

Google *Paideia* for more information about this design that has been implemented by more than 80 elementary and secondary schools across the country.

Understanding by Design, created by educators Grant Wiggins and Jay McTighe (2005), is another popular tool for curriculum planning. Its focus is "teaching for understanding." The core of UbD is "backward teaching," meaning looking at outcomes before designing curriculum units, performance assessments, and classroom instruction.

This design places emphasis on creating big ideas (enduring understandings—foundational concepts), determining acceptable evidence (worth being familiar with), then planning learning activities that promote understanding, interest, and excellence.

Questions to consider as big ideas:

- If you were emigrating to America in the late 1800s, where would you go to start a new life?
- How would you address the current economic crisis if you were President Obama?

Can you come up with a learning activity for the two questions posed?

Note that additional models exist. Consult, for instance, Pinar, Reynolds, Slattery, and Taubman's 1995 work.

There are eight key steps to consider when designing curriculum.

1. Context
   a. For whom are you designing curriculum?
      i. Grade level
      ii. Content area—subject matter
      iii. Type of educational setting
      iv. Demographics of student body
      v. Time and place
   b. With whom are you designing curriculum?
   c. What resources are available?

2. What are the needs of the students, teachers, and society?

3. What is the vision and/or mission statement of the school?

4. What are the state, local, and school standards?

5. What are the benchmarks? Benchmarks subdivide standards on grade level.

   a. By the end of _____ students will be able to _____.

6. Assessments

   a. What do I want my students to be able to do and know?
   b. Base lessons on what you are going to assess.

7. Framework

   a. How will you accomplish your benchmarks? Creation on learning activities and lesson plans.

8. Implementation of activity, revision of activity

   a. Understand that components of the curriculum continuously change.

Of Quality

Allan Glatthorn (2000, pp. 11–12) highlights several guidelines for developing quality curriculum, some of which are reviewed below.

- Structure the curriculum to allow for greater depth and less super-ficial coverage. Teachers should engage students in meaningful and detailed lessons that involve problem-solving projects and activities and critical-thinking teaching strategies. Such activities and strategies form the basis for any topic to be covered during the course of the school year. Rather than rushing to "cover" topics or "teaching for the test," teachers should give students the problem-solving and critical-thinking skills that they, on their own, can apply to any topic.
- Structure and deliver the curriculum so that it facilitates the mastery of essential skills and knowledge of the subjects. Providing students a rich and deep knowledge base is primary but should be incorporated with problem-solving strategies that are realistic and meaningful to students.
- Structure the curriculum so that it is closely coordinated. Coordinating content within lessons and among units over the course of the school year is imperative so that curriculum is sequential and well organized.
- Emphasize both the academic and the practical. Relating content to the lived experiences of students is important to increase student learning. Hands-on activities, when feasible, are very much warranted.

> The curriculum is the school's description of what it will teach its students.

According to Charlotte Danielson (2002, p. 83), a "curriculum in a school organized for high-level learning by all students must first of all be rigorous and should demand high levels of cognitive engagement from students." The curriculum, Danielson continues, is the "school's description of what it will teach its students; it gives meaning to the school's academic goals." Curriculum must be connected to state or district content standards and the school's goals for student learning. A poor curriculum bears no relation to state or district standards or to the schools' goals for student learning.

STANDARDS IDEA #2: SUGGESTIONS FOR IMPLEMENTING STANDARDS

Below are some practical suggestions for implementing state and local curriculum standards.

1. *Seek assistance*—You are probably unfamiliar with your local curriculum standards. Seek advice from the assistant principal. Assistant principals and principals play a key role in curriculum standards implementation as they challenge and lead teachers to consider:

> Implementation of Curriculum
>
> Seek assistance from administrators and colleagues.
>
> Use scope and sequence guides.
>
> Review curriculum goals.
>
> Use content area performance outcomes.
>
> Integrate curriculum.

- Content matched to the developmental level of students.
- Prerequisite knowledge and skills before undertaking a new unit of instruction.
- Inductive and deductive teaching approaches.
- Selection and appropriateness of learning experiences.
- Sequencing of learning experiences.
- Selection and appropriateness of assessment instruments.

Teachers should be provided with standards-based scope and sequence charts and the performance standards for the particular grade and/or subject. Simply distributing these booklets is insufficient. Teachers should be provided with professional development workshops on how the school wishes teachers to use the standards.

2. *Refer to the district curriculum guides*—Schools and districts design and select curriculum materials across grades to make the course of study consistent from year to year. Scope and sequence charts serve as valuable reference tools for teachers in planning appropriate individual, small-group, and whole-class instruction.

As you refer to a district curriculum guide that outlines the scope and sequence of various curriculum units, make certain that the curriculum guide meets the following criteria, among others (Glatthorn, 2000, p. 42).

- Guide is organized for easy use, is up to date, and is "teacher-friendly."
- Guide reflects current thinking about the subject.
- Guide focuses on key objectives.
- Objectives are developmentally appropriate.
- Objectives are developed and coordinated from grade to grade without repetition.

In addition, review the scope and sequence (e.g., see http://schools.nyc.gov/Teachers/QuickLinks/scopesequence.htm) of expected knowledge and skills to obtain a sense of the overall curriculum in each content area in which you teach. Think about which formal and/or informal assessment instruments you will apply to determine student achievement.

Example: You are a fourth-grade teacher and you discover the following objectives stated in the scope and sequence document.

Science: Examine, describe, investigate, and measure the effects of erosion and other natural events on Earth materials, such as on land, water, and air.

Social Studies: Locate information by investigating different types of primary and secondary sources, such as maps, globes, graphs, charts, newspapers, magazines, cartoons, media, and brochures.

Mathematics: Use knowledge of place value to read and write numbers up to the hundred millions.

English/Language Arts: Keep a record of what has been read, reflecting goals and accomplishments.

As an elementary school teacher, you are responsible to teach each of these content areas. Referring to the scope and sequence chart, you know in advance what knowledge and skills are expected of students at the end of the year. In each of the four cases above, for example, you will develop lesson plans that address the particular outcome. You also will identify assessment instruments that will measure student success in meeting these objectives.

3. *Review curriculum goals*—Review the types of curriculum goals established by your district. According to Charlotte Danielson (2002) they may include the following:

- *Knowledge*—What should students know and understand after the unit? Students should know facts, for instance, but also be able to apply their knowledge to different situations or settings.
- *Thinking and Reasoning Skills*—Though conceptual knowledge is important, students must be able to reason, draw conclusions, compare and contrast, interpret information, and think deeply about a topic.
- *Communication Skills*—Though reading and writing are paramount, students must also become conversant in other means of communication (e.g., visual representation and the performing arts).
- *Social Skills*—Students should learn to get along with others and interact effectively.
- *Physical Skills*—Skills developed as part of a physical education program are important, as are physical skills developed in other curriculum areas, such as handwriting and the playing of musical instruments.

4. *Familiarize yourself and utilize content area performance outcomes (standards)*—Thoroughly review performance standard guides in each content area you teach. Use the guides every day you plan lessons. Specify how your lesson plan addresses a particular standard. The performance standard curriculum guide gives you the details while the scope and sequence charts give you the overview of what is expected by the end of the year in a given subject.

For example, here's an excerpt of a lesson plan that identifies specific standards front and center:

Diagnosis:

- Grade Level: 4
- Subject: Mathematics
- Topic: Equivalent fractions
- Sequence: Second lesson (one out of four)
- Class Composition: Inclusive classroom, 20 students, 1 student with ADHD, 1 visually impaired student
- Duration: Full lesson will take about 45 minutes to one hour.

Goal: To use visual models and manipulatives to understand equivalent fractions.

Aim: What portion of the pizza will you eat? (discovering equivalent fractions)

Objectives:

1. Students will *describe* how fractions relate to everyday life. (Knowledge)

2. Students will *distinguish* equivalent fractions. (Comprehension)

3. Students will *manipulate* materials to form fractions and show understanding of equivalent fractions. (Synthesis)

Standards:

From http://ncrtl.msu.edu/http/craftp/html/pdf/cp902.pdf

4.N.7—Develop an understanding of fractions as locations on number lines and as divisions of whole numbers.

4.N.8—Recognize and generate equivalent fractions (halves, fourths, thirds, fifths, sixths, and tenths) using manipulatives, visual models, and illustrations.

4.N.9—Use concrete materials and visual models to compare and order unit fractions or fractions with the same denominator (with and without the use of a number line).

4.CM.4—Organize and accurately label work.

4.CM.5—Share organized mathematical ideas through the manipulation of objects, drawing, pictures, charts, graphs, tables, diagrams, models, symbols, and expressions in written and verbal form.

5. *Integrate curriculum through use of thematic units and interdisciplinary study*—Integrating curriculum has a number of substantial educational advantages, including teaching students to become independent problem solvers and understanding the interrelationships among varied disciplines or subjects (Roberts & Kellough, 1996). Teachers may plan subject-specific material in a scope and sequence outline on tropical rain forests, for instance. Teachers can then develop thematic units that address the topic from various disciplines, such as language arts, social studies, mathematics, and science. Identify, specify, and implement standards that cut across these various disciplines.

The following is an example of a curriculum design based on an interdisciplinary thematic unit plan.

Unit Topic: Geography and Customs of Republic of China

Course/Subject: Social Studies/Technology—Grade 3

Approximate Time Required: Six weeks—weekly, 40-minute periods

Overarching Goals:

- To imbue students with an appreciation for the skillful use of technology as a significant modality for educational and/or personal success
- To acquaint students with the geography and culture of the Republic of China and to imbue students with an appreciation of cultures other than their own (social studies)

- To introduce students to the Internet and KidPix software as tools that will enable them to enhance their knowledge base and educational and/or personal products (technology)
- To accomplish these goals through a project-based unit integrating social studies and technology

Rationale:

Note: This integrated activity is the result of a collaborative effort of third-grade classroom teachers, the technology coordinator, and the principal. Students will begin learning about China in their classes and take notes in a format prescribed by teacher. Lessons will be based on the unit plan, which is subject to change based on students' needs, behaviors, comments, and teachers' observations and formative assessments. The overarching goals will remain constant; however, modifications to content and/or approach to teaching might occur.

Planning for this product-based unit is based on the philosophies of Bruner (spiral curriculum), Dewey (experiential learning), Bloom's Taxonomies (hierarchy of intellectual behavior), Gardner's Multiple Intelligences (visual/spatial, verbal/linguistic, bodily kinesthetic, logical/mathematical, musical/rhythmic, intrapersonal, interpersonal), NETS Standards (for technology literate students), and state social studies standards, as well as teacher, technology coordinator and principal input.

	Social Studies	Technology
Week 1	Introduction to the geography of China (Lesson 1) Map of China rivers, mountain ranges, the sea, capital (Lesson 2)	Introduction to the Internet and http: //www.enchantedlearning.com/ Map of China (review and support Social Studies class work—Week 1)
Week 2	Introduction to different products that come from different regions in China Bridging the relationship between the geography of China and the types of jobs people have in different regions (Lesson 3)	Introduction to KidPix software Creating a picture using new tools presented and/or additional tools that students have prior knowledge of to create rivers, mountain ranges, the sea, capital (review, support, enhance Social Studies class work—Week 1)

	Social Studies	Technology
Week 3	Introduction to the different symbols that represent China—flag, flower, bird, tree, emblem (Lesson 4)	Introduction to additional KidPix tools Continuation of picture using new tools and/or tools that students have prior knowledge of to represent and describe different products and occupations associated with China (review, support, enhance Social Studies class work—Week 2)
Week 4	Introduction to Chinese holidays and customs (Lesson 5)	Introduction to additional Kid Pix tools Continuation of picture using new tools and/or tools that students have prior knowledge of to represent and describe different symbols of China (review, support, enhance Social Studies—Week 3)
Week 5	Evaluation Geography and culture of China (Lesson 6)	Introduction of additional Kid Pix tools Continuation of picture using new tools and/or tools that students have prior knowledge of to represent and describe different holidays and customs of China (review, support, enhance Social Studies—Week 4)
Week 6		Completion of project and/or creation of new project representing anything about China using your knowledge, imagination, and choice of tools

Lessons 2 through 6 have been created to integrate the knowledge that the learners have gained in their general studies classroom and technology. In this case, technology serves as a catalyst for further learning in the forms of remediation, reinforcement, and/or enhancement. Additionally, from this knowledge the learners should be able to construct new knowledge on their own.

The following is a copy of the first of six lessons. Subsequent lessons are dependent on the assessment of lesson 1.

Lesson 1

Goal: Introduction to the Internet and Enchanted Learning (http://www .enchantedlearning.com/)

Aim: To use the Internet to answer questions about the geography of China

Instructional Objectives: Students will be able to

- Describe how to access the Internet and how to access a Web site (Knowledge)
- Access the Internet and the following URL: http://www.kidport.com/ Reflib/WorldGeography/China/China.htm
- Create a Map-quiz printout and print (Application)
- Utilize the Internet as a research/learning/review tool to locate a map-quiz of China, print it, and use it as a primary source to answer questions about the geography of China (Comprehension/application)

Standards and Taxonomies:

- Social Studies—Standard 3
- Technology—Standards 2, 4
- Bloom's Taxonomy—Levels 1, 2, 3

Rationale: This lesson is important because it bridges the gap between different learning modalities. In the classroom, the students learned about the geography of China through direct teaching, textbooks, a map, and handout sheets. In technology, the same information was very quickly accessed on a Web site. For a student with attention deficit challenges, the immediate feedback makes a huge difference between sitting and fiddling around and being actively engaged in a task with a visually engaging screen.

For students who are not comfortable with the computer, this lesson lends itself to partner or group efforts. This lesson reinforces the skillful use of computers as a life skill.

Instructional Strategies and Learning Activities:

Motivation (5 minutes)

- Teacher will explain that one of the reasons we use the Internet is to access information very quickly.

- Teacher will ask the class to think about if they used the computer to learn something or to learn about something, and to explain what it was.
- Students will be given a few moments to respond.
- Teacher will then explain that today the class is going to see how one site on the Internet will give them a lot of information about a topic they are learning about in their class—the geography of China. This will tie the technology goals with the social studies goals.
- Teacher will explain that she is going to demonstrate how to access the Internet and find online the same activity that the students worked on in their class. (Direct instruction)

Students are familiar with the China Map Quiz (handouts from their teacher) from class. They have already answered the questions and reviewed the answers with their teachers. In Computers, they are being introduced to another modality of learning, as well as reviewing and reinforcing content.

Direct Instruction (5 minutes)

- Utilizing a computer, multimedia projector, and large screen, teacher will demonstrate how to access the Internet, where and how to type a URL, and how to find information on a Web page. Teacher will demonstrate how to print from a Web page.
- Teacher will ask students to return to their seats. They will not be seated according to their different needs today. Teacher is planning to observe and take notes during the learning activity today. Students will be repositioned at the next session, if necessary.

Learning Activity (20 minutes)

- Student learning activity is hands-on, task-related. The task is to access the Internet, type the requested URL, find the appropriate map, and print the map/quiz. (Knowledge, Understanding, Application)
- Students will be asked to answer the questions on the map/quiz printout.
- Teacher will circulate, observe the ease or difficulty students are experiencing in completing the task, interact with students or assist when requested, take notes, and pace class.

Differentiation of Instruction: Though not every intelligence can be addressed at every session, this session can include a few.

Interpersonal or intrapersonal—Students may work in pairs or independently.

Verbal/linguistic—Some students will be encouraged to answer the questions as if they were going to present to class.

Spatial—Some students will be encouraged to explain how to read the map.

Bodily/kinesthetic—Some students will be encouraged to take a quick break by walking around the room, getting out of seat, and moving around (bodily/kinesthetic).

Naturalist—Some students will be encouraged to focus on the different regions of China and the landforms inherent to the region.

Additionally, the teacher will prepare an *additional question sheet* about China for students who complete the task quickly. The questions will become increasingly more complex to answer, but will all require using the same Web site for the answers.

All lessons will be product based, utilizing social studies content previously presented in the classroom. Different activities and levels of activities will be prepared for each session, based on reflections and formative assessments.

Assessment of Student Learning

Teacher will circulate and observe. Teacher will assist students when needed. Teacher will listen to student responses and comments during activity. Teacher will assess students' printed work, looking for

- Completion of assignment
- Level or depth of answers

Teacher will take notes.

Culminating or Follow-Up Activity (10 minutes)

Students will be asked to gather at the demonstration area where they will

- Share their answers with the class
- Explain the process of finding answers
- Compare the process with that of finding answers in the classroom

Unit Reflection

After completion of this lesson, teacher should have an initial idea about

- Skillfulness of students
- Motivation level of students

- Compatibility of the partners or groups of students
- Changes to make in the next lesson

CONCLUSION

Implementing and teaching to the numerous statewide and local standards-based reforms while at the same time developing creative, interdisciplinary lessons is a challenge, but one that's not insurmountable. The standards, you will find, are useful to guide and reinforce instruction. Following them is a way to make sure that as a classroom teacher you are on the right track to ensure your students are meeting rigorous standards. Certainly, I'm not advocating simply "teaching to the standards" without developing relevant and worthwhile lessons. Though you are required to adhere to the standards, you can still create interesting lessons and units of instruction. Try to maintain your positive attitude, despite those around you who might decry the imposition of standards. Use them wisely to enrich the educational experiences of your students.

Follow-Up Questions/Activities

1. Interview an experienced teacher and ask how he or she has integrated standards-based reforms.

2. Develop an interdisciplinary curriculum unit that incorporates district standards.

3. What is the connection between assessment and standards?

4. Give advice to a teacher newer than yourself on how best to incorporate district standards.

5. What more do you need to know about standards? Ask your assistant principal, curriculum coordinator, or principal.

ACTIVITY 9

Go to http://www.iste.org/. In the search box, type *Social Studies Standards*.

You are a third-grade teacher and would like to use technology to support a social studies unit on "communities."

Based on the technology standards and profiles that you have just reviewed, how would you use technology to support this unit?

Ask your colleagues how they would use technology to support this unit?

Explain other ways that you have used technology to support a lesson or unit?

Ask your colleagues the same.

If you have never used technology to support a lesson/unit, use Google to search for *technology integrated lessons*.

_____

_____

_____

_____

_____

_____

_____

_____

_____

_____

_____

_____

_____

_____

_____

_____

_____

_____

_____

_____

How Can I Begin to Incorporate Technology Into My Teaching?

Technology is a necessary and useful tool to bring content alive to our students. Technology literate teachers are familiar with the technology standards, can evaluate web sites and educational software for their appropriateness and value for their students, can use PowerPoint effectively, as well as incorporate the newest technologies to enhance the learning experiences of all students.

—Jeffrey Glanz

What our students understand (and that we, as teachers, seem blind to) is that the very nature of information has changed. It's changed in what it looks like, what we look at to view it, where we find it, what we can do with it, and how we communicate it. We live in a brand new and dynamically rich information environment, and if we are going to reach our students in a way that is relevant to their world and their future (and ours), then we must teach them from this new information environment.

—David Warlick

Focus Questions

1. What are some major advantages of incorporating technology in teaching?

2. Are you familiar with ISTE and NETS standards?

3. Are you adequately prepared to include technology as a teaching tool in your lesson plans? If so, describe.

4. Are you familiar with modalities such as the SMART Board, Promethean board, iPod, or LCD projectors and their uses?

5. Have you ever created or used an e-portfolio, a school Web site for communicating with students or parents, or recorded your grades electronically?

6. Do you know how to use the Microsoft Office suite as a productivity and/or teaching tool? Do you know the Office suite programs?

Over the course of the past 20 years, changing technology has resulted in the changing needs of businesses, schools, students, professional and nonprofessional working people, and ordinary citizens. It has also changed the way in which teachers teach and learners learn.

To address the role you play as an educator in today's digital age, we must look at the needs of society and the different technologies (software and hardware) that are available, and at your students who are not only familiar with the latest technologies, but use them on a daily basis as part of their regular routine. They were born into a highly technical world and know of nothing else. We must acknowledge the fact that many educators are less familiar or comfortable with technology than their students, therefore, resulting in anxiety about using it in the classroom, integrating it into their curriculum, or using it as a support tool. When using technology in the classroom, many teachers must shift from their traditional role of teacher, with the comfort of being the expert to that of learner. For the teacher who is not comfortable with this ideology, dealing with technology can be a most traumatic experience.

Nevertheless, teachers are put in the position of having to equip students with the social, vocational, and intellectual tools needed to work and contribute, and to prosper in the world. This means teaching them basic skills, and the ability to use those skills successfully. It also means understanding the importance of technology in society as well as understanding why it's imperative for students to become technologically literate in and out of school. (Paraphrased from http://www.ed.gov/rschstat/eval/tech/20years.pdf.)

Preparing students for the global workplace by teaching them to use computers productively and safely has been imperative. Teachers model technology's practicality and usefulness when they incorporate it in their teaching.

Teachers have found that technology is a powerful means to promote teaching and learning. Though technology can never replace a competent teacher, it can aid the instructional process. Today's teachers must feel comfortable using technology to promote learning when and wherever feasible. Knowing what is available and how and when to employ technology in the classroom is the essence of good teaching with technology.

Much has been done in this realm by state and national agencies, as well as professionals in the field (compiling best practices, generating books and creating Web sites as a resource and support for educators, administrators, students and parents), but ultimately it's the teacher who is responsible for using technology in the classroom.

The purpose of this chapter is to help you get started using technology in your classrooms by sharing with you practical instructional technology strategies and ideas based on national technology standards, introducing you to current technologies and favorite Web sites, empowering you with Web site and software evaluation guidelines, and showing you how to use the Microsoft Office suite to the benefit of your students and yourself.

Respond

How technologically competent are you? Are you up on new technologies and how to apply them to benefit your students as well as yourself?

Check off below the technologies and software you feel most proficient at as a teaching modality or for personal/professional use.

Software	The Internet	Peripheral Devices
Microsoft Office suite	Search engines	Digital camera
• Word	• Professional	Video camera
• Excel	• Educational	LCD projector
• Access	• Subject area	Scanner
• PowerPoint		DVD player
• Publisher	E-mail/communications	External hard drive
WordPerfect	• Handling attachments	Flash drive
Other Web Page Design	• Netiquette	SMART Board
• FrontPage, Adobe GoLive, other	• Text, digital pictures, videos, etc.	Promethean board
Instructional Software	• Facebook/MySpace	
Electronic grade book	• School Web site	
	• YouTube	

How many programs did you check off under Microsoft Office suite? Did you check off Microsoft Word? Typing, using grammar and spell-checks, merging documents, using the thesaurus, cutting and pasting—all familiar to you? Do you encourage students to use the computer for assignments? Do you accept student work where the computer has been used as a productivity tool? What about using a spreadsheet (Excel) to record and manage student grades? Have you placed all your students in a database file (Access) for easy access to information on each student? Have you supported your teaching with instructional software? If so, in what curriculum areas? Did instructional software improve student learning of the material? Although you may regularly use cassette players/recorders and televisions (VCR and/or DVD), have you ever used an electronic encyclopedia, atlas, or dictionary? If not, what about use of e-mail or an intraschool Web site or portal as a form of communication and discussion?

Though this sounds like quite a bit, it's only the tip of the iceberg. But let me assure you that there are ways to handle and manage technology so that it becomes one of your most valued productivity tools.

Current literature suggests setting reasonable goals for integrating technology into the teaching and learning process and taking small steps to meet them; for example, focusing on one or a few learning objectives in a single discipline or course and thinking about how students would better meet those objectives through the use of technology.

Ask yourself if students' learning would be enhanced through the use of a PowerPoint presentation, a Web quest, or the Internet. Setting small, realistic goals while piloting the use of technology in the classroom, it seems to me, is perceived as something attainable, resulting in willingness to try. (Paraphrased from http://connect.educause.edu/Library/EDUCAUSE+Quarterly/ThinkSmallABeginnersGuide/40019?time=1202251550.)

TECHNOLOGY IDEA #1:
A FEW SIMPLE WAYS TO INTEGRATE
TECHNOLOGY FOR BEGINNERS AND MORE

Here are a few ideas that can be carried out just as easily by novices as experts in technology integration.

Why not encourage your students to visit the Australian rain forests? Send them to http://www.fieldstudies.org/pages/131_center_for_rainforest_studies_australia.cfm. Say you just completed that topic and wish students to compare and contrast rain forests around the world. Guide them to the Internet. Acquainting them with various search engines or links is critical. Although many search engines exist (e.g., Yahoo!, Ask.com, or Dogpile.com), why not lead them to my favorite, Google? Students can simply type in the information they are seeking. Here is another option: http://www.srl.caltech.edu/personnel/krubal/rainforest/Edit560s6/www/where.html.

Similarly, if the class has read a novel, the teacher may gather information for herself from the Internet as well as lead students to follow-up information on the Web. For instance, if fifth- or sixth-grade students have read *The Devil's Arithmetic*, they may be guided to various relevant Web sites as a follow-up activity. Students are generally enthused about learning more about a topic on the Web that was first discussed in class.

Try this Internet search: In Google, type in *The Devil's Arithmetic*. At least ten different Web sites can he explored for more ideas on using this novel with students. Some sites include interactive lesson plans and online discussion groups for students who have read the book. See, for example, http://www.janeyolen.com/tchrsideas.html. This site is composed of shared ideas and experiences in relation to this novel. It. includes child-created artwork, thoughts, and e-mails reacting to the novel. Easy enough?

You can enhance students' opportunities for writing by using e-mail as a teaching tool. While most students know very well how to communicate via e-mail, unfortunately, they develop poor habits of writing when they use what my daughter calls shortcuts, as in

hey sup?

nm hows skewl?

lol me 2 ill brb . . . back

so wats doin?

o kool wat u doin in the summer?

o well idk yet prob work btw wanna go 2 the park tom?

ur so mean!! jk go 4 me ok? ok w/e well neways

omg ppl are annoying me!! wats ur # again?

k well srry i gtg gn ttyl mb ill c u tom i dunno k bb oh b4 i go happy b-day!!! lol!

Got it? If not, see below:

Hey what's up?

Nothing much. How's school?

(laughing out loud) Me too. I'll be right back . . . I'm back.

So what's doing?

Oh cool. What are you doing in the summer?

Oh, well, I don't know yet. I will probably work. By the way, want to go to the park tomorrow?

You're so mean! Just kidding. Go for me, OK? OK, whatever. Well, anyway.

Oh, my gosh, people are annoying me! What's your number again?

Okay. Well sorry, I have to go. Good night. Talk to you later. Maybe I'll see you tomorrow. I don't know. Okay, bye-bye. Oh, before I go, "Happy Birthday!" (laughing out loud!)

Why not send and receive homework assignments via e-mail. Teach students various skills you want to reinforce, such as writing in complete sentences. In fact, use e-mail to improve writing in general (e.g., punctuation, sentence structure). Although e-mail is generally used without attention to writing standards, it can be an ideal way to motivate your students. Also, teach them other skills, such as attaching files. You can require students, for instance, to submit their assignments and papers via e-mail as attachments.

Before planning a lesson or unit, it's a good idea to review content-rich Web sites. Just Google your content area. The Internet can be an invaluable resource for planning instructional activities and units for your students. Many sites exist.

Here are a few of my favorite sites.

The International Society for Technology in Education (ISTE) (http://www.iste.org/)

- Click on *Educator Resources.*
- Click on *Curriculum.*
- Select the subject area and grade level you are interested in.

Or, clicking on *NETS* gives you *NETS for Students 2007* or *NETS for Teachers 2008.*

After years of research, data collection, and collaboration with educators from around the world, ISTE has created technology standards for students, teachers, and administrators based on the needs of society. These standards offer a framework and benchmarks that education professionals must become familiar with if they are going to use technology as it should be used in the 21st century.

"NETS for students: the next generation" describes what students should know and be able to do to learn effectively and live productively in our information environment.

"NETS for teachers (NETS.T)" was introduced in 2008.

"NETS for administrators (NETS.A)" was introduced in 2009.

More Examples

Using the Microsoft Office Suite in the Classroom: Word, Excel, Access, PowerPoint, Publisher

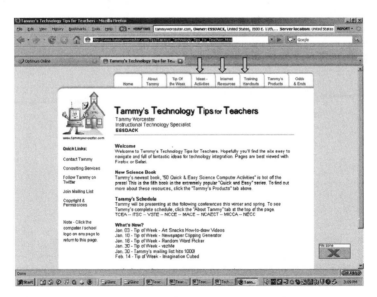

At http://www.tammyworcester.com/Tips/Tammys_Technology_Tips_
for_Teachers.html, peruse the following categories: Ideas-Activities, Internet
Resources, Training Handouts.

In "Ideas-Activities" you will find

All-About-Me Scavenger Hunt

Bar Graph—Pt. 1—Basics

Bar Graph—Pt. 2—Pictogram

Brochure—Tri-Fold

Gift Bag—From an Envelope

Idiom Slide Show

Multiplication Chart

Name Tents

Number Autobiography

Point of View

Pop-Up Greeting Card

Poster—How to Design and Print

Sense Poetry

Shape Poetry

Sticky Notes—How to Print

TALL Tales

Transformations

Venn Diagram

In "Internet Resources" you will find

Creativity Tools

Cool Tech Tools

K–2 Teachers & Students

Internet Basics

Teacher Resources

Student Resources & Games

Math Resources

Science Resources

Language Arts Resources

Social Studies Resources

Other Subjects

In "Training Handouts," click on the archive of old handouts and you will find

Building Integrated Technology Projects

Cool Web Tools for Teaching and Learning

Electronic Portfolios

EMTL Grant

Galena Park ISD

Inspiration & Kidspiration in the Classroom

Internet Resources for Teaching & Learning

Isle of Wight County Schools

Is This Really PowerPoint?

ITSC 2008—Portland

K–2 Computer Activities

Language Arts Computer Activities

Literacy & Technology Symposium 2008

MACE Manhattan 2008

Math Computer Activities

Math + Technology = Learning

MICCA 2008

Mitchell, SD Laptop Institute

Multiple Intelligences and Technology

NCaect 2008

NCCE 2008

NCETC 2007

NECC 2007

NECC 2008

NWOET 2008 Wapakoneta, OH

PowerPoint Basics

Quick & Easy Computer Activities

Rev Up Your Reading & Writing Classrooms!

Riddle Mixup File

Science & Social Studies Computer Activities 2

Tammy's Favorite Technology Tips, Tricks & Tools

TCEA 2008

Valley Center

VSTE 2008

Walkertown

Winchester Feb. 22, 2008

See http://www.education-world.com/a_tech/tech/tech176.shtml to read *Technology Integration: Ideas That Work* for wonderful ideas.

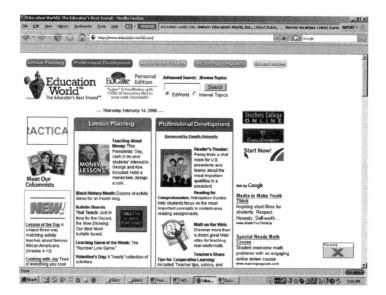

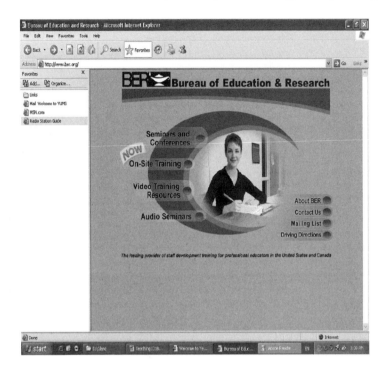

The Bureau of Education and Research (BER) (http://www.ber.org/) offers excellent workshops and manuals that enable and empower teachers, coordinators, and administrators who are seeking to become more proficient in the use of technology.

Once you have accessed the BER Web site, click on *Seminars and Conferences*, then click on your state on the map. Choose a course group (pre-K–6 or 6–12) and click on a city/choose a workshop.

You will find that most administrators are very happy to foot the bill for this kind of professional development.

> Do you have your own favorite Web sites for content-related material or for technology integration ideas?
>
> Think about why you continue to return to those sites.

TECHNOLOGY IDEA #2: CRITERIA FOR EVALUATING WEB SITES

As we use sources on the Web for ourselves or to enhance student learning, we must remain cognizant of the fact that not all Web sites contain accurate information or are useful. Teachers should always preview a Web site prior to use in the classroom.

Educators revisit Web sites for good reasons. Many of the reasons are found in the criteria for evaluating Web sites.

Table 9.1 contains some guidelines to assist you in determining the authenticity and usefulness of a site.

Table 9.1   Criteria for Evaluating World Wide Web Sites

Authoritativeness	Poor	Fair	Excellent
The authors are respected authorities in the field.			
The authors are knowledgeable.			
The authors provide a list of credentials and/or educational background.			
The authors represent respected, credible institutions or organizations.			
Complete information on references (or sources) is provided.			
Information for contacting the authors and webmaster is provided.			
Comprehensiveness			
All facets of the subject are covered.			
Sufficient detail is provided at this site.			
Information provided is accurate.			
Political, ideological, and other biases are not evident.			
Presentation			
Graphics serve an educational, rather than decorative, purpose.			
Links are provided to related sites.			
What icons stand for is clear and unambiguous.			
The Web site loads quickly.			
The Web site is stable and seldom, if ever, nonfunctional.			

Authoritativeness	Poor	Fair	Excellent
Timeliness			
The original Web site was produced recently.			
The Web site is updated and/or revised regularly.			
Links given at the Web site are up to date and reliable.			

Source: From *Becoming a Teacher,* 5th ed., by F. W. Parkay and B. H. Stanford. Copyright © 2000 by Pearson Education. Reprinted by permission of the publisher.

Internet Safety in the Schools

We are all aware that the Internet is here to stay. Most people agree that the Internet has changed the way in which they research a topic, communicate, and perceive how long it should take to access and transmit information. Most people also agree that if not handled appropriately, the Internet can be a very dangerous place, especially for the young population.

When I think of the Internet in relation to young people, I think of a child being out in the streets alone at night. With the proper supervision and understanding of the risks, he's okay. Without it, he can be in grave danger.

This brings us to the issue of how schools can enable students to use the Internet and its rich sources of information, as well as using it to communicate while keeping them safe from objectionable language, inappropriate visual material, and bullying.

In addition to using filtering and antivirus systems to ensure that outside predators do not enter, schools must address additional problems such as improper usage of language and cyberbullying. Cyberbullying is a common occurrence that must be taken very seriously and must be addressed with students prior to their engaging in activities that involve communications via the Internet. Students should be made aware that they can hurt others' feelings or scare people with e-mail or any kind of electronic messaging. They should not write anything that they would not want written to them. They also can be the recipients of threatening or hurtful messages. They should immediately speak to a parent or responsible adult if they are the recipients of frightening messages. Students must be taught to show respect to others on the Internet by respecting their privacy—do not enter chat rooms just for fun or to distract others. Try these additional sites for more information:

Kids' Rules for Online Safety (http://www.safekids.com/kidsrules.htm)

The Ten Commandments of Computer Ethics (http://www.tekmom.com/tencommand/index.html)

TECHNOLOGY IDEA #3: CRITERIA FOR EVALUATING SOFTWARE PROGRAMS

Equipped with knowledge of achievable instructional technology ideas in the classroom, professional support Web sites, NETS standards, and Internet safety tips, we are ready to take a serious look at software. Educational software on CDs or DVDs can be a very effective means to support learning.

Why do you prefer using one CD to another for teaching purposes?

Why do your students prefer one CD or DVD to another?

There are good reasons why one program is more popular than another, and why educators and students prefer using them. Many of the reasons are found in the criteria for evaluating Web sites.

Don't be surprised if you find your answers in these criteria for evaluating software (Table 9.2).

Table 9.2   Criteria for Evaluating Software Programs

	Poor	Fair	Excellent
User Friendliness			
How easy is it to start the program?			
Is there an overview or site map for the program?			
Can students easily control the pace of the program?			
Can students exit the program easily?			
Can students create their own paths through the program and develop their own links among elements?			
After first-time use, can student bypass introductory or orientation material?			
Does the program include useful hotlinks to Internet sites?			

	Poor	Fair	Excellent
Inclusiveness			
Can students with hearing or visual impairments make full use of the program?			
Can students navigate the program by making simple key strokes with one hand?			
Does the material avoid stereotypes and reflect sensitivity to racial, cultural, and gender differences?			
Textual Material			
How accurate and thorough is the content?			
Is the content well organized and clearly presented?			
Is the textual content searchable?			
Can the content be integrated into the curriculum?			
Images			
Is the image resolution high quality?			
Is the layout attractive, user friendly, and uncluttered?			
Do the graphics and colors enhance instruction?			
How true are the colors of the images?			
Are the images large enough?			
Does the program have a zoom feature that indicates the power of magnification?			
Does the program make effective use of video and animation?			
Audio			
Are the audio clips high quality?			
Does the audio enhance instruction?			

(Continued)

Table 9.2 (Continued)

	Poor	Fair	Excellent
Technical			
Is installation of the program easy and trouble-free?			
Are instructions clear and easy to follow?			
Is user-friendly online help available?			
Are technical support people easy to reach, helpful, and courteous?			
Motivational			
Does the program capture and hold students' interest?			
Are students eager to use the program again?			
Does the program give appropriate, motivational feedback?			
Does the program provide prompts or cues to promote students' learning?			

Source: From *Becoming a Teacher,* 5th ed., by E. W. Parkay and B. H. Stanford. Copyright © 2000 by Pearson Education. Reprinted by permission of the publisher.

Based on the above criteria for evaluating quality software, I have compiled a list of reputable software retailers that offer software for teacher planning and for student use. I have also listed names of programs that educators across the country have used successfully and that students find engaging. Retailers often send desk copies free of charge for teachers to try out or have trials online that can be accessed or downloaded for a period of time. Additionally, I have included Internet sites that offer free downloadable software.

Broderbund (http://www.broderbund.com/)—*The Print Shop, Kid Pix, Oregon Trail, Carmen San Diego, Cluefinders,* and *Reader Rabbit*

Sunburst Technology (http://www.sunburst.com/)—*Type to Learn, Hyperstudio, Hot Dog Stand, Numbers Undercover, Learn About Science* Series

Internet sites for free downloadable software:

Educational Freeware (http://www.educational-freeware.com/freeware/)

OpenOffice.org (http://www.openoffice.org/)

Owl & Mouse (http://www.yourchildlearns.com/owlmouse.htm)

OpenOffice is a great free download for those who purchase a computer that's not loaded with applications. OpenOffice includes applications such as a word processor, spreadsheet, presentation manager, and drawing program that are compatible with Microsoft Office.

How do you suppose educators have used some of these resources in the teaching and learning process?

Where would you use some of these resources listed in your classroom or in the school?

TECHNOLOGY IDEA #4: PRACTICAL INTEGRATED PROJECTS WITH MICROSOFT OFFICE

We have shared some technology suggestions, Web sites, and software that support teaching and learning, and we are ready to see what educators have done with the resources that are available to them.

The following examples of integrated projects resulted from collaborative planning and implementation efforts of grade-level classroom teachers, specialists, the computer teacher, and myself, the instructional technology coordinator.

Project: Using Microsoft Word to Create a Cookbook in Hebrew Language and Technology

This project was a culmination of a food unit in Language class.

- Each student brought a recipe to class and was asked to write a composition in Hebrew which included the name, ingredients, and preparation instructions. (This can be done in any language.)

(Continued)

(Continued)

- Students were then brought into the Computer Lab, where they were given instruction on how to type in Hebrew using Microsoft Word software. Microsoft Word has the capacity to type in many different languages. Students were also taught how to add graphics to their documents and how to proofread for spelling and grammar errors.
- On completion of the task, each student read the recipe to the class in the Hebrew language, omitting the name of the recipe. Class listeners guessed the names of the recipe.
- Finally, the recipes were compiled and bound to create a class cookbook.
- Each student took a class cookbook home.

Project: Using Microsoft Excel to Create a Spreadsheet

Math and Technology

- In Math, each student was asked to come up with a question and three to five answers to the question that each classmate would be given the opportunity to answer. For example:
  o What is your favorite kind of chocolate? white, dark, milk, other
  o What video game system do you like best? GameCube, Xbox 360, Nintendo DS

  Each student was responsible for keeping track of the data collected on a sheet of paper.

- Students were brought into the Computer Lab, where they learned how to use Excel, a spreadsheet program, to post, manage, and graph the data they collected from the class. They were taught how to add graphics, proofread, and spell-check.
- On completion of the task, students presented their Excel spreadsheets to the class on a large screen with the aid of an LCD projector hooked up to a computer.
- Finally, the spreadsheets were compiled and bound to create a "Class Survey Results Book."

Project: Using Microsoft Publisher to Create a Newspaper

Social Studies, English, and Technology

- In the classroom, students were learning about the Revolutionary War and pretending that they were living in that time period. They were all writers for a newspaper that they named called The Revolutionary Gazette. Each student was given the job of writing an article for the paper. Some students were hard news writers, including writing about topics such as the Massacre at Boston, Battle of Bunker Hill, or British Surrender at Saratoga. Other students wrote about people of the time; for example, Benedict Arnold. Some students wrote book reviews on books such as *Trouble River, Westward to Home,* and *Sign of the Beaver.* Others wrote poetry about the Revolution. And still others wrote advertisements of the time.
- Students were brought into the Computer Lab, where they were introduced to Microsoft Publisher, a desktop-publishing program. Using this medium, they could type their articles, as well as format them using their creativity. They were taught how to add graphics, proofread, and spell-check.
- On completion, student work was saved, combined into one publication, printed, and assembled as a newspaper would be assembled. The newspaper was distributed to the entire grade.

Project: Using Microsoft Access to Create an Address/Telephone Book

This was an end-term project that taught the skill of using Access as a database program for personal use.

- In the classroom, students were asked to compile a list of names, camp or home addresses, and phone numbers of each student in the class, in addition to friends or relatives they want to keep in contact with over the summer.
- Students were then brought into the Computer Lab, where they were given instruction on how to create a simple database using Microsoft Access.
- On completion of task, each student printed the database of names, ordered alphabetically by surname, and took home a custom-made address book.

Project: Using Microsoft PowerPoint to Create a Slideshow Presentation

Science and Technology—An Internet Research Project

- This was truly a computer-assisted learning activity. All learning took place in the Computer Lab. Although the topics were not covered by the classroom teachers, together, as a team, they decided what the topics would be. The topics were landforms and natural disasters. Two Web quests, created by the computer teacher, were the source of learning for the students.
- Students had never done a Web quest before; therefore, they were introduced to what a Web quest was and how to go about completing it.
- Students were familiar with creating PowerPoint presentations and were directed to create slides for each question and answer.
- Web quests lend themselves to students working collaboratively; therefore, students worked in pairs. Directions on the Web quest prompted the students to go from one task to another. Appropriate Internet links were embedded onto the "quest" so that students could answer the questions and complete the tasks. While one student might be navigating through the Web quest, the other student might be setting up the PowerPoint presentation.
- Student PowerPoint projects were printed, presented by the students to the class, compiled, and bound to create a research book.

See http://www.apples4theteacher.com/science.html for free interactive educational elementary science activities for teachers and kids

Here's how one of my excellent students integrated PowerPoint in teaching.

TECHNOLOGY IDEA #5: USE OF POWERPOINT IN THE CLASSROOM

By Anthony Vavallo

Abstract and Rationale

This unit plan takes students through a five-step process to teach them how to compile a PowerPoint project. It will be implemented to do the following:

1. Enhance writing skills.

2. Enhance computer skills.

3. Promote social interaction in the classroom.

4. Introduce what a PowerPoint project is.

5. Promote the use of technology in the classroom.

Lesson 1

Goals and Objectives:

- Students will be given an opportunity to compile a PowerPoint project.
- Students will prepare the materials to use for their slide project.

Activities:

- Students are shown what a PowerPoint project looks like.
- Students are given the opportunity to compile an eight-slide template out of folded card stock paper.

Lesson 2

Goals and Objectives:

- Students will have a final draft of their eight-slide template.
- Students will critique each other's work.

Activities:

- Students are required to finish the final draft of their eight-slide template.
- Students are shown how to "bullet" an idea instead of typing long sentences.
- Students are also given the opportunity to critique each other's work.

Lesson 3 Aim: To create a slideshow using PowerPoint

Goals and Objectives:

- Students are given an introduction in how to type a PowerPoint project.
- Students will be able to transfer their templates to the actual PowerPoint slides.

Activities:

- Students are assigned their own computers to use for the project.
- Students are given a tutorial on how to begin a basic PowerPoint project.

Lesson 4 Aim: To format the slideshow

Goals and Objectives:

- Students will be given an introduction to improving their PowerPoint projects.
- Students will be able to change the font, font style, font size, and color.

Activities:

- Students are shown how they can change the font, font style, font size, and color in their slide show.
- Students are also given an opportunity to add a picture of themselves in the project.

Lesson 5

Goals and Objectives:

- Students will be able to change the format of the slides in their project.
- Students are given the opportunity to refine their projects for submission.

Activities:

- Students are given the knowledge and the opportunity to reformat their slide show.
- Students will have ample time to complete their projects.

Below is the text file (without the actual PowerPoint slides) of a student who followed Mr. Vavallo's lessons. You can probably figure out the types of slides the student developed based on the text. Counting the title, the student created eight slides.

MY YEAR OF THE ROOSTER *By Jacky Yan*	Contents Celebrating Chinese New Year Chinese Zodiac Dance of the Dragon and Lion Food Clothing About the Author

Celebrating Chinese New Year People celebrate Chinese New Year, well, to celebrate the New Year. Money is given to their family members. The money represents good luck. In the New Year festival, the color red appears everywhere. That's why red is a lucky color.	*Chinese Zodiac* People are born in different years. There is an order of each animal. It goes like this: rat, rabbit, horse, rooster, ox, dragon, goat, dog, tiger, snake, monkey, and pig. February 1, 2003, is the Year of the Goat. The goat is artistic and shy.
Dance of the Dragon and Lion People believe that the dance of the dragon and the lion scare away evil spirits. Some people believe that firecrackers scare away evil spirits. People that work in stores put lettuce at the top of the store for the lion. Sometimes, the lettuce has a red envelope inside. The money is to help the environment.	*Food* People have a big feast with lots of food. People eat the food to celebrate Chinese New Year. These are some examples of the food of Chinese New Year: fish, noodles, duck, chicken, pig, rice, and seafood.
Clothing People wear red to represent the color of China. They also wear red to celebrate the Chinese New Year. The idea of wearing red is taken from the red money envelopes.	*About the Author* Hi, my name is Jacky Yan. My favorite year is the Year of the Rooster. I was born in the Year of the Rooster. I am 10 years old. I am in fourth grade. I was born in 1993. I think Chinese New Year is cool. I live in New York.

Learning to use PowerPoint is relatively easy. I suggest you use a tutorial and join the crowd who use PowerPoint effectively as a teaching tool. Research indicates higher levels of student motivation and excitement in learning when PowerPoint is judiciously used (not overused) in teaching.

TECHNOLOGY IDEA #6: NEW TECHNOLOGIES

We are finally ready to look at how new technologies that you might not be very familiar with, but which are impacting teaching and learning are being used in 21st-century classrooms.

The SMART Board is an interactive whiteboard. It's a large, touch-controlled screen that works with a computer and an LCD projector. The projector sends the image that is showing on the desktop of the computer to the whiteboard. Users can write on the interactive whiteboard using a special wand or a finger to control computer applications by pointing, clicking, and dragging, just as with a desktop mouse. To emphasize a point, users can also write or type over a presentation on the screen. Users can add clipart or animated objects to engage students or for emphasis. Anything you can do on the computer can be done on the screen. SMART Boards are used in education as an interactive presentation modality. (Paraphrased from http://www2.smarttech.com/st/en-US/Products/SMART+Boards/.)

Two Examples of How to Teach Keyboarding Using the SMART Board

1. In the one-computer classroom

2. In the Computer Lab

Aim: To type the letters *m* and *o* using the SMART Board keyboard tool and a word processing program

Objectives: Students will be able to
- Access a word processing program
- Type the letters *m* and *o* independent of other letter or words, in small words, in phrases, in short sentences consisting of letters with which they are familiar
- Save and/or print document

Review: Using the SMART Board, review how to access a document, access the keyboard tool, and review where the old keys are located and correct finger placement.

Presentation 1: Locate the new keys on the keyboard and demonstrate correct finger placement.

Application 1: Students can alternate practicing the keys, accessing a word processing program, saving, and printing. Students can observe while each student is typing. This lesson is excellent for students who learn visually or bodily/kinesthetically.

Aim: To type the letters *m* and *o* using the SMART Board and Type To Learn software

Objectives: Students will be able to

- Access Type To Learn software
- Type the letters *m* and *o* independent of other letters, in small words, in phrases, in short sentences using letters with which they are familiar
- Save and/or print document

Review: Using the SMART Board, review how to access a document, access the keyboard tool, and review where the old keys are located and correct finger placement

Presentation 2: Demonstrate how to access Type To Learn software. Demonstrate how to run the software and watch with students how the lesson unfolds.

Application 2: Students will begin using the program and following the prompts for learning the new keys.

Unlike the one computer classroom, in the Computer Lab, each student has a computer to use.

Go to http://www.juliethompson.com/SMART.html to take a look at different ways that teachers are using SMART Board technology in schools.

The Promethean board is an enhanced digital whiteboard system. Where the whiteboard allows teachers and students to view different applications and Web sites and write notes or add clipart or animated graphics, the Promethean board (in addition to all SMART Board functions) allows students to interact with it. For example, students are given a handheld device with buttons on it, which enables them to answer questions. The responses are analyzed and the teacher can determine whether pupils are following a lesson. Results can also be saved or exported to Excel for record keeping and further analysis.

An Example of How to Use a Promethean Board in the Classroom
Twelfth Grade American History

Topic: America before Columbus

Objectives: Student will be able to

- Describe the civilizations of the south
- Describe the civilizations of the north

(Continued)

(Continued)

- · Describe the first English settlements
- Explain why the English came to the New World

Presentation: Students will watch a video that addresses the topic or link to a Web site such as the ones at http://www.ibiblio.org/expo/1492.exhibit/Intro.html or http://www.mcallen.lib.tx.us/library/child/homework/am1799.htm.

Review and Reflection/Application: A question sheet will be distributed that encourages students to reflect on the video or Web site and answer questions relating to the topic, or the teacher can verbalize the questions.

Questions are created by the teacher. Varying levels of questions should reflect different levels of thinking.

An answer sheet is created on the computer and transferred to the Promethean board technology.

As questions are posed to students, they answer using a mouselike device that syncs with the Promethean board technology.

Answers are assessed immediately, and the teacher and students are made aware of how many students are grasping the information presented in the lesson.

The teacher then can pace the lesson appropriately.

Go to http://www.greenville.k12.sc.us/oakview/dept/media/teacher.asp and take a look at different ways that teachers are using Promethean board technology in schools.

The iPod is a palm-sized, electronic device primarily created to record and play music.

One Way to Use an iPod in the Classroom
Foreign Language—Middle to Upper Grade Levels

Topic: Speaking Hebrew

Objectives: Students will be able to converse using basic Hebrew words, phrases, and sentences.

The review and presentation will be recorded using a microphone connected to the iPod. Voice memos can be manually copied on the iPod so that they can be played back. Voice memos can be synchronized to iTunes on the computer and played back from the Music menu on the iPod.

Presentation: After a brief review of key words, the teacher will begin a conversation in Hebrew with the class. The teacher will begin by asking simple questions using one or more of the key words and other familiar words.

Students will be called on to answer the questions.

Once all students have participated, the activity will change to the teacher asking and answering the same question followed by one student asking the same question and another student answering while the rest of the class listens. All students will have the opportunity to be listeners and speakers.

Teacher will then present new words.

Application: Students will create their own questions and answers and share them with class. Students will ask class members questions and class members will answer.

Homework/Reinforcement: Students will be asked to play back the conversations of the day on their iPod. This will serve as a review and reinforcement.

Go to http://support.apple.com/kb/HT2396?viewlocale=en_US to learn more about voice recording using the iPod. Go to http://www.apple.com/au/education/ipod/lessons/ to learn more about using the iPod in the classroom.

YouTube and Microsoft Soapbox are just two examples of Internet-based video sharing sites.

Since young people seem to be so engaged when creating or watching videos, why not use online videos as a teaching/learning modality. Videos can be used in the classroom to enhance instruction in any subject area and at any grade level. The auditory or visual learner could benefit greatly from this form of learning. It can also benefit learners with special needs; for example, learners who have difficulty writing or who have difficulty paying attention for long periods. Videos can be paused, played back, or viewed from home at an entirely different time and in a different environment, perhaps one that is less stressful to the student and more conducive for concentration. Additionally, student projects can be uploaded to YouTube or Microsoft Soapbox, and linked to the school's Web site for viewing. Saved documents serve as an e-portfolio.

One Way to Use YouTube or Microsoft Soapbox in the Classroom

Social Studies/Current Events/Presidential Debates—Middle to Upper Grade Levels

Topic: Presidential Democratic candidates Clinton and Obama debates

Objectives: Students will be able to describe some of the issues that the candidates are talking about and that the country is concerned with.

Review: Who is running for president on the Democratic ticket? What do you think Americans are concerned with?

Presentation: Students will listen to the two candidates speak on important issues and will take notes on what they perceive as being important.

Application: Students will engage in conversation about campaign issues and who they think has better answers and why. They will reflect on whom they would vote for, if they were voting on the Democratic ticket, and the reasons why.

Access the following link to view a debate between Hillary Clinton and Barak Obama: http://youtube.com/watch?v=MD9F1t9GQzA.

To see how teachers are using e-portfolios, check out the following:

A Classroom Wiki Webquest (http://blog.wikispaces.com/2008/02/a-classroom-wiki-webquest.html)—Great example of a seventh and eighth grade Web quest.

Electronic Portfolios (http://www.west.asu.edu/achristie/eportfolios/main.html)—Click on Student Writing Samples.

Electronic portfolios, also known as e-portfolios or digital portfolios, are collections of electronic documents assembled and managed on the Web.

E-portfolios are online spaces used to display student or class work. E-portfolios enable teachers and students to share, reflect, and work together in and outside of the classroom. E-portfolios, like traditional portfolios, document work over the course of time and track growth. They serve as an assessment instrument for teachers as well as a self-assessment instrument for students.

MySpace and Facebook are Web sites that were initially created as social networks.

MySpace was established in 1999 by eUniverse and for eUniverse employees only. The company was later renamed Intermix Media.

Facebook was created in 2004 by Mark Zuckerberg, a Harvard student, for Harvard students only.

Because of the huge interest exhibited by people who accessed these Web sites, business strategists, students, educators, and special interest groups realized the impact that MySpace or Facebook could make if used wisely. Because of the enormous need, the Web sites allowed more people to log on.

Today, millions and millions of people log on to either MySpace or Facebook daily and view whatever is posted on the home page or the Wall. Users communicate with friends, colleagues, or coworkers by sending messages, joining groups, or posting pictures and comments. Through this medium, friends, colleagues, and coworkers get to know each other and keep up with "what's happening." Users often follow favorite music and videos together, share and compare movie reviews, and exchange all kinds of information that they have in common.

MySpace	Facebook
Open to anyone who wants to log on. Allows users to post as many as ten photos. Privacy settings can be set or changed. Videos can be added to page.	Access limited to registered users whose e-mail addresses are chosen by the owner of the "Wall." Allows users to post photos. Privacy settings can be set or changed.

How Can Facebook or MySpace Be Used in the Classroom?

Teachers would be more likely to use a site such as Facebook because they can work or communicate within a safe environment, such as a work group of peers only. Facebook can be used as a tool for developing a sense of community with students where students feel free to post their ideas on a variety of topics.

At the beginning of the school year, assignments can be placed on the group Wall, such as

"Who are you?"

"What are your favorite subjects?"

"What are your outside interests?"

"Express yourself in a creative way."

Hot topics can be addressed within the group throughout the year. During an election year, questions such as

"What does it mean to be a Republican?"

"What does it mean to be a Democrat?"

"Do you consider yourself a Republican or a Democrat and why?"

"Do you consider yourself anything else?"

The Clinton/Obama run for the presidency is of particular interest. Questions such as "Who is your favorite Democratic candidate and why?" can be posted on the Wall as an assignment. Or, "What are the issues that we should be looking for presidential hopefuls to answer and what do the answers mean to us?" can be posted. Students will answer and be able to view each other's responses. YouTube footage or digital pictures can be attached to enhance clarity. The teacher can make comments each day on students' progress. The teacher can post current articles and offer students additional insights. Toward the end of the election process, the teacher can post the following question: "Who is your choice for the next president of the United States and why?" The teacher can post a pie chart showing how the class as a whole voted.

Reflection

Which of the following technologies do you think would benefit you most in the classroom or personally/professionally?

How would you use them?

- SMART Board
- Promethean board
- iPod
- YouTube and/or Soapbox
- E-portfolios
- Facebook

CONCLUSION

We can't ignore technology. Technology is a tool we can use as educators to enhance the educational experiences of our students. As a professional educator, you are obligated to become technology proficient to the extent to which you can model best practices with students and use technology as a viable teaching tool. It is important to understand that your students may be light-years ahead of you technologically. They are not intimidated by new smartphones, digital cameras, iPods, with all the bells and whistles. They are not intimidated by new versions of software run by the latest version of

Windows or Mac platforms. They just dive right in. As educators, we might be unable to stay one step ahead of our students, but we should be open to learning from students when necessary, and it is incumbent on us to keep abreast of best practices in the classroom associated with the use of new technologies.

To be able to use technology as a teaching tool, Bernie Poole, educational technology professor at The University of Pittsburgh, mentions six essential technology-related skills all teachers should possess:

1. Knowing what the Microsoft Office suite is

2. Basic technology problems in the classroom troubleshooting skills

3. Technical assistance resources

4. Familiarity with subject-area Web sites

5. Web searching skills

6. Interest and flexibility regarding change

http://www.educationworld.com/a_tech/tech/tech227.shtml.

Although I advocate technological integration in your teaching, you are still the most critical element in the classroom. Technology cannot, by itself, transform lives. Only you can do so. As bell hooks (1994) reminds us, "To teach in a manner that respects and cares for the souls of our students is essential if we are to provide the necessary conditions where learning can most deeply and intimately begin."

Follow-Up Questions/Activities

1. Interview a more experienced teacher and ask how he or she integrates technology in teaching, or visit another school that is known for technology integration (if you are really interested in technology, ask your principal to release you for a morning to go visit that school). Find out what technologies are used and how they promote student learning.

2. Create a PowerPoint presentation in a specific content area. Be sure to include Internet links.

3. Try to find information from YouTube to present to your class.

4. Become a Facebook user.

5. Which ideas presented in this chapter were of most value? Explain.

6. What further professional development technology activities would you be interested in pursuing? Find most useful?

Closing Comments

Recollection

Thinking about succeeding, I recall a great story told by Dr. Charles Garfield, author of *Peak Performance*, as related by the "The Executive Speechwriter Newsletter." The story and its interpretation address our professional commitment as educators.

A very wealthy man bought a huge ranch in Arizona, and he invited some of his closest associates in to see it. After touring some of the 1,500 acres of mountains and rivers and grasslands, he took everybody into the house. The house was as spectacular as the scenery, and out back was the largest swimming pool you have ever seen. However, this gigantic swimming pool was filled with alligators. The rich owner explained it this way: "I value courage more than anything else. Courage is what made me a billionaire. In fact, I think that courage is such a powerful virtue that if anybody is courageous enough to jump in that pool, swim through those alligators, and make it to the other side, I'll give him anything he wants, anything— my house, my land, my money." Of course, everybody laughed at the absurd challenge and proceeded to follow the owner into the house for lunch . . . when suddenly they heard a splash. Turning around, they saw this guy swimming for his life across the pool, thrashing at the water, as the alligators swarmed after him. After several death-defying seconds, the man made it, unharmed to the other side. The rich host was absolutely amazed, but he stuck to his promise. He said, "You are indeed a man of courage and I will stick to my word. What do you want? You can have anything—my house, my land, my money—just tell me what and it's yours." The swimmer, breathing heavily, looked up at his host and said, "I just want to know one thing—who the hell pushed me into that pool?"

(Continued)

(Continued)

Well, no one is going to, nor can, "push" you to do anything you don't want to do. But, each of us has enormous resilience, tenacity, grit, guts, and determination to accomplish anything despite difficult circumstances. Not unlike the swimmer, you may need that extra push or encouragement, but once you get going you can achieve success at anything you put your mind to! Teaching is fraught with challenges that may lead to feelings of despair and a sense of failure. But such feelings are short-lived because teaching has so many positives to offer. The excitement of seeing a young mind become aware of something new is incredible. The thrill of working with young people and making a real difference in their lives is unparalleled. As lifelong learners and professionals, good teachers continually strive to achieve excellence and professional growth.

Those of you who strive for professional excellence will realize inevitably, as you gain more teaching experience, that teaching as a field of study and practice is a complex enterprise. Those who teach well are in the minority. Teaching is both an art and a science. Those of you who conceive it as such realize there is much to learn. Michael Fullan (1995) makes the point even stronger: "Quality learning for all students depends on quality learning for all educators" (p. 5). As you gain experience, you will learn more about critical pedagogy, content area strategies, advanced cooperative learning groupings, reflective practice, peer coaching, action research, transformative teaching practice, literacy development—oh, there is so much more to learn and do. But that is what makes this field so exciting and growth oriented. Each day is different and new, and those who envision teaching as a lifelong growth process will hone their skills and continually learn. The best teachers are the best learners.

In *Teaching 101* I have highlighted the importance of taking your study and practice of teaching seriously by viewing yourself as an esteemed professional. Learning as much as you can about your chosen field is as necessary as it is empowering professionally. Understanding the essential knowledge, skills, and dispositions to good teaching is imperative. Knowing the learning needs of your students, understanding how children learn, and appreciating and accommodating the diverse abilities of your students are all critical. Creating effective lessons and developing the ability to communicate well is foundational to good teaching practice. Assisting your students through study skills instruction is significant. No matter how knowledgeable and skillful you are, you can't succeed in the classroom without a systematic approach to classroom management and the skills to work effectively with students. Developing a comprehensive student assessment plan, incorporating technology as a teaching tool, and working to meet local or state standards are further challenges. But above all else, remain proud of your profession. Feel empowered and grow as a professional. Continued success . . .

Appendix A

Annotated Bibliography

T he literature on teaching is extensive. The list below is not meant to serve as a comprehensive resource by any means. The titles I have selected to annotate are few but, in my opinion, are among the most useful references on the subject. I may have missed, of course, many other important works. Nevertheless, the list below is a good start. Don't forget that life is a long journey of continuous learning. Continue to hone your skills by reading good books and articles on the topic. No one is ever perfect and everyone can learn something new by keeping current with the literature in the field. Share your readings and reactions with a colleague.

Assessment

Gronlund, N. E. (2003). *Assessment of student achievement* (7th ed.). Boston: Allyn & Bacon.

Clearest, most concise work on the subject.

Becoming a Teacher

Abbey, O. F., Jr. (2003). *A practical guide for new teachers: Getting started, surviving, and succeeding.* Norwood, MA: Christopher-Gordon.

A short, practical guide for new teachers that includes advice on how to obtain a teaching position, an introduction to what life in school is like, and tips on how to survive in the classroom.

Armstrong, T. (1998). *How to awaken genius in the classroom.* Alexandria, VA: Association for Supervision and Curriculum Development.

Some may consider this book "far out," but I think its thesis is true and it is a must-read—a really short book.

Ayers, W. (2001). *To teach: The journey of a teacher.* New York: Teachers College Press.

Inspiring introduction to teaching.

Feeney Jonson, K. (2001). *The new elementary teacher's handbook.* Thousand Oaks, CA: Corwin.

Nice, brief, and easy-to-use handbook to guide a teacher.

Kane, P. R. (Ed.). (1996). *My first year as a teacher.* New York: Signet.

Short, practical stories from new teachers.

Kohl, H. (1989). *Growing minds: On becoming a teacher.* New York: Harper & Row.

Classic book that greatly affected my own teaching practice.

Kottler, J. A., & Zehm, S. J. (2000). *On being a teacher: The human dimension* (2nd ed.). Thousand Oaks, CA: Corwin.

Inspirational, practical, and current—reminds you why you went into teaching in the first place.

Palmer, P. J. (2007). *The courage to teach: Exploring the inner landscape of a teacher's life.* San Francisco: Jossey-Bass.

Clear, refreshing work to get you going when you don't feel particularly inspired.

Brain-Based Education

Sousa, D. A. (2006). *How the brain learns* (3rd ed.). Thousand Oaks, CA: Corwin.

Practical and easy-to-understand volume devoted to synthesizing brain research to assist educators in maximizing student learning—packed with teaching ideas.

Wolfe, P. (2001). *Brain matters: Translating research into classroom practice.* Alexandria, VA: Association for Supervision and Curriculum Development.

Practical classroom applications and brain-compatible teaching strategies.

Classics

Anyon, J. (1981). Social class and school knowledge. *Curriculum Inquiry, 11*(1), 3–41.

Required reading for every education student—insights into prejudice, discrimination, and differential treatment.

Banks, J. A. (2008). *Teaching strategies for ethnic studies* (8th ed.). Boston: Allyn & Bacon.

An important and popular work by a noted educator.

Bloom, B. S. (Ed.). (1956). *Taxonomy of educational objectives: The classification of educational goals. Handbook I: Cognitive domain.* New York: David McKay.

One of the most familiar educational books of all time—Bloom identified six levels of intellectual behavior within the cognitive domain.

Cremin, L. (1964). *The transformation of the school.* New York: Vantage.

One of the 20th century's noted educational historians.

Dewey, J. (1929). *The sources of a science of education.* New York: Liveright.

How can one not include a work by the foremost educator in the previous century? This work is short and clear, unlike many of his other works.

Giroux, H. A. (2001). *Theory and resistance in education: A pedagogy for the oppression.* Hadley, MA: Bergin & Garvey.

Although not an easy read, his views are avant-garde and insightful.

Goodlad, J. I. (2004). *A place called school.* New York: McGraw-Hill.

Prolific and noted educator.

Greene, M. (1988). *The dialectic of freedom.* New York: Teachers College Press.

One of the greatest educational philosophers of our time—her other work, *Teacher as Stranger*, shaped my beliefs about teaching.

hooks, b. (1994). *Teaching to transgress: Education as the practice of freedom.* New York: Routledge.

A wonderful read.

Howard, J. (1991). *Getting smart: The social construction of intelligence.* The Efficacy Institute.

Groundbreaking work on the social construction of intelligence—every teacher must read this piece.

Hunter, M. (1982). *Mastery teaching.* Thousand Oaks, CA: Corwin.

How can one not read a book by Madeline Hunter, who influenced teaching practice almost more than anyone else?

James, W. (1902). *Talks to teachers on psychology, and to students on some of life's ideals.* New York: Henry Holt.

One of the most influential works on teaching.

Katz, M. B. (1971). *Class, bureaucracy, and schools: The illusion of educational change in America.* New York: Praeger.

A classical treatise on bureaucracy in American education.

Kozol, J. (1991). *Savage inequalities: Children in America's schools.* New York: Crown.

Classic work on school inequities.

Lortie, D. (1975). *Schoolteacher: A sociological study.* Chicago: University of Chicago Press.

The classic study on becoming a teacher.

Noddings, N. (1992). *The challenge to care in schools: An alternative approach to education.* New York: Teachers College Press.

Noted educational philosopher—her "ethic of caring" has become axiomatic.

Oakes, J. (1995). *Keeping track: How schools structure inequality.* New Haven, CT: Yale University Press.

A belief-changing work—greatly influenced me.

Pyne, S. L. (1951). *The art of asking questions.* Princeton, NJ: Princeton University Press.

The essence of good teaching—practical.

Rist, R. C. (1970). Student social class and teacher expectations: The self-fulfilling prophecy in ghetto education. *Harvard Educational Review, 40*(3), 411–451.

Classic article on the influence of teacher expectations.

Sadker, D., & Sadker, M. (1999). *Failing at fairness: How our schools cheat girls.* New York: Simon & Schuster.

An eye-opener to gender inequities—also affected me deeply.

Sarason, S. B. (1971). *The culture of the school and the problem of change.* Boston: Allyn & Bacon.

The classic on educational change.

Schlechty, P. C. (1990). *Schools for the 21st century.* San Francisco: Jossey-Bass.

Futurists must read this one.

Vygotsky, L. (1978). *Thought and language.* Cambridge: MIT Press.

Vygotsky, along with Dewey, is among the elder statesmen of education.

Wong, H. K., & Wong, R. T. (1998). *How to be an effective teacher: The first days of school.* Mountain View, CA: Harry K. Wong.

National bestseller—Wong is an inspirational speaker and his book is a must-read, not only for every beginning teacher, but even for experienced teachers to remind them of the basics and to inspire them.

Classroom Management

Arnold, H. (2000). *Succeeding in the secondary classroom: Strategies for middle and high school teachers.* Thousand Oaks, CA: Corwin.

One of the better resources for the upper grades—as a teacher in the upper grades, I could have used this practical book. Hands-on strategies and practical techniques, especially for prospective and beginning teachers, make this book a must-read.

Belvel, P. S., & Jordan, M. M. (2002). *Rethinking classroom management: Strategies for prevention, intervention, and problem solving.* Thousand Oaks, CA: Corwin.

Few resources deal effectively with preventive, supportive, and corrective stages of discipline—this work does the trick. Encouraging reflective thinking, this useful resource reviews excellent intervention techniques and problem-solving strategies.

Burden, P. R. (2000). *Powerful classroom management strategies: Motivating students to learn.* Thousand Oaks, CA: Corwin.

Nice combination of theory and practical strategies for effective classroom management. I especially like its easy reading style. Emphasizing the importance of motivation theory, this compact work is very user-friendly.

Canter, L. (2001). *Assertive discipline.* Santa Monica, CA: Canter & Associates.

The very best book on corrective discipline out there. One of three books I require my teaching students to read. Learn and practice the three response styles. It's controversial; some hate the system, others swear by it—I'm in the latter camp. Use it! A lifesaver!

Charles, C. M. (2001). *Building classroom discipline.* New York: Longman.

Best textbook on the subject.

Curwin, R. L., & Mendler, A. N. (2008). *Discipline with dignity.* Alexandria, VA: Association for Supervision and Curriculum Development.

Classic—most useful. It's one of three books I require my students to read in a course I teach on classroom management. Their creative ideas have caught on nationally and their work is used extensively at all levels. A must-read.

Gill, V. (2001). *The eleven commandments of good teaching: Creating classrooms where teachers can teach and students can learn* (2nd ed.). Thousand Oaks, CA: Corwin.

Really concise and useful. Don't let the catchy, perhaps simplistic, title fool you—this book is excellent. Full of tactics and strategies, this resource is written by a veteran teacher who has practical and wise advice.

Ginott, H. G. (1972). *Between teacher and child.* New York: Macmillan.

If I could recommend only one book, this is it! Sensitive, insightful, and practical, this work is a classic in the field. An "oldie but goodie."

Gootman, M. E. (2000). *The caring teacher's guide to discipline: Helping young students learn self-control, responsibility, and respect* (2nd ed.). Thousand Oaks, CA: Corwin.

Another Corwin favorite of mine—I believe a good classroom manager is above all else a *caring* human being. Thoughtful, practical, and extremely sensitive.

Rosenblum-Lowden. R. (2000). *You have to go to school . . . you're the teacher: 200 tips to make your job easier and more fun* (2nd ed.). Thousand Oaks, CA: Corwin.

One of my favorites—I read a tip a day. Filled with pearls of wit and wisdom, this very brief resource will help you develop rapport with students and manage everyday school problems.

Cognitive Strategy Instruction (Study Skills)

Mangrum, C. T., II, Iannuzzi, P., & Strichart, S. S. (1998). *Teaching study skills and strategies in grades 4–8.* Needham, MA: Allyn & Bacon.

Easy and ready-to-use strategies to effectively teach students study skills.

Pressley, M., & Woloshyn, V. (1995). *Cognitive strategy instruction that really improves children's academic performance.* Brookline, MA: Brookline Books.

Classic book that reviews many study skill strategies in various content areas. Offers specific suggestions for teaching cognitive learning strategies.

Scheid, K. (1993). *Helping students become strategic learners: Guidelines for teaching.* Brookline, MA: Brookline Books.

A most practical guide that helps beginning or experienced teachers adopt practical teaching tools for learning in the basic skill areas.

Critical Pedagogy

Freire, P. (1974). *Pedagogy of the oppressed.* New York: Seabury.

Also a classic on innovative teaching practices.

Freire, P. (1994). *The pedagogy of hope: Reliving pedagogy of the oppressed.* New York: Continuum.

Classic follow-up to previous work.

Kohl, H. (1998). *The discipline of hope: Learning from a lifetime of teaching.* New York: Simon & Schuster.

How can a "best book" list not include a work by Kohl?

McLaren, R (2006). *Life in schools: An introduction to critical pedagogy in the foundations of education* (5th ed.). New York: Longman.

A guru of critical pedagogy.

Wink, J. (2004). *Critical pedagogy: Notes from the real world* (3rd ed.). New York: Addison Wesley Longman.

Powerful and accessible, opens doors on a broad and deep perspective of teaching and learning.

Diversity

Banks, J. A. (2007). *An introduction to multicultural education* (4th ed.). Needham Heights, MA: Allyn & Bacon.

Classic overview of the subject.

Delpit, L. (2006). *Other people's children: Cultural conflict in the classroom.* New York: The New Press.

One of most widely read books on the subject.

Jelloun, T. B. (2006). *Racism explained to my daughter.* New York: The New Press.

A small book—contributors include William Ayers, Lisa Delpit, and Bill Cosby.

Nieto, S. (2007). *Affirming diversity: The sociopolitical context of multicultural education.* New York: Longman.

Also a classic on diversity.

Nieto, S. (1999). *The light in their eyes: Creating multicultural learning communities.* New York: Teachers College Press.

Her superb follow-up to the previous work—just as good.

Paley, V. (2000). *White teacher.* Cambridge, MA: Harvard University Press.

A moving personal account of her experiences as a kindergarten teacher in an integrated school in a predominantly white middle-class area.

Shapiro, A. (1999). *Everybody belongs: Changing negative attitudes toward classmates with disabilities.* New York: Routledge Falmer.

A colleague of mine, and a great, detailed book with practical suggestions.

Sleeter, C. E. (1996). *Multicultural education as social activism*. Albany: State University of New York Press.

Clear and useful.

Stalvey, L. M. (1989). *The education of a wasp*. Madison: University of Wisconsin Press.

Honest and passionate, a white woman's chronicle of discovering racism—disturbing.

Tatum, D. B. (2003). *Why are all the black kids sitting together in the cafeteria?* New York: Basic Books.

Phenomenal, life-changing, and practical.

West, C. (2001). *Race matters*. New York: Vintage.

Classic treatise on the topic from one of the most brilliant and controversial thinkers of our time.

General Education

Berliner, D., & Biddle, B. (1995). *The manufactured crisis: Myths, fraud, and the attack on America's public schools*. New York: Addison Wesley Longman.

Defend yourself as an educator—read this one.

General Teaching

Brause, R. S., Donohue, C. P., & Ryan, A. W. (2002). *Succeeding at your interview: A practical guide for teachers*. Mahwah, NJ: Erlbaum.

One of the most practical and detailed books on the topic.

Jackson, P. (1968). *Life in classrooms*. New York: Holt, Rinehart & Winston.

The classic on classroom life—insightful.

Joyce, B., & Weil, M. (1996). *Models of teaching*. Boston: Allyn & Bacon.

A classic on teaching strategies.

Morrison, G. S. (2003). *Teaching in America* (3d ed.). Boston: Allyn & Bacon.

A comprehensive textbook—one of best.

Nagel, G. (1994). *The Tao of teaching*. New York: Primus.

Esoteric yet practical—pithy advice such as "obey your instincts," "have compassion, practice frugality, be willing to follow."

Parkay, F. W., & Hardcastle Stanford, B. (2007). *Becoming a teacher* (7th ed.). Boston: Allyn & Bacon.

Appendixes are great and include a list of many professional teacher organizations you should become familiar with, if not join.

Warner, J., & Bryan, C. (1995). *The unauthorized teacher's survival guide.* Indianapolis, IN: Park Avenue.

Handy, easy to read, and really practical.

Warner, J., & Bryan, C. (1997). *Inside secrets of finding a teacher's job: The unauthorized teacher's survival guide.* Indianapolis, IN: Park Avenue.

Among the best on the topic.

Inclusion

Peterson, J. M., & Hittie, M. M. (2003). *Inclusive teaching: Creating effective schools for all learners.* Boston: Allyn & Bacon.

Comprehensive, up to date, and practical.

Sapon-Shevin, M. (2007). *Widening the circle: The power of inclusive classrooms.* Boston: Beacon Press

Winebrenner, S. (1996). *Teaching kids with learning difficulties in the regular classroom: Strategies and techniques every teacher can use to challenge and motivate struggling students.* Minneapolis, MN: Free Spirit.

Packed with practical tips, this book is a must-read for all teachers.

Inspirational

Bluestein, J. (Comp.). (1995). *Mentors, masters and Mrs. MacGregor stories of teachers making a difference.* Deerfield Beach, FL: Health Communications.

Delightful book that reminds me why I became a teacher—to deeply and profoundly affect the lives of others—inspirational.

Whitaker, T., & Whitaker, B. (2002). *Teaching matters: Motivating and inspiring yourself.* Larchmont, NY: Eye on Education.

Inspirational—taking care of yourself.

Journals and Newspapers

The Clearing House	*Education Week*
The Educational Forum	*The Elementary School Journal*
Educational Leadership	*Equity & Excellence in Education*
Educational Studies	*Harvard Educational Review*

Journal of Curriculum & Supervision   *Phi Delta Kappa Fastbacks*

Kappan   *Teachers College Record*

Multicultural Education

Legal Issues

Imber, M., & van Geel, T. (2004). *A teacher's guide to education law* (3rd ed.). Mahwah, NJ: Erlbaum.

Primer including sections on student's rights, discipline, discrimination, special education, negligence, hiring, due process, and tenure.

Literacy

Beaty, J. J., & Pratt, L. (2003). *Early literacy and preschool and kindergarten.* Columbus, OH; Upper Saddle River, NJ: Merrill/Prentice Hall.

An invaluable textbook for early childhood educators focusing on preschool learning. Superb treatments of the foundations of literacy specific strategies for reading.

National Board Certification

Berg, J. H. (2003). *Improving the quality of teaching through national board certification: Theory and practice.* Norwood, MA: Christopher-Gordon.

Nuts-and-bolts approach for prospective National Board candidates.

Personal Growth

Glanz, J. (2000). *Relax for success: An educator's guide to stress management.* Norwood, MA: Christopher-Gordon.

My suggestions for a successful life and career.

Whitaker, T., & Winkle, J. (2001). *Feeling great: The educator's guide for eating better, exercising smarter, and feeling your best.* Larchmont, NY: Eye on Education.

A wonderful reference work.

Practical Strategies

Chuska, K. R. (1995). *Improving classroom questions: A teacher's guide to increasing student motivation, participation, and higher-level thinking.* Bloomington, IN: Phi Delta Kappa Educational Foundation.

The key to effective teaching is posing *good* questions—this is a short practical guide.

Gregory, G. H., & Chapman, C. (2002). *Differentiated instructional strategies: One size doesn't fit all.* Thousand Oaks, CA: Corwin.

Practical strategies and techniques.

Harmin, M. (1994). *Inspiring active learning: A handbook for teachers.* Alexandria, VA: Association for Supervision and Curriculum Development.

If I could only recommend one book for you to read on practical strategies to promote learning, then this book would be the one! Don't miss it. See http://www.inspiringonline.com/History.html.

Raffini, J. P. (1996). *150 ways to increase intrinsic motivation in the classroom.* Boston: Allyn & Bacon.

Action-packed with great ideas.

Scruggs, T. E., & Mastropieri, M. A. (1992). *Teaching test-taking skills: Helping students show what they know.* Brookline, MA: Brookline Books.

One of the clearest and most useful brief books packed with practical ways of helping students develop skills necessary to do well on tests, including essay, short answer, multiple choice, and so on.

Silver, H. E, Strong, R. W, & Perini, M. J. (2000). *So each may learn: Integrating learning styles and multiple intelligences.* Alexandria, VA; Association for Supervision and Curriculum Development.

Fascinating and useful.

Spreyer, L. (2000). *Teaching is an art: An A–Z handbook for successful teaching in middle and high schools.* Thousand Oaks, CA: Corwin.

Geared for the upper grades—this is a practical book loaded with practical teaching strategies and resources.

Tauber, R. T. (1997). *Self-fulfilling prophecy: A practical guide to its use in education.* Westport, CT: Praeger.

Invaluable tool for introducing and summarizing the vast literature into the impact of the self-fulfilling prophecy.

Tomlinson, C. A. (2004). *How to differentiate instruction in mixed-ability classrooms* (2nd ed.). Alexandria, VA: Association for Supervision and Curriculum Development.

Provides easy-to-read and useful practical strategies for how teachers can navigate a diverse classroom. If you want to learn how to teach students of different abilities at the same time, read this book—great case studies of classrooms at all levels in which instruction is differentiated successfully.

Whitaker, T., & Fiore, D. J. (2001). *Dealing with difficult parents: And with parents in difficult situations.* Larchmont, NY: Eye on Education.

Great resource—practical.

Professional Development

Glickman, C. D. (2002). *Leadership for learning: How to help teachers succeed.* Alexandria, VA: Association for Supervision and Curriculum Development.

Practical guidance to help teachers improve classroom teaching and learning.

Reflective Thinking

Schon, D. A. (1995). *The reflective practitioner: How professionals think in action.* New York: Basic.

Advocates reflection on the practice of teaching.

Special Education

Shelton, C. E, & Pollingue, A. B. (2000). *The exceptional teacher's handbook: The first-year special education guide for success.* Thousand Oaks, CA: Corwin.

Practical guide for the new special education teacher—includes checklists, forms, and so on.

Teaching Characteristics

McEwan, E. K. (2003). *10 traits of highly effective teachers.* Thousand Oaks, CA: Corwin.

Outstanding work that identifies 10 traits of effective teachers: passionate, positive, leader, with-it, style, motivational expert, instructional effective, learned, street smart, and reflective.

Rosenshine, B. (1971). *Teaching behaviors and student achievement.* London: National Foundation for Education Research in England and Wales.

A classic book in the field.

Teaching Effectiveness

Danielson, C. (2007). *Enhancing professional practice: A framework for teaching.* Alexandria, VA: Association for Supervision and Curriculum Development.

Author has developed a framework or model for understanding teaching based on current research in the field.

Marzano, R. J., Pickering, D. J., & Pollock, J. E. (2004). *Classroom instruction that works: Research-based strategies for increasing student achievement.* Alexandria, VA: Association for Supervision and Curriculum Development.

Authors examine decades of research in education to come up with nine teaching strategies that have positive effects on student learning—one of the books that is a must-read.

Stronge, J. H. (2002). *Qualities of effective teachers.* Alexandria, VA: Association for Supervision and Curriculum Development.

Most recent and one of the best summaries of current research on teacher effectiveness.

Technology in Teaching

Bitter, G., & Pierson, M. (2008). *Using technology in the classroom* (7th ed.). Boston: Allyn & Bacon.

Very helpful, comprehensive, and packed with practical ways to help teachers incorporate technology into teaching.

Jukes, I., Dosaj, A., & Macdonald, B. (2000). *NetSavvy: Building information literacy in the classroom.* Thousand Oaks, CA: Corwin.

Easy-to-follow guide for assisting students to use the Internet.

Leu, D. J., Jr., & Leu, D. D. (2004). *Teaching with the Internet: Lessons from the classroom* (3rd ed.). Norwood, MA: Christopher-Gordon.

Easy-to-use guide to teaching with the Internet, packed with great Web sites in content areas.

Appendix B

Some of the Best Web Sites for Teachers

B elow are some of the best resources on the Web. I offer them as suggestions because the voluminous material that exists on the Web can actually turn you off. Begin with the sites below. You will find them enormously helpful and they'll lead you to others.

The best book for resources for the Internet and the World Wide Web is Eugene E. Provenzo's *The Internet and the World Wide Web for Teachers,* published in 2002 by Allyn & Bacon—you won't believe how many great resources are listed.

Alphie Kohn home page (http://www.alfiekohn.org/). Useful site packed with the ideas and writings of a noted critic of public education.

Association for Supervision and Curriculum Development (ASCD) Home (http://www.ascd.org/). Consult *Educational Leadership,* ASCD journal (see Appendix A)—"Web Wonders"—great resources on a plethora of topics.

Corwin (http://www.corwinpress.com/). Refer to the veritable storehouse of wisdom contained in other Corwin publications. Ask for a catalog at 1-800-818-7243.

EffectiveTeachers.com (http://www.effectiveteachers.com/). Harry Wong's site (see Appendix A) is packed with information.

Google (http://www.google.com/). Great advice: Search Google by typing in *classroom management*—now, spend the day exploring. (Also, try typing in *discipline.* Because many nonschool discipline sites are included, you'll have to pick and choose. It's worth exploring though.) Google is the most accessible, easy-to-use, and current search engines.

Inspiring Teachers (http://www.inspiringteachers.com/). A great action-packed site that includes tips for new teachers, resources, and an opportunity to interact with colleagues.

The MASTER Teacher (http://www.masterteacher.com/). This for-profit Web site is a phenomenal storehouse of educational resources (some for free) that includes videos, books on a host of relevant topics (e.g., leadership, inclusion, mentoring)—a must to browse, with loads of teaching ideas. Subscribe for free materials at list@masterteacher.com, or get a great free catalog from 1-800-669-9633.

The New Teacher Center (http://www.newteachercenter.org/). Promotes excellence and diversity in schools—very teacher friendly.

ProTeacher! and Innovative Classroom (http://www.proteacher.com, http://www .innovativeclassroom.com/). Both sites contain many useful ideas and tools (including lesson plans in content areas) on a variety of educational topics— easy to navigate.

Soupserver.com (http://soupserver.com/). Daily inspirational sayings that uplift the soul.

Southern Poverty Law Center (http://www.splcenter.org/). Covers tolerance and diversity issues.

Teachers Network (http://teachersnetwork.org/). The site connects innovative teachers with one another. Loads of useful information. Click on the site's "For New Teachers" link for access to a Helpline, which allows you to ask a question of veteran teachers, and you receive a response within 72 hours.

Teaching Tips Index (http://honolulu.hawaii.edu/intranet/committees/FacDevCom/ guidebk/teachtip/teachtip.htm). One of the most comprehensive sites, with a host of topics that provide ready-to-use materials for practical use in the classroom.

U.S. Department of Education (http://www.ed.gov/). The home page of the U.S. Department of Education provides timely news regarding the state of education in our country, answers to frequently asked questions, links to related governmental officials, updates on legislation, application information for federal grants, and links to federally funded publications.

WebQuest.Org (http://webquest.org/). Web-questing is hot. Do a Google search for *WebQuest*. The WebQuest Portal. Find links for "Top," "Middling," and "New."

Appendix C

Self-Assessment Instrument

Charlotte Danielson, in a 1996 work titled *Enhancing Professional Practice: A Framework for Teaching,* published by the Association for Supervision and Curriculum Development (see Appendix A), developed a framework or model for understanding teaching based on current research in the field. She identified "components" clustered into four domains of teaching responsibility: *planning and preparation, classroom environment, instruction,* and *professional responsibilities.* I developed the questionnaire below based on her framework. Please take the questionnaire because it will serve as an important reflective tool. A short activity to assess your responses can be found at the end of the questionnaire.

Analyzing Your Responses

Note that the items draw on research that highlights good educational practice. Review your responses and circle responses that concern you. For instance, if you checked *Strongly Agree* for "I ask multiple questions that sometimes confuse students," ask yourself, "Why is this is a problem?" "How can I remedy the situation?" and "What additional resources or assistance might I need?" If you agree, share and compare responses with another educator; the dialogue that will ensue will serve as a helpful vehicle to move toward more effective teaching practice.

SELF-ASSESSMENT INSTRUMENT

Directions: Using the key below, check the appropriate box for each item.

SA = Strongly Agree ("For the most part, yes")
A = Agree ("Yes, but . . . ")
D = Disagree ("No, but . . . ")
SD = Strongly Disagree ("For the most part, no")

Planning and Preparation	SA	A	D	SD
1. I make many errors when I teach in my content area.				
2. I display solid content knowledge and can make connections with the parts of my discipline or with other disciplines.				
3. I rarely consider the importance of prerequisite knowledge when introducing new topics.				
4. I actively build on students' prior knowledge and seek causes for students' misunderstanding.				
5. Although I am content knowledgeable, I need additional assistance with pedagogical strategies and techniques.				
6. I'm familiar with pedagogical strategies and continually search for best practices to emulate in my teaching.				
7. I don't know too much about the developmental needs of my students.				
8. I know the typical developmental characteristics of the age groups I teach.				
9. I'm unfamiliar with learning styles and multiple intelligences theories.				
10. I have a solid understanding of learning styles and multiple intelligences theories and can apply them to instructional practice.				
11. I do not fully recognize the value of understanding students' skills and knowledge as a basis for my teaching.				
12. I understand the importance of students' skills and knowledge, even those students with exceptional needs.				
13. I don't believe that setting goals for my class is ever helpful because they may influence my expectations for them in a potentially negative way.				

14. Goal setting is critical to my success in planning and preparing for my class.				
15. I am unfamiliar with teaching resources to assist me in the classroom.				
16. I am very aware of teaching resources and seek to use them in preparing for lessons.				
17. I don't develop appropriate learning activities suitable for my students.				
18. I plan for a variety of meaningful learning activities matched to my instructional goals.				
19. I teach the whole class most of the time without utilizing instructional groups.				
20. I use varied instructional grouping.				
21. My lessons, generally, have no clearly defined structure.				
22. My lessons are well planned, organized, and matched to my instructional goals, most of the time.				
23. I usually don't have a systematic plan for assessment of student learning.				
24. I have a well-defined understanding of how I will assess my students after a unit of instruction.				

Classroom Environment	SA	A	D	SD
1. I realize I sometimes use poor interaction skills with my students, such as use of sarcastic or disparaging remarks.				
2. My interactions with students are generally friendly and demonstrate warmth and caring.				
3. Students in my class, generally, don't get along with each other and conflicts are not uncommon.				
4. Student interactions are generally polite and friendly.				

(Continued)

(Continued)

Classroom Environment	SA	A	D	SD
5. I convey a negative attitude toward the content suggesting that the content is mandated by others.				
6. I convey a genuine enthusiasm for the subject.				
7. Students in my class demonstrate little or no pride in their work and don't perform to the best of their ability.				
8. Students meet or exceed my expectations for high-quality work.				
9. I don't always communicate high expectations for all my students.				
10. I communicate high expectations for all my students.				
11. Students in my class are sometimes on-task, but often off-task behavior is observed.				
12. Students in my class are highly engaged and on-task.				
13. I have difficulty managing my class during transitions; e.g., change of subjects or at dismissals.				
14. Transitions in my class occur smoothly, with little loss of instructional time.				
15. Routines for handling materials and supplies in my class are not well organized, causing loss of instructional time.				
16. Routines for handling materials and supplies in my class are well organized, with little, if any, loss of instructional time.				
17. I have not established a well-defined system of rules and procedures.				
18. I pride myself on the well-established system of rules and procedures in my class.				

19. I have difficulty enforcing standards for acceptable conduct in my class.				
20. Standards for conduct are clear to all students.				
21. I monitor student behavior and I am aware of what students are doing.				
22. I am alert to student behavior at all times.				
23. I have difficulty responding effectively to student misbehavior, and consequently students are disruptive.				
24. My response to misbehavior is appropriate and successful most of the time.				
25. I don't consider safety issues in my classroom in terms of room arrangement.				
26. My classroom is safe and the furniture arrangements are a resource for learning.				

Instruction	SA	A	D	SD
1. My directions are not clear to students, often causing confusion.				
2. My directions are clear and appropriate.				
3. My spoken language is often inaudible and crude.				
4. I speak clearly and appropriately, according to the grade level of my students.				
5. My use of questions needs improvement.				
6. My questions are uniformly of high quality.				
7. I mostly lecture (talk) to my students without enough student participation.				
8. I encourage students to participate and prefer for students to take an active role in learning.				

(Continued)

(Continued)

Instruction	SA	A	D	SD
9. Only a few students participate in class discussions.				
10. I engage all students in class discussions.				
11. My ability to communicate content is poor.				
12. My ability to communicate content is sound and appropriate.				
13. Activities and assignments are inappropriate to students and don't engage students mentally.				
14. Activities and assignments are appropriate to students and encourage student understanding.				
15. I don't know how to group students appropriately for instruction.				
16. I'm very familiar with grouping strategies to promote instruction.				
17. I select inappropriate and ineffective instructional materials and resources.				
18. Instructional materials and resources are suitable and engage students mentally.				
18. Instructional materials and resources are suitable and engage students mentally.				
19. My lessons have little, or no structure and my pacing of the lesson is too slow, rushed, or both.				
20. My lessons are highly coherent and my pacing is consistent and appropriate.				
21. I rarely provide appropriate feedback to my students.				
22. Feedback to my students is consistent, appropriate, and of high quality.				
23. When I do provide feedback, it's inconsistent and not timely.				

24. Feedback is consistently provided in a timely manner.				
25. I rely heavily on the teacher's manual for instruction.				
26. I rarely, if ever, rely on the teacher's manual because I can adjust a lesson to make it appropriate to the needs and level of my students.				
27. I often ignore students' questions or interests.				
28. I consistently encourage student questions.				
29. I often blame my students for their inability to learn by attributing their lack of success to their background or lack of interest or motivation.				
30. I don't give up with slow learners and try to encourage them all the time.				
31. I tend to go off on tangents.				
32. I ask multiple questions that sometimes confuse students.				
33. I use wait time effectively.				

Professional Responsibilities	SA	A	D	SD
1. I have difficulty assessing my effectiveness as a teacher.				
2. I can accurately assess how well I'm doing in my classroom.				
4. I am aware of what I need to do in order to become an effective teacher.				
5. I don't have a system for maintaining information on student completion of assignments.				
6. My system for maintaining information on student completion of assignments is effective.				

(Continued)

(Continued)

Professional Responsibilities	SA	A	D	SD
7. I don't have a system for maintaining information on student progress in learning.				
8. My system for maintaining information on student progress is sound.				
9. I rarely encourage parental involvement in my class.				
10. I actively and consistently engage parents in my classroom.				
11. I rarely reach out to parents.				
12. I reach out to parents consistently.				
13. I have difficulty relating to my colleagues in a cordial and professional manner.				
14. I collaborate with my colleagues in a cordial and professional manner.				
15. I rarely participate in school events.				
16. I often volunteer to participate in school events.				
17. I avoid becoming involved in school and district projects.				
18. I volunteer to participate in school and district projects.				
19. I rarely seek to engage in professional development activities.				
20. I seek out opportunities for professional development to enhance my pedagogical skills.				
21. I am rarely alert to students' needs.				
22. I am active in serving students.				
23. I'm not an advocate for student's rights.				
24. I am an advocate for student's rights.				
25. I rarely desire to serve on a school-based committee.				
26. I volunteer to serve on departmental or schoolwide committees.				

In summary, review your responses for each of the four domains and circle your summary response (SA, A, D, or SD) for each of the domains below.

Respond

Domain 1: Planning and Preparation. This domain demonstrates your content and pedagogical knowledge, knowledge of students and resources, ability to select instructional goals, and the degree to which you assess student learning.

SA   A   D   SD

I am satisfied that my planning and preparation knowledge and skills are satisfactory.

Domain 2: The Classroom Environment. This domain assesses the degree to which you create an environment of respect and caring, establish a culture for learning, manage classroom procedures, manage student behavior, and organize physical space.

SA   A   D   SD

I am satisfied that my knowledge and skills of classroom environment are satisfactory.

Domain 3: Instruction. This domain assesses the ability to communicate with clarity, use questioning and discussion techniques, engage students in learning, provide feedback to students, and demonstrate flexibility and responsiveness to student's instructional needs.

SA   A   D   SD

I am satisfied that my knowledge and skills of instruction are satisfactory.

Domain 4: Professional Responsibilities. This domain assesses the degree to which you reflect on teaching, maintain accurate records, communicate with parents, contribute to the school/district, grow and develop professionally, and show professionalism.

SA   A   D   SD

I am satisfied that I am professionally responsible.

Appendix D

Teacher's Suggestions Exchange Forum

I hope you enjoyed reading *Teaching 101*. In order to keep readers in communication with more teaching information and suggestions, I am starting an e-mail exchange forum. Please e-mail me any great teaching ideas (e.g., curriculum materials, sample lesson plans, good Web sites, quotations, books, articles, or any other resources) that you feel other teachers would appreciate. I may then use them for future editions of this book, but would more likely first e-mail them to our e-mail list.

In order to join the list, simply send me an e-mail at glanz@yu.edu stating that you want to be included, and I will add you to the e-mail group list. When I receive suggestions, I will send them to you.

References

Adler, M. J. (1998). *The Paideia proposal: An educational manifesto.* New York: Touchstone.

Allan, J. (1999). *Actively seeking inclusion.* London: Falmer Press.

Barton, L. (1998). *The politics of special educational needs.* Lewes, UK: Falmer.

Beach, D. M., & Reinhartz, J. (2000). *Supervisory leadership: Focus on instruction.* Boston: Allyn & Bacon.

Bolotin, J. P., & Burnaford, G. E. (2001). *Images of schoolteachers in America* (2nd ed.). Mahwah, NJ: Erlbaum.

Bolt, R. (1962). *A man for all seasons.* New York: Basic Books.

Brezak, D. (2002). *Education in turbulent times: Practical strategies for parents and educators.* Brooklyn, NY: Mesorah.

Canter, L. (1989). *Assertive discipline for secondary school teachers: Inservice video package and leader's manual.* Santa Monica, CA: Canter & Associates.

Capper, C. A., Frattura, E., & Keyes, M. (2000). *Meeting the needs of students of all abilities: How leaders go beyond inclusion.* Thousand Oaks, CA: Corwin.

Card, N. A. (2003, April). *Victims of peer aggression: A meta-analytic review.* Presented at Society for Research in Child Development biennial meeting. Tampa, FL.

Charles, C. M. (2001). *Building classroom discipline* (7th ed.). New York: Longman.

Clough, P., & Corbet, J. (2000). *Theories of inclusive education.* Thousand Oaks, CA: Sage.

Cochran-Smith, M. (2002). Reporting on teacher quality: The politics of politics. *Journal of Teacher Education, 53*(5), 379–382.

Coloroso, B. (2004). *The bully, the bullied, and the bystander: From preschool to high school—How parents and teachers can help break the cycle of violence.* New York: Collins.

Danielson, C. (2002). *Enhancing student achievement: A framework for school improvement.* Alexandria, VA: Association for Supervision and Curriculum Development.

Darling-Hammond, L. (2000). *Studies of excellence in teacher education.* Washington, DC: American Association of Colleges for Teacher Education and National Commission on Teaching and America's Future.

Darling-Hammond, L. (2003). Keeping good teachers: Why it matters what leaders do. *Educational Leadership, 60,* 6–13.

Darling-Hammond, L., Chung, R., & Frelow, E. (2002). Variation in teacher preparation: How well do different pathways prepare teachers to teach? *Journal of Teacher Education, 53*(4), 286–302.

Davis, O. L., Jr. (1998). Beyond beginnings: From "hands-on" to "minds-on." *Journal of Curriculum and Supervision, 13,* 119–122.

Dewey, J. (1899). *The school and society.* Chicago: University of Chicago Press.

Dunn, R., & DeBello, T. C. (Eds.). (1999). *Improved test scores, attitudes, and behaviors on America's schools: Supervisors' success stories.* Westport, CT: Bergin & Garvey.

Dunn, R., Giannitti, M. C., Murray, J. B., Rossi, I., Geisert, G., & Quinn, P. (1990). Grouping students for instruction: Effects of learning style on achievement and attitudes. *Journal of Social Psychology, 130,* 485–494.

Elliott, D., & McKenney, M. (1998). Four inclusion models that work. *Teaching Exceptional Children, 30*(4), 54–58.

Fisher, D., Frey, N., & Williams, D. (2002). Seven literacy strategies that work. *Educational Leadership, 60,* 70–73.

Freire, P. (1974). *Pedagogy of the oppressed.* New York: Seabury.

Freire, P. (1994). *The pedagogy of hope: Reliving pedagogy of the oppressed.* New York: Continuum.

Fullan, M. (1995). Contexts: Overview and framework. In M. J. O'Hair & S. J. Odell (Eds.), *Educating teachers for leadership and change* (pp. 1–10). Thousand Oaks, CA: Corwin.

Gardner, H. (2000). *Intelligence reframed: Multiple intelligences for the 21st century.* New York: Basic Books.

Ginott, H. (1993). *Teacher and child: A book for parents and teachers.* New York: Macmillan.

Glanz, J. (2002). *Finding your leadership style: A guide for educators.* Alexandria, VA: Association for Supervision and Curriculum Development.

Glasser, W. A. (1975). *Reality therapy.* New York: HarperCollins.

Glatthorn, A. A. (2000). *The principal as curriculum leader: Shaping what is taught and tested* (2nd ed.). Thousand Oaks, CA: Corwin.

Good, T. L., & Brophy, J. E. (1997). *Looking in classrooms* (7th ed.). New York: Addison-Wesley.

Goodlad, J. (1970). *Behind the classroom door.* Belmont, CA: Wadsworth.

Gronlund, N. E. (2003). *Assessment of student achievement* (7th ed.). Boston: Allyn & Bacon.

Herrell, A., & Jordan, M. C. (2004). *Fifty strategies for teaching English language learners* (2nd ed.). Upper Saddle River, NJ: Pearson/Prentice Hall.

Holmes Group. (1986). *Tomorrow's teachers: A report of the Holmes Group.* East Lansing, MI: Author.

hooks, b. (1994). *Teaching to transgress: Education as the practice of freedom.* New York: Routledge.

Huber, T. (2002). *Quality learning experiences for ALL students.* San Francisco: Caddo Gap.

Irvine, J. J., & Armento, B. J. (2003). *Culturally responsive teaching.* Boston: McGraw-Hill.

Kessler, R. (2000). *The soul of education: Helping students find connection, compassion, and character at school.* Alexandria, VA: Association for Supervision and Curriculum Development.

Kochhar, C. A., West, L. L., & Taymans, J. M. (2000). *Successful inclusion: Practical strategies for a shared responsibility.* Upper Saddle River, NJ: Merrill.

Kohl, H. (1998). *The discipline of hope: Learning from a lifetime of teaching.* New York: Simon & Schuster.

Kottler, E., & Kottler, J. A. (2002). *Children with limited English: Teaching strategies for the regular classroom* (2nd ed.). Thousand Oaks, CA: Corwin.

Kounin, J. (1977). *Discipline and group management in classrooms.* New York: Holt, Rinehart & Winston.

Kubiszyn, T., & Borich, G. (2003). *Educational testing and measurement: Classroom application and practice* (7th ed.). New York: Wiley.

Ladson-Billings, G. (1994). *The dreamkeepers.* San Francisco: Jossey-Bass.

Lauria, J. (2005). Effects of learning-style-based homework prescriptions on the achievement and attitudes of middle school students. *NASSP Bulletin, 89*(642), 67–89.

Lortie, D. (1977). *Schoolteacher: A sociological study.* Chicago: University of Chicago Press.

MacDonald, R. E., & Healy, S. D. (1999). *A handbook for beginning teachers* (2nd ed.). New York: Longman.

Macedo, D. (Ed.). (1994). *Literacies of power.* Boulder, CO: Westview.

Mangrum, C. T., II, Iannuzzi, P., & Strichart, S. S. (1998). *Teaching study skills and strategies in grades 4–8.* Needham, MA: Allyn & Bacon.

McLaren, P. (1994). Critical pedagogy: Constructing an arch of social dreaming and a doorway to hope. In L. Erwin & D. MacLennan (Eds.), *Sociology of education in Canada: Critical perspectives on theory, research, and practice* (pp. 137–160). Toronto: Copp Clark Longman.

McLeskey, J., & Waldron, N. (2001). *Inclusive schools in action: Making differences ordinary.* Alexandria, VA: Association for Supervision and Curriculum Development.

Merton, R. K. (1948). The self-fulfilling prophecy. *Antioch Review, 8,* 193–210.

Morse, T. E. (2002). Designing appropriate curriculum for special education students in urban schools. *Education and Urban Schools, 34*(1), 4–17.

Novick, R. M. (2000). *BRAVE instructor manual.* New Hyde Park, NY: Alliance for School Mental Health.

Oakes, J., & Lipton, M. (1999). *Teaching to change the world.* New York: McGraw-Hill.

O'Day, J. A. (2002). Complexity, accountability, and school improvement. *Harvard Educational Review, 72*(3), 293–329.

Ogle, D. (1986). The K-W-L: A teaching model that develops active reading of expository text. *The Reading Teacher, 39,* 564–570.

Ornstein, A. C. (1990). *Institutionalized learning in America.* New Brunswick, NJ: Transaction.

Osterman, K. E., & Kottkamp, R. B. (1993). *Reflective practice for educators: Improving schooling through professional development.* Newbury Park, CA: Corwin.

Parkay, F. W., & Stanford Hardcastle, B. (2001). *Becoming a teacher* (5th ed.). Boston: Allyn & Bacon.

Pinar, W. E., Reynolds, W. M., Slattery, P., & Taubman, E. M. (1995). *Understanding curriculum: An introduction to the study of historical and contemporary curriculum discourses.* New York: Peter Lang.

Popham, W. J. (2002). *Classroom assessment: What teachers need to know* (3rd ed.). Boston: Allyn & Bacon.

Pressley, M., & Woloshyn, V. (1995). *Cognitive strategy instruction that really improves children's academic performance.* Brookline, MA: Brookline Books.

Rist, R. C. (1970). Student social class and teacher expectations: The self-fulfilling prophecy in ghetto education. *Harvard Educational Review, 40,* 411–451.

Roberts, P. L., & Kellough, R. D. (1996). *A guide for developing an interdisciplinary thematic unit.* Englewood Cliffs, NJ: Merrill.

Rosenthal, R., & Jacobson, L. (1968). *Pygmalion in the classroom.* New York: Holt, Rinehart & Winston.

Schubert, W. H. (1993). Curriculum reform. In *Challenges and achievements of American education: The 1993 ASCD yearbook* (pp. 80–115). Washington, DC: Association for Supervision and Curriculum Development.

Slattery, P. (1995). *Curriculum development in the postmodern era.* New York: Garland.

Slavin, R. (1994). *Cooperative learning: Theory, research, and practice.* Boston: Allyn & Bacon.

Smith, M. S., Fuhrman, S. H., & O'Day, J. (1994). National curriculum standards: Are they desirable and feasible? In R. E Elmore & S. H. Fuhrman (Eds.), *The governance of curriculum* (pp. 12–29). Alexandria, VA: Association for Supervision and Curriculum Development.

Smith, P. K., Cowie, H., Olafsson, R., & Liefoogle, A. P. D. (2002). Definitions of bullying: A comparison of terms used, and age and sex differences in a 14-country international comparison. *Child Development, 73,* 1119–1133.

Stronge, J. H. (2002). *Qualities of effective teaching.* Alexandria, VA: Association for Supervision and Curriculum Development.

Tauber, R. T. (1997). *Self-fulfilling prophecy: A practical guide to its use in education.* Westport, CT: Praeger.

Tyler, R. W. (1949). *Basic principles of curriculum and instruction.* Chicago: University of Chicago Press.

Walber, H. J., Paschal, R. A., & Weinstein, T. (1985). Homework's powerful effects on learning. *Educational Leadership,* 76–79.

Wiggins, W., & McTighe, J. (2005). *Understanding by design.* Englewood Cliffs, NJ: Prentice Hall.

Wolfendale, S. (2000). *Special needs in the early years: Snapshots of practice.* London: Routledge.

Zukav, G. (2000). *Soul stories.* New York: Simon & Schuster.

Index

Abbreviations and symbols, 160
Academic allocated time
    (AAT), 23
Academic engaged time (AET), 23
Academic instructional time (AIT), 23
Academic success time
    (AST), 24
Accelerated learners, 55–56
Access, 245
Accountability, 168
Acronyms, 164
Active learning, 36–37
Activity sheets
    assessment strategies, 176
    best and worst teachers, xxii
    cognitive learning strategies, 150
    curriculum development, 206
    effective teachers, 10
    lesson plans, 80
    role-play activity, 124
    student characteristics, 42
    technology integration
        strategies, 226
Adams, Henry Brooks, 1
Adler, M. J., 213–214
Aggression, 128
Allan, J., 70
Alternative assessments, 181
Analytical learning style, 61
Annotated bibliography, 261–273
Anticipatory sets, 85
Armento, B. J., 58, 60
Assertiveness, 132–133
Assessment strategies
    activity sheets, 176
    classroom requirements, 186–188
    fairness, 188–190

focus questions, 177–178
follow-up activities, 205
fundamental principles, 182–183
grades, 180, 184–185, 186, 204–205
implementation and analysis,
    184–186
parental involvement, 188
portfolio assessments, 181, 200–204
purpose, 178
recollection activities, 179–180
reflective activities, 178
reliability tests, 191–192
resources, 261, 271
respond questionnaires, 182
self-assessment instrument, 277–285
terminology, 180–181
test construction guidelines,
    192–200
traditional assessments, 178–179
validity tests, 190–191
Attention spans, 45
Auditory skills, 54
Authentic assessments, 181

Backward teaching, 214
Barton, L., 70
Barzun, Jacques, 11
Basic interpersonal communication
    skills (BICs), 56
Beach, D. M., 211
Behavior assessment, 127
Belief systems, 17, 18, 137
Benchmarks, 208–209
Berry, Shawn Allen, 48
Bias, 25–26, 48–50
Bigotry, 48–50
Bloom's Taxonomy, 86–88, 220

Bodily/kinesthetic intelligence, 68
Bolotin, J. P., 9
Bolt, R., 1
Borich, G., 183
Brain-based education resources, 262
Breathing exercises, 157, 163
Brewer, Lawrence Russell, 48
Brezak, D., 7
Brophy, J. E., 12, 125
Browning, Robert, 8
Bruner, J., 220
Bullying, 50–51, 239
Bureau of Education & Research
     (BER), 237
Burnaford, G. E., 9
Byrd, James, 48

Canter, L., 132, 174
Capper, C. A., 70
Card, N. A., 50
Charles, C. M., 127, 132
Cheating, 189
Chinese proverb, ix
Chung, R., 17
Civic responsibility, 210
Classroom management strategies
     basic concepts, 127–128
     classroom characteristics, 128–129
     discipline strategies, 126–127,
          129–141
     effective teachers, 17, 19, 46–47
     focus questions, 125
     follow-up activities, 148–149
     reflective activities, 127
     resources, 265–266
     respond questionnaires, 142–148
     role-play activity, 124
Class work questions, 89
Clough, P., 70
Cochran-Smith, M., 11, 17
Cognitive academic language
     proficiencies (CALP), 56
Cognitive learning strategies
     activity sheets, 150
     cooperative learning, 167–172
     early grades, 157
     focus questions, 151
     follow-up questions, 175

influencing factors, 152–153
learning improvement guidelines,
     158–161
reading skills, 166–167
reflective activities, 154, 158, 162,
     166, 167
self-fulfilling prophecy, 171–175
study skill instruction, 153–156,
     162–166
Coloroso, B., 50
Commitment, 30–31
Communication skills, 56
Compassion, 28–29
Completion questions, 195
Consensual validity, 191
Constructivist learning, 37
Content validity, 190–191
Contracts, 133
Convergent questions, 33–34
Conway, Linda, 151
Cooperative group rules, 138–139
Cooperative learning, 62, 64, 68, 130,
     156, 167–172
Corbet, J., 70
Corrective discipline, 128,
     132–134, 141
Cowie, H., 50
Criscuolo, Dana, 5–6
Culturally relevant teaching strategies,
     57–60
Curriculum development
     activity sheets, 206
     basic concepts, 210–211
     definitions, 211–212
     development models, 212–214
     district standards, 208–210
     focus questions, 208
     follow-up activities, 225
     integrated activities, 219–222
     quality curricula, 215–216
     standards implementation guidelines,
          216–225
     Tyler Rationale model, 212–213
Cyberbullying, 239

Danielson, C., 207, 216, 217, 277
Darling-Hammond, L., 12, 17, 152
Davis, Barbara Gross, 204

Davis, O. L., Jr., 36–37
DeBello, T. C., 72
Defiance of authority, 128
Dewey, J., 36, 213, 220
Differentiating instruction
    effective teachers, 20
    resources, 271
    student needs, 63–69
    see also Curriculum development
Digital portfolios, 254
Discipline strategies, 17, 126–127,
        129–141
    see also Classroom management
        strategies
Discrimination, 48
Discussion-based teaching approach,
        15, 21–22
Disposition assessment, 40
    see also Effective teachers
Disruptive behaviors, 128
Distractibility, 54
Divergent questions, 33–34
Diversity resources, 267–268
Driscoll, Amy, 81
Dunn, R., 72

Economic efficiency, 210
Education, purpose of, 210–211
Education World, 236
Effective teachers
    activity sheets, 10
    character traits, 24–32
    critical concepts, 23–24
    evaluation guidelines, 13–14
    focus questions, 11
    follow-up activities, 40–41
    hands-on/minds-on learning
        strategies, 36–37
    influencing factors, 14–15, 17, 19,
        46–47, 152–153
    K-W-L strategy, 37–38
    literacy strategies, 34–36
    parental involvement, 38–39
    questioning strategies, 33–34
    recollection activities, 16–17
    reflective activities, 12, 15–16,
        62–63, 72
    research-based findings, 19–20

resources, 272–273
respond questionnaires, 18
self-assessments, 19, 20–21
teaching approaches, 21–22, 62–63
training effects, 17
wait time, 32–33
Eisner, Elliot, xiii
Electronic portfolios, 254
Elliott, D., 70
E-mail skills, 231–232
Empathy, 28–29
Empowerment, 46
Energy levels, 31
English language learners (ELLs),
        56–57
Enhanced digital whiteboards,
        251–252
Enrichment activities, 56
Enthusiasm, 30–32
Erasmus, ix, xiii
Essay questions, 198–200
Ethical conduct, 27
Ethnicity, 47–48
eUniverse, 254
Excel, 244
Exchange forum, 287
External assessments, 184

Facebook, 254–256
Face-to-face interaction, 169
Face validity, 191
FACT (focus, act, connect, try)
        strategy, 161
Fairness, 27
Field-independent/field-dependent
        learning style, 62
Fisher, D., 34
Focus questions
    assessment strategies, 177–178
    classroom management, 125
    cognitive learning strategies, 151
    curriculum development, 208
    effective teachers, 10
    lesson plans, 81
    student needs, 43
    teaching as a profession, 1
    technology integration
        strategies, 228

Following directions, 157
Follow-up questions
 assessment strategies, 205
 classroom management, 148–149
 cognitive learning strategies, 175
 curriculum development, 225
 effective teachers, 40–41
 lesson plans, 120–123
 student needs, 79
 teaching as a profession, 9
 technology integration
  strategies, 257
Forbes, Malcolm S., ix
Frattura, E., 70
Freedom, 46
Freiberg, H. Jerome, 81
Freire, P., 70
Frelow, E., 17
Frey, N., 34
Fuhrman, S. H., 208
Fullan, M., 260
Fun, 46

Game-based questions, 89–90
Gardner, H., 67, 220
Garfield, Charles, 259
Gartner, A., 70
Geisert, G., 72
Gender, 47–48
Giannitti, M. C., 72
Ginott, H., 4–5
Glanz, J., 3, 151, 207, 227
Glasser, W., 45
Glasser, W. A., 45
Glatthorn, A. A., 215, 217
Global learning style, 61
Goals and objectives for lesson plans,
 84–85
Goodlad, J., 17
Good teachers
 see Effective teachers
Good, T. L., 12, 125
Goofing off, 128
Grades, 180, 184–185, 186, 204–205
Graphic organizers, 34
Graphic reinforcers, 131
Gronlund, N. E., 183, 184, 189,
 190, 200
Group learning, 55

Hands-on learning, 36–37
Hatred, 48–50
Healy, S. D., 192–200
Herrell, A., 56
Highlighters, 166–167
High-stakes testing, 183
Holistic assessments, 181
Homework assignments, 92–94
Homework questions, 89
hooks, b., 257
Huber, T., 70
Human relationships, 210
Hyperactivity, 53

Iannuzzi, P., 154
Immorality, 128
Impartiality, 25–27
Impulsive learning style, 62
Inclusive educational practices,
 70–79, 269
Inflexibility, 26
Inspirational resources, 269
Instructional strategies
 accelerated learners, 55–56
 assessment strategies, 183–184
 culturally relevant teaching
  strategies, 57–60
 differentiating instruction, 63–69
 effective teachers, 19–20
 hands-on/minds-on learning
  strategies, 36–37
 inclusive educational practices,
  70–79
 K-W-L strategy, 37–38
 learning disabled students,
  52–57
 learning styles, 61–63
 literacy strategies, 34–36
 parental involvement, 38–39
 questioning strategies, 33–34
 resources, 262–264, 271–272
 student characteristics, 44
 underachievers, 54–55
 wait time, 32–33
 see also Curriculum development
Integrated projects, 219–222
Interactive whiteboards, 250–251
International Society for Technology in
 Education (ISTE), 232–233

Internet-based video sharing sites, 253–254
Internet safety, 239–240
Internet searches, 230–231
Interpersonal intelligence, 68
Interrater reliability, 192
Intrapersonal intelligence, 68
iPods, 252–253
Irvine, J. J., 58, 60

Jacobson, L., 171
Johnson, Samuel, 81
Jordan, M. C., 56
Journalist-style questions, 89
Journals and newspapers, 269–270

Kellough, R. D., 219
Kessler, R., 4
Keyes, M., 70
Key words, 164–166
King, John William, 48
Knowledge assessment, 40
    see also Effective teachers
Kochhar, C. A., 70
Kohl, H., 70
Kottkamp, R. B., 17
Kottler, E., 58–59
Kottler, J. A., 58–59
Kounin, J., 132
KR-21 (Kuder-Richardson formula), 192
Kubiszyn, T., 183
K-W-L strategy, 37–38

Ladson-Billings, G., 59
Lauria, J., 72
Learning disabilities, 44, 52–57, 70–79
Learning environments, 130, 158–159
Learning styles, 61–63
Lecture-based teaching approach, 15, 21–22
Legal resources, 270
Lesson plans
    activity sheets, 80
    assessment strategies, 183–184
    characteristics, 91
    components, 84–94
    cooperative learning, 170
    critiques, 98–101

discipline strategies, 130
evaluation guidelines, 94
focus questions, 81
follow-up activities, 120–123
guidelines, 82–84
homework assignments, 92–94
procedures, 91
reviews, 91
sample plans, 101–120
strengths and weaknesses, 94–98
tests, 92
Liefoogle, A. P. D., 50
Links, 164
Lipsky, D. K., 70
Lipton, M., 70
Listening skills, 155, 157, 159
Literacy strategies, 34–36, 270
Logical/mathematical intelligence, 67
Lortie, D., 1

MacDonald, R. E., 192–200
Macedo, D., 70
Mandino, Og, 43
Mangrum, C. T., II, 154
Matching questions, 197–198
McKenney, M., 70
McLaren, P., 70
McLeskey, J., 70
McTighe, J., 214
Mead, Margaret, 8
Mental planning, 82
Merton, R. K., 171
Microsoft Access, 245
Microsoft Excel, 244
Microsoft Office, 229, 230, 243–246
Microsoft PowerPoint, 246–249
Microsoft Publisher, 245
Microsoft Soapbox, 253–254
Microsoft Word, 243–244
Minds-on learning, 36–37
Misbehavior, 127–128
Mnemonics, 164–166
Morse, T. E., 70
Motivation, 31, 45, 85, 270
Multicultural education resources, 267–268
Multiple-choice questions, 195–197
Multiple intelligences, 67–69, 220, 223–224

Murray, J. B., 72
Musical/rhythmic intelligence, 67
MySpace, 254–256

National Board Certification
    resources, 270
Naturalist intelligence, 68
Negative consequences, 140
NETS Standards, 220
Newspapers, 269–270
Nonverbal signals, 132
Note-taking skills, 155, 160–161
Novick, R. M., 50

Oakes, J., 70
Objective tests, 194–197
O'Day, J. A., 208
Ogle, D., 37
Olafsson, R., 50
Online videos, 253–254
Open-mindedness, 26–27
Optimism, 31, 32
Ornstein, A. C., 23
Osterman, K. E., 17
Outlines, 161, 163, 167

Paideia model, 213–214
Paper-and-pencil testing, 184
Parallel forms method, 192
Paraphrasing, 160
Parental involvement, 38–39, 188
Parkay, F. W., 239, 242
Paschal, R. A., 93
Pasternak, Boris, 8–9
Past experiences, 15–16
Pedagogy resources, 266–267
Peer tutoring, 55–56
Pegs, 164–166
Performance assessments, 181, 184
Personalized discipline plan,
    135–141
Physical proximity, 132
PIGS FACE technique, 168–169
Pinar, W. E., 214
Plato, 125
Play-based questions, 89–90
Poole, Bernie, 257
Poor questions, 90
Popham, W. J., 178, 183

Portfolio assessments,
    181, 200–204, 254
Positive interdependence, 168
Positive reinforcement strategies,
    131, 139
PowerPoint, 246–249
Prejudice, 25, 48–50
Preparation skills, 158
Pressley, M., 153
Preventive discipline,
    128, 129–131, 140
Problem-solving skills, 157
Professional development, 272
Professional excellence and success,
    259–260
Promethean boards, 251–252
Provenzo, E. E., 275
Public Law 94-142, 70

Questioning strategies, 33–34, 85–90,
    159, 163, 167
Quinn, P., 72

Race, 47–48
Read-alouds, 34
Reading skills, 34, 156, 166–167
Reciprocal teaching, 35
Recollection activities
    assessment strategies, 179–180
    cognitive learning strategies,
        172–173
    discipline strategies, 134–135
    effective teachers, 16–17
    hatred and bigotry, 49–50
    past experiences, 15–16
    professional excellence and success,
        259–260
    teaching as a profession, 2
Reflective activities
    assessment strategies, 178
    classroom management, 127
    cognitive learning strategies, 154
    cooperative learning, 171
    differentiating instruction, 69
    early grade study strategies, 158
    effective teachers, 12
    hands-on/minds-on learning
        strategies, 37
    inclusive educational practices, 72

learning improvement
   guidelines, 162
literacy strategies, 36
past experiences, 15–16
questioning strategies, 34
reading skills, 167
self-assessments, 21
standards, 209
student-teacher relationship, 47
study skill instruction, 154, 166
teaching approaches, 22, 62–63
technology integration
   strategies, 256
Reflective learning style, 62
Reflective thinking resources, 272
Reinhartz, J., 211
Reliability tests, 191–192
Resources, 261–273
Respond questionnaires
   assessment strategies, 182
   classroom management, 142–148
   effective teachers, 14–15, 18, 24–25,
     27–28, 30
   lesson plans, 98–101
   self-assessment instrument, 285
   teaching as a profession, xi–xii, 3
   technology integration
     strategies, 229
Rewriting notes, 160, 162
Reynolds, W. M., 214
Rhymes, 164
Rist, R. C., 173
Roberts, P. L., 219
Role-play activities, 124, 157
Rosenthal, R., 171
Rossi, I., 72
Rubrics, 181, 203–204

Sacred tasks, 8
Sample discipline plan, 137–139
Sample lesson plans, 101–120
Schubert, W. H., 211
SEA technique, 168
Security, 46
Self-assessment instrument, 277–285
Self-esteem, 54
Self-fulfilling prophecy, 171–175, 271
Self-realization, 210
Sense of belonging, 45

Sense of control, 46
Sensory modality learning style, 61
Sexual orientation, 47–48
Shared reading, 34
Shepard, Matthew, 48
Sitting up front, 158–159
Skills assessment, 40
   see also Effective teachers
Slattery, P., 4, 214
Slavin, R., 156, 167
Slepian, Barnett, 48
SMART Boards, 250–251
Smith, M. S., 208
Smith, P. K., 50
Social class, 47–48
Social networks, 254–256
Social reinforcers, 131
Social skills, 168–169
Social studies curriculum development
   sample, 219–222
Socratic teaching approach, 15, 21–22
Software program evaluation
   criteria, 240–243
Special needs, 44, 70–79, 272
Split-half method, 192
SQ4R (Survey, Question, Read,
   Reflect, Recite, Review)
   technique, 166
Standards, 208–210, 216–225
Standards for Teacher Competence in
   Educational Assessment of
   Students, 184
Stanford Hardcastle, B., 239, 242
State Social Studies standards, 220
Stress management, 157, 270
Strichart, S. S., 154
Stronge, J. H., 12, 19–20
Student learning
   cognitive learning strategies,
     150–151
   critical concepts, 23–24
   effective teachers, 14–15, 46–47
Student needs and characteristics
   accelerated learners, 55–56
   activity sheets, 42
   bullying, 50–51
   culturally relevant teaching
     strategies, 57–60
   differentiating instruction, 63–69

effective teachers, 46–47
English language learners (ELLs),
    56–57
essential needs, 45–46
focus questions, 43
follow-up activities, 79
hatred and bigotry, 48–49
inclusive educational practices,
    70–79
learning disabilities, 44, 52–57
learning styles, 61–63
recollection activities, 49–50
reflective activities, 47, 69, 72
student backgrounds, 47–48
student-teacher relationship, 44–45
underachievers, 54–55
Student-oriented questions, 90
Student response strategies, 86–90
Study skill instruction, 153–156,
    162–166, 266
Suggestions exchange forum, 287
Supportive discipline, 128,
    131–132, 141
Symbols and abbreviations, 160

Tammy's Technology Tips for Teachers,
    233–236
Tangible reinforcers, 131
Tape recorder usage, 159, 162
Tauber, R. T., 173–174
Taubman, E. M., 214
Taymans, J. M., 70
Teacher-made tests, 180, 181,
    184–185, 201
Teaching as a profession
    follow-up activities, 9
    making a difference, 4–9
    meaningfulness, 1–4
    recollection activities, 2
    resources, 261–262, 268–269,
        271–272
    student-teacher relationship,
        44–45
Teaching suggestions exchange
    forum, 287
Technology integration strategies
    activity sheets, 226
    e-mail skills, 231–232

focus questions, 228
follow-up activities, 257
importance, 228–230, 256–257
Internet safety, 239–240
Internet searches, 230–231
Microsoft Office-based integrated
    activities, 243–246
new technologies, 249–256
PowerPoint presentations,
    246–249
reflective activities, 256
resources, 273
respond questionnaires, 229
software program evaluation criteria,
    240–243
Web sites, 232–239, 275–276
Test construction guidelines,
    192–200
Testing
    see Assessment strategies
Test-retest method, 191
Thinking skills, 157
Time-outs, 133–134
Tomlinson, C. A., 63
Traditional assessments, 178–179, 180
Training effects, 17
True-false questions, 194
Tyler Rationale model, 212–213
Tyler, R. W., 212–213

Underachievers, 54–55
Understanding by Design (UbD)
    model, 213, 214

Validity tests, 190–191
Verbal/linguistic intelligence, 67
Verbal skills, 54
Vested interests, 26
Visual skills, 54
Visual/spatial intelligence, 67
Vocabulary instruction, 35

Wait time, 32–33, 90
Walber, H. J., 93
Waldron, N., 70
Warlick, David, 227
Web sites
    evaluation criteria, 237–239

Internet safety, 239–240
planning resources, 232–237
recommendations, 275–276
Weinstein, T., 93
West, L. L., 70
Whiteboards, 250–252
Wiggins, Grant, 177
Wiggins, W., 214
Williams, D., 34

With-it-ness, 132
Wolfendale, S., 70
Woloshyn, V., 153
Writing skills, 35, 160

YouTube, 253–254

Zuckerberg, Mark, 254
Zukav, G., 8